Ancient
Civilizations
Almanac

VOLUME **2** China–Rome

Ancient Civilizations Almanac

Judson Knight

Stacy A. McConnell and
Lawrence W. Baker, Editors

U·X·L®

AN IMPRINT OF THE GALE GROUP

DETROIT · SAN FRANCISCO · LONDON
BOSTON · WOODBRIDGE, CT

Ancient Civilizations: Almanac

Judson Knight

Staff

Stacy A. McConnell, Lawrence W. Baker, *U•X•L Editors*
Carol DeKane Nagel, *U•X•L Managing Editor*
Tom Romig, *U•X•L Publisher*

Rita Wimberley, *Senior Buyer*
Evi Seoud, *Assistant Production Manager*
Mary Beth Trimper, *Composition Manager*

Margaret A. Chamberlain, *Permissions Specialist (pictures)*

Martha Schiebold and Michelle DiMercurio, *Senior Cover Art Directors*
Pamela A.E. Galbreath, *Senior Page Art Director*
Cynthia Baldwin, *Product Design Manager*
Barbara J. Yarrow, *Graphic Services Supervisor*

Linda Mahoney, LM Design, *Typesetting*

Front cover: (top photo) The Parthenon. Reproduced by permission of Susan D. Rock. (bottom photo) Terra cotta statues from the tomb of Shih-huang-ti. Reproduced by permission of AP/Wide World Photos.

Library of Congress Cataloging-in-Publication Data

Knight, Judson
    Ancient Civilizations: Almanac / Judson Knight; edited by Stacy A. McConnell and Lawrence W. Baker
      p. cm.
    Includes biographical references and index.
    Summary: Provides historical information and interpretation on ancient civilizations in Egypt, Mesopotamia, Asia Minor, China, Africa, Israel, and elsewhere.
    ISBN 0-7876-3982-6 (set), —- ISBN 0-7876-3983-4 (v. 1). —- ISBN 0-7876-3894-2 (v. 2);
    Civilization, Ancient-Juvenile literature. 2. Civilization, Ancient-Miscellanea-Juvenile literature. [1. Civilization, Ancient.] I. McConnell, Stacy A. II. Title
    CB311 .K594 1999

930-dc21   99-046791
[B]-DC21   CIP

To Tyler, from her ancient daddy;
and to Deidre, from her modern husband.

Contents

Egyptian workers depicted on a frieze. *(Archive Photos. Reproduced by permission.)*

Volume 1

Volume 2

Advisory Board

Special thanks are due to U•X•L's Ancient Civilizations Reference Library advisors for their invaluable comments and suggestions:

- Jonathan Betz-Zall, Children's Librarian, Sno-Isle Regional Library, Edmonds, Washington

- Nancy Guidry, Young Adult Librarian, Santa Monica Public Library, Santa Monica, California

- Karen Shugrue, Junior High Media Specialist, Agawam Junior High School, Feeding Hills, Massachusetts.

Reader's Guide

Reader's Guide

Civilization in its purest form is universal, something available to all people. The wisdom that went into the building of the Egyptian pyramids, the creation of Greek democracy, or the construction of the Mesoamerican metropolis Teotihuacán does not belong to any race or nation: it is a part of the human legacy, something all people can appreciate regardless of their heritage. *Ancient Civilizations: Almanac* focuses on twelve civilizations and cultures, beginning with the ancient Egyptians and covering the Sumerians of Mesopotamia, the Shang of China, the Olmec of the Americas, and the Minoan of ancient Greece, among others, and concludes with the rise and fall in A.D. 476 of the Roman Empire. While concentrating on each culture's unique history and customs, *Ancient Civilizations: Almanac* also highlights the similarities between cultures that existed thousands of years—and sometimes thousands of miles—apart from each other.

Arranged into chapters by geographic region, *Ancient Civilizations: Almanac* features more than 110 black-and-white photographs that help bring the civilizations to life. Maps in each chapter place the civilization in a geographic context as well as highlight landmarks relating to that civilization. Numerous sidebar boxes provide lists of words to know or in-depth coverage of topics of high interest, such as the legacy of Saharan rock art. Cross references point the user to related information, while a "For More Information" section concludes each chapter. *Ancient Civilizations: Almanac* also features a glossary of terms used throughout the volumes, a timeline containing significant milestones from each civilization, and an index covering the people, places, and events discussed throughout *Ancient Civilizations: Almanac.*

Comments and Suggestions

We welcome your comments on *Ancient Civilizations: Almanac,* as well as your suggestions for persons to be featured in future editions. Please write, Editors, *Ancient Civilizations: Almanac,* U•X•L, 27500 Drake Rd., Farmington Hills, Michigan, 48331-3535; call toll-free: 1-800-877-4253; fax to 248-414-5043; or send e-mail via http://www.galegroup.com.

Words to Know

A

Acropolis: An elevated fortress in Greek cities.

Ancestor: An earlier person in one's line of parentage, usually more distant in time than a grandparent.

Anoint: To pour oil over someone's head as a symbol that God has chosen that person to fill a position of leadership.

Apostle: A religious figure who is sent out to teach, preach, and perform miracles.

Archaeology: The scientific study of past civilizations.

Architect: Someone who designs a building or other structure.

Aristocrat: A very wealthy and/or powerful person.

Assassination: Killing, usually of an important leader, for political reasons.

B

Baptism: To be lowered into water as a symbol of death and rebirth.

Bureaucracy: A network of officials who run a government.

Bust: A sculpture of a human head, neck, and shoulders.

C

Caravan: A company of travelers, usually with pack animals, traveling through a desert or other forbidding region.

Caste system: A system of ranking people into very social groups, which prevailed in India from ancient times to the modern day.

Census: A count of the people living in any defined area.

Civil servant: Someone who works for the government.

Civil war: A military conflict that occurs when a group of citizens within a nation attempts to break away from the rule of the government.

Commoner: Someone who is not a member of a royal or noble class.

Concubine: A woman whose role toward a man is like that of a wife, but without the social and legal status of a wife.

Constitution: A set of written laws governing a nation.

Contemporary (n.): Someone who lives at the same time as another person.

Cremation: The burning, as opposed to burial, of a dead body.

Crucifixion: A Roman punishment in which the victim was nailed or tied up to a cross until he died.

Cult: A small religious group, most often with specialized beliefs.

D

Deify: To turn someone or something into a god.

Deity: A god.

Democracy: A form of government in which the people, usually through elected representatives, rule.

Descendant: Someone who is related to an earlier person, or *ancestor.*

Disciple: A close follower of a religious teacher.

E

Edict: A command.

Epic: A long poem that recounts the adventures of a legendary hero.

Epistle: A letter.

Eunuch: A man who has been castrated, thus making him incapable of sex or sexual desire.

F

Famine: A period when there is not enough food in a region to feed all its people.

Fasting: Deliberately going without food, often but not always for religious reasons.

G

Gentile: Someone who is not a Jew.

H

Hellenic: Greek.

Hellenistic: Influenced by Greece.

Heresy: Something that goes against established religious doctrine.

Hoplite: A heavily armed foot soldier.

I

Islam: A faith that arose in Arabia in the A.D. 600s, led by the prophet Muhammad (A.D. 570?-632.)

L

Legacy: Something that is left to a later generation.

Legitimacy: The right of a ruler to hold power.

M

Martyr: Someone who dies for their faith.

Medieval: Relating to the Middle Ages.

Mercenary: A professional soldier who will fight for whoever pays him.

Middle Ages: The period from the fall of the Roman Empire to the beginning of the Renaissance, roughly A.D. 500 to 1500.

Middle Class: A group in between the rich and the poor, or the rich and the working class.

Millennium: A period of a thousand years.

Mint (v.): To produce currency.

Missionary: Someone who goes to other lands to convert others to their religion.

Moat: A trench, filled with water, which surrounds a castle or city.

Monarch: A king.

Monotheism: Belief in one god.

Muslim: A believer in Islam.

N

Noble: A ruler within a kingdom who has an inherited title and lands, but who is less powerful than the king or queen.

O

Obelisk: A tall, free-standing column of stone.

Oligarchy: A government ruled by a few people.

P

Pagan: Someone who worships many gods; also used as an adjective.

Papyrus: A type of reed from which the Egyptians made the first type of "paper."

Peasant: A farmer who works a small plot of land.

Phalanx: A column of *hoplites* designed for offensive warfare.

Pharisee: A member of a group of Jewish religious scholars who demanded strict adherence to religious law.

Philosophy: A discipline which seeks to reach a general understanding of values and of reality.

Plague: A disease or other disaster that spreads among a group of people.

Proportion: The size of one thing in relation to something else, and the proper representation of their relationship.

R

Rabbi: A Jewish teacher or priest.

Radical (adj.): Thorough or sweeping changes in society; used as an noun for a person who advocates such changes.

Regent: Someone who governs a country when the monarch is too young, too old, or too sick to lead.

Reincarnation: The idea that people are reborn on Earth, and live and die, again and again.

Relief: In sculpture, a carved picture, distinguished from regular sculpture because it is two-dimensional.

Renaissance: A period of renewed interest in learning and the arts which began in Europe in the 1300s and continued to the 1700s.

Revolution: In politics, an armed uprising against the rulers of a nation or area.

S

Sack (v.): To destroy a city.

Satrap: A governor in the Persian Empire.

Scribes: A small and very powerful group in ancient society who knew how to read and write.

Siege: A sustained military attack against a city.

Stele (or stela): A large stone pillar, usually inscribed with a message commemorating a specific event.

Stupa: A dome-shaped Buddhist temple.

T

Theorem: A statement of fact in logic or mathematics, derived from other formulas or propositions.

Totalitarianism: A political system in which the government exerts total, or near-total, control.

U

Usurp: To seize power.

Utopia: A perfect society.

V

Vassal: A ruler who is subject to another ruler.

Vineyard: A place where grapes are grown for making wine.

Vizier: A chief minister.

W

Western: The cultures and civilizations influenced by ancient Greece and Rome.

Z

Ziggurat: A Mesopotamian temple tower.

Pronunciation Guide

a = h*a*t

ah = t*o*p, f*a*ther

ai or *ay* = h*a*ze, w*ay*s, d*ai*sy

ee = p*ea*ce, fl*ee*ce, an*y*

eh = h*e*lp, s*ai*d, h*ea*d, s*ay*s

g = *g*ood (compare *j*)

hw = *wh*at

ie or *i[consonant]e* or *igh* or *y* = h*i*de, sp*y*

i = l*i*p

j = *j*ust, a*dj*ust, *g*ym (compare *g*)

ks = ta*x*, ta*ck*s

oh = h*o*pe, r*oa*m

oo = z*oo*m, pl*u*me

s = *s*ay, pea*c*e (compare *z*)

ts = dan*c*e, pan*ts*

ü = g*oo*d, c*ou*ld

uh = h*u*sh, d*o*ne

z = thing*s*, *z*one (compare *s*)

zh= occa*si*on, lei*s*ure, a*z*ure, unu*su*al

Timeline

c. 2,000,000-c. 10,000 B.C.: Paleolithic Age.

c. 10,000 B.C.: Last ice age ends.

c. 10,000-c. 4000 B.C.: Neolithic Age.

c. 3500 B.C.: Beginnings of Sumerian civilization.

c. 3100 B.C.: Pharaoh Menes unites the kingdoms of Upper and Lower Egypt.

c. 3000 B.C.: Babylon established.

c. 2950 B.C.: First examples of hieroglyphs in Egypt.

c. 2920 B.C.: First Dynasty begins in Egypt.

c. 2800 B.C.: Mycenaeans leave the Black Sea area, moving toward Greece.

c. 2650 B.C.: Beginning of Old Kingdom in Egypt.

c. 2650 B.C.: Step Pyramid of Saqqara, designed by Imhotep, built under reign of pharaoh Zoser.

c. 2550 B.C.: Great Pyramid of Cheops built in Egypt.

c. 2500 B.C.: Indus Valley civilization begins in India.

c. 2300 B.C.: Early Dynastic Period ends in Sumer; Sargon of Akkad, first great Mesopotamian ruler, establishes Akkadian Empire.

c. 2200 B.C.: Hsia, semi-legendary first dynasty of China, begins.

2150 B.C.: End of Old Kingdom in Egypt; beginning of First Intermediate Period.

c. 2150 B.C.: Akkadian Empire ends with Gutian invasion of Mesopotamia; rise of Ur.

c. 2000 B.C.: Origins of Gilgamesh Epic in Sumer.

c. 2000 B.C.: Phoenician civilization established.

c. 2000 B.C.: Beginnings of Mayan civilization in Mesoamerica.

c. 2000 B.C.: Establishment of Kushite civilization in Africa.

c. 2000 B.C.: Beginnings of Minoan civilization in Crete.

1986 B.C.: Pharaoh Mentuhotep II unites all of Egypt; end of First Intermediate Period and beginning of Middle Kingdom.

c. 1900 B.C.: Indus Valley civilization begins to decline.

1813 B.C.: Shamshi-Adad, first important Assyrian ruler, takes throne.

1792 B.C.: End of Old Babylonia in Mesopotamia; Hammurabi, who later establishes first legal code in history, takes throne.

1766 B.C.: Shang Dynasty, first historic line of Chinese kings, begins.

c. 1760 B.C.: Hammurabi of Babylonia takes control of Assyria.

1759 B.C.: Middle Kingdom ends in Egypt; beginning of Second Intermediate Period.

c. 1750 B.C.: Beginning of Hittite civilization, establishment of capital at Hattush in Asia Minor.

c. 1700 B.C.: Crete experiences earthquake; later the Minoans rebuild their palaces at Knossos and other sites.

c. 1700-1500 B.C.: Phoenicians develop the world's first alphabet.

c. 1670 B.C.: Hyksos invade Egypt.

c. 1650 B.C.: Beginnings of Mycenaean civilization in Greece.

1539 B.C.: Second Intermediate Period ends in Egypt; beginning of New Kingdom.

c. 1500 B.C.: Indo-Europeans invade India; beginning of Vedic Age.

c. 1500 B.C.: Thebes founded on Greek mainland.

c. 1500-c. 1300 B.C.: Kingdom of Mitanni flourishes in Mesopotamia.

1473 B.C.: Pharaoh Hatshepsut assumes sole power in Egypt; becomes first significant female ruler in history.

c. 1450 B.C.: Minoan civilization in Crete comes to an end, probably as a result of volcanic eruption on Thera.

1363 B.C.: Ashur-uballit, who establishes the first Assyrian empire, begins reign.

c. 1347: Pharaoh Amenhotep IV changes his name to Akhenaton and introduces sweeping religious reforms.

1323 B.C.: Death of Tutankhamen in Egypt; power struggle follows, along with effort to erase memory of Akhenaton.

c. 1300 B.C.: City of San Lorenzo established in Mesoamerica.

1200s B.C.: Moses dies.

1279 B.C.: Beginning of Pharaoh Ramses II's reign in Egypt.

1285 B.C.: Battle of Kadesh between Egyptians and Hittites.

c. 1200 B.C.: Sea Peoples bring an end to Hittite civilization in Asia Minor.

c. 1200 B.C.: Aramaeans, after briefly controlling Babylonia, conquer Syria.

c. 1200 B.C.: Olmec civilization established in what is now Mexico.

c. 1200 B.C.: Bantu peoples migrate southward from what is now Nigeria.

c. 1200 B.C.: Trojan War.

c. 1200 B.C.: Etruscans settle on Italian peninsula.

c. 1200-900 B.C.: Carving of giant heads by Olmec in Mesoamerica.

c. 1140 B.C.: Macedonians move southward, displacing the Dorians from northern Greece.

1125 B.C.: King Nebuchadnezzar I begins reign in Babylon.

c. 1100 B.C.: Dorians bring an end to Mycenaean civilization; beginning of Dark Ages in Greece, which last for four centuries.

1070 B.C.: End of New Kingdom in Egypt; Third Intermediate Period Begins.

1027 B.C.: Revolt led by Prince Wu Wang brings an end to Shang Dynasty, and the establishment of Chou Dynasty, in China.

c. 1000 B.C.: Saul killed; David becomes ruler of Israel.

c. 1000 B.C.: End of Vedic Age, beginning of Epic Age, in India.

c. 1000 B.C.: Beginnings of Chavín civilization in South America.

c. 1000 B.C.: Celts begin to spread from Gaul throughout Europe.

900s B.C.: Phoenicians begin establishing trade routes and overseas colonies.

c. 960 B.C.: David dies; Solomon becomes ruler of Israel.

934 B.C.: Beginning of Assyrian conquests which will lead to establishment of Neo-Assyrian Empire.

922 B.C.: End of Solomon's reign, and of unified kingdom of Israel.

800s B.C.: Dorians establish Sparta.

883 B.C.: Ashurnasirpal II assumes throne in Assyria, establishes Neo-Assyrian Empire.

879 B.C.: Beginning of King Ben-Hadad II's reign in Syria.

c. 850 B.C.: Greeks start trading with other peoples; beginning of the end of the Dark Ages.

c. 850-750 B.C.: Rise of city-states in Greece.

c. 800 B.C.: Carthage established by Phoenicians.

c. 800 B.C.: Poets Homer and Hesiod flourish in Greece.

776 B.C.: First Olympic Games held.

771 B.C.: Invasion by nomads from the north forces Chou Dynasty of China to move capital eastward; end of Western Chou period.

753 B.C.: Traditional date of Rome's founding; Romulus first of seven legendary kings.

c. 751 B.C.: Piankhi takes throne in Kush.

722 B.C.: Spring and Autumn Period, a time of widespread unrest, begins in China.

c. 732 B.C.: Assyrians gain control of Syria.

c. 725 B.C.: King Mita, probably the source of the Midas legend, unites the Phrygians.

721 B.C.: Sargon II of Assyria conquers Israel and carries off its people, who become known as the Ten Lost Tribes of Israel.

715 B.C.: End of war with Messenia brings a rise to Spartan militarism.

712 B.C.: Kushites under Shabaka invade Egypt, establish Twenty-Fifth Dynasty; end of Third Intermediate Period, and beginning of Late Period.

c. 700 B.C.: End of Dark Ages, beginning of two-century Archaic Age, in Greece.

c. 700 B.C.: City-state of Athens, established centuries before, dominates Attica region in Greece.

600s B.C.: State of Magadha develops in eastern India.

600s B.C.: Important developments in Greek architecture: establishment of Doric order, first structures of stone rather than wood.

695 B.C.: Cimmerians invade Phrygia, ending Phrygian civilization.

689 B.C.: Assyrians sack Babylon.

c. 685 B.C.: Gyges founds Mermnad dynasty in Lydia.

681 B.C.: Sennacherib dies; Esarhaddon takes Assyrian throne.

672 B.C.: Assyrians first drive Kushites out of Egypt, install Necho I as pharaoh.

669 B.C.: Beginning of Ashurbanipal's reign; last great Assyrian king.

667 B.C.: Assyrian troops under Ashurbanipal complete conquest of Egypt from Kushites.

Mid-600s B.C.: Meröe Period begins when Kushites, removed from power in Egypt, move their capital southward.

Mid-600s B.C.: Establishment of Ionian Greek trading colony at Naucratis in Egypt.

Mid-600s B.C.: Age of tyrants begins in Greece.

c. 650 B.C.: Scribes in Egypt develop demotic script.

648 B.C.: Ashurbanipal of Assyria subdues Babylonian revolt; his brother Shamash-shum-ukin reportedly commits suicide.

625 B.C.: Nabopolassar establishes Chaldean (Neo-Babylonian) Empire.

621 B.C.: Draco appointed by Athenian oligarchs; creates a set of extremely harsh laws.

616 B.C.: Power-sharing of Sabines and Latins in Rome ends with Etruscan takeover under legendary king Tarquinius Priscus.

613 B.C.: First recorded sighting of Halley's Comet by Chinese astronomers.

612 B.C.: Babylonians and Medes destroy Nineveh; end of Neo-Assyrian Empire.

605 B.C.: Nabopolassar dies; his son Nebuchadnezzar II, the greatest Babylonian ruler, takes throne.

c. 600 B.C.: Pharaoh Necho II of Egypt sends a group of Carthaginian mariners on voyage around African continent.

c. 600 B.C.: Nebuchadnezzar builds Hanging Gardens in Babylon, one of the Seven Wonders of the Ancient World.

Late 600s, early 500s B.C.: Romans wage series of wars against Sabines, Latins, and Etruscans.

500s B.C.: Careers of Lao-tzu and Confucius, Chinese philosophers.

500s B.C.: High point of Etruscan civilization in Italy.

594 B.C.: Solon appointed archon of Athens.

586 B.C.: Nebuchadnezzar II destroys Israelites' capital at Jerusalem; beginning of Babylonian Captivity for Israelites.

585 B.C.: Thales, first Western philosopher, comes to fame in Greece for correctly predicting a solar eclipse on May 28.

c. 560 B.C.: Beginning of Croesus's reign in Lydia.

Mid-500s: Israelite prophet Daniel, a captive in Babylon, flourishes.

559 B.C.: Cyrus the Great of Persia takes the throne.

550 B.C.: Cyrus the Great of Persia defeats the Medes, establishes Persian Empire.

c. 550 B.C.: King Croesus of Lydia conquers Greek city-states of Ionia.

c. 550 B.C.: Temple of Artemis at Ephesus, one of the Seven Wonders of the Ancient World, is built.

546 B.C.: Persian armies under Cyrus the Great depose King Croesus and take over Lydia.

546 B.C.: Cyrus the Great of Persia conquers Ionian city-states of Greece.

538 B.C.: Persians conquer Babylonia; end of Chaldean (Neo-Babylonian) Empire, and of Israelites' Babylonian Captivity.

529 B.C.: Cyrus the Great of Persia dies, succeeded by his son, Cambyses II.

c. 528 B.C.: In India, Gautama Siddartha experiences his enlightenment; becomes known as the Buddha.

527 B.C.: Peisistratus, tyrant of Athens, dies; he is replaced by his sons, Hippias and Hipparchus, who prove unpopular.

522 B.C.: Returning to Persia to deal with rebellious forces, Cambyses II dies, and is succeeded by Darius the Great.

521 B.C.: Darius the Great of Persia conquers Punjab region of western India.

510 B.C.: Four years after the assassination of his brother Hipparchus, Athenians remove Hippias from power.

509 B.C.: Traditional date of Roman overthrow of Etruscan rule.

507 B.C.: Founding of Roman Republic.

502 B.C.: Athenians adopt a new constitution based on reforms of Cleisthenes, ending the age of tyrants; birth of democracy.

c. 500 B.C.: End of Epic Age in India.

c. 500 B.C.: Kingdom of Aksum established in Africa.

c. 500 B.C.: End of Archaic Age, beginning of Classical Age, in Greece.

c. 500 B.C.: Celts (Gauls) enter northern Italy, while other Celtic tribes settle in Britain.

499 B.C.: Persian Wars in Greece begin with revolt of Ionian city-states against Persians.

490 B.C.: Persian troops under Darius the Great burn Ionian Greek city-state of Eretria.

490 B.C.: Battle of Marathon: Greeks defeat Persians.

486 B.C.: Darius the Great of Persia dies and is succeeded by his son Xerxes, the last powerful emperor of Persia.

481 B.C.: End of Spring and Autumn Period of Chou Dynasty in China.

480 B.C.: King Xerxes of Persia launches massive attack against Greece.

480 B.C.: Battle of Thermopylae in Greece; Persians victorious despite heroic Spartan defense.

480 B.C.: Xerxes burns Athens.

480 B.C.: Battle of Salamis: Athenian-led Greek naval force defeats Persians under Xerxes.

479 B.C.: Battle of Plataea: Spartan-led force overwhelms Persians under Mardonius.

479 B.C.: Battle of Mycale: naval victory by Greeks expels Persians from mainland Greece for good.

479 B.C.: Golden Age of Greece begins.

478 B.C.: Delian League founded in Greece, with Athens as its leading city-state.

474 B.C.: Carthaginians end Etruscan dreams of empire with defeat at Cumae; Etruscan civilization begins to decline.

468 B.C.: Delian League of Greece defeats Persian fleet off Ionian coast.

462 B.C.: Pericles and Ephialtes institute a series of democratic reforms in Athens.

460 B.C.: Pericles becomes sole archon of Athens, beginning the Age of Pericles.

450s B.C.: Athenian Empire subdues various Greek city-states, wages wars throughout Mediterranean and Aegean seas.

459 B.C.: Spartans and Athenians clash over control of Megara; first of conflicts leading to Peloponnesian War in 431 B.C.

453 B.C.: Warring States Period begins in China, only ending when Ch'in Dynasty replaces the Chou dynasty in 221 B.C.

453 B.C.: Pericles of Athens becomes first leader to establish pay for jurors.

451 B.C.: The "Twelve Tables," the first Roman legal code, established.

449 B.C.: Persian Wars officially come to an end.

c. 440 B.C.: Parthenon built in Athens.

c. 440 B.C.: Phidias sculpts Statue of Zeus at Olympia, one of the Seven Wonders of the Ancient World.

431 B.C.: Peloponnesian War between Athens and Sparta begins in Greece.

430 B.C.: Herodotus begins publishing *The History*.

429 B.C.: Plague breaks out in war-torn Athens.

425 B.C.: Athens defeats Sparta in battle, bringing temporary end to Peloponnesian War.

420 B.C.: Because it broke Olympic truce by attacking Athens, Sparta keeps it athletes out of the Olympic Games.

412 B.C.: Ionian revolt effectively ends power of Delian League.

404 B.C.: Athens surrenders to Sparta, ending Peloponnesian War.

404 B.C.: Golden Age of Classical Greece comes to an end.

c. 400 B.C.: Decline of Chavín civilization in South America.

300s B.C.: Ch'in state emerges in western China.

300s-200s B.C.: Romans conquer most Etruscan cities.

396 B.C.: Rome breaks a century-long peace treaty by conquering Etruscan city of Veii.

395 B.C.: Athens, Corinth, and Thebes revolt against Sparta, beginning Corinthian War.

390 B.C.: Celts (Gauls) invade Rome.

390 B.C.: Beginnings of Roman military buildup after expulsion of Gauls.

386 B.C.: Spartans put down revolt of Athens and other city-states, ending Corinthian War.

Mid-380s B.C.: Plato establishes Academy in Athens.

371 B.C.: Theban commander Epaminondas defeats Spartans at Leuctra, bringing an end to Spartan power over Greece.

Mid-300s B.C.: Mausoleum at Halicarnassus, one of the Seven Wonders of the Ancient World, is built.

359 B.C.: Philip II takes throne in Macedon, and five years later begins conquest of Balkan peninsula.

346 B.C.: Philip II of Macedon brings an end to war between Greek leagues over control of Delphi, calls for Hellenic unity.

339 B.C.: Philip II of Macedon completes conquest of Balkan peninsula.

338 B.C.: Macedonian forces under Philip II defeat Greek city-states at Charonea; Macedonia now controls Greece.

336 B.C.: Philip II assassinated; 20-year-old Alexander III (Alexander the Great) becomes king of Macedon.

335 B.C.: Alexander consolidates his power, dealing with rebellions in Macedon and Greek city-states.

335 B.C.: Aristotle establishes the Lyceum, a school in Athens.

334 B.C.: Alexander begins his conquests by entering Asia Minor.

334 B.C.: Beginning now and for the last twelve years of his life, Aristotle writes most of his works.

333 B.C.: In April, Alexander's forces defeat Persian armies under Darius III in Cilicia; Darius flees.

332 B.C.: Alexander conquers Syria, Phoenicia, and Palestine.

332 B.C.: Alexander invades Egypt.

332 B.C.: End of Late Period in Egypt; country will not be ruled by Egyptians again for some 1,500 years.

331 B.C.: Alexander establishes city of Alexandria in Egypt.

331 B.C.: Alexander's army completes defeat of Persians under Darius III at Gaugamela in Assyria; Darius is later assassinated.

331 B.C.: Alexander conquers Mesopotamia.

330 B.C.: Persepolis, capital of the Persian Empire, falls to Alexander the Great.

330 B.C.: Alexander embarks on four-year conquest of Iran, Bactria, and the Punjab.

324 B.C.: Chandragupta Maurya, the founder of Mauryan dynasty, takes the throne of Magadha in eastern India.

323 B.C.: Beginning of Hellenistic Age, as Greek culture takes root over the next two centuries in lands conquered by Alexander.

323 B.C.: Ptolemy, one of Alexander's generals, establishes dynasty in Egypt that lasts for three centuries.

312 B.C.: Seleucid empire established over Persia, Mesopotamia, and much of the southwestern Asia.

c. 310 B.C.: Greek explorer Pytheas sets off on voyage that takes him to Britain and Scandinavia.

c. 300 B.C.: Composition of *Mahabharata,* an Indian epic, begins; writing will continue for the next six centuries.

c. 300 B.C.: Hinduism develops from the Vedic religion brought to India by the Aryans.

290 B.C.: Romans defeat Samnites, establish control over much of southern Italy.

287 B.C.: Plebeians establish power over Roman Senate.

282 B.C.: Colossus of Rhodes, one of the Seven Wonders of the Ancient World, completed; destroyed in earthquake fifty-four years later.

c. 280 B.C.: Lighthouse of Alexandria, last of the Seven Wonders of the Ancient World, built.

279 B.C.: Celts invade Greece, but are driven out by Antigonus Gonatas.

275 B.C.: Romans defeat Greek colonists in southern Italy, establishing control over region.

272 B.C.: Bindusara, ruler of Mauryan dynasty of India, dies; his son Asoka, the greatest Mauryan ruler, later takes throne.

264 B.C.: First Punic War between Rome and Carthage begins.

262 B.C.: Mauryan king Asoka, disgusted by his killings in battle with the Kalinga people, renounces violence.

260 B.C.: Asoka begins placement of rock and pillar edicts throughout India.

c. 250 B.C.: Kushite civilization reaches its height. It will remain strong for the next four centuries.

247 B.C.: Beginning of Parthian dynasty in Iran.

246 B.C.: End of Shang Dynasty in China.

241 B.C.: First Punic War ends with Roman defeat of Carthage; Rome controls Sicily, Corsica, and Sardinia.

230s B.C.: Asoka loses power over Indian court as rebellious advisors gain influence over his grandson Samprati.

229 B.C.: Rome establishes military base in Illyria; first step in conquest of Greece.

223 B.C.: Antiochus the Great, most powerful Seleucid ruler, begins reign in Syria.

221 B.C.: Ch'in Shih Huang Ti unites China, establishes Ch'in Dynasty as first Chinese emperor.

221 B.C.: Chinese under Ch'in Shih Huang Ti begin building Great Wall.

221 B.C.: Unification of China under Ch'in Shih Huang Ti begins driving the nomadic Hsiung-Nu and Yüeh-Chih tribes westward.

218 B.C.: Hannibal of Carthage launches Second Punic War against Romans, marching from Spain, over Alps, and into Italy.

216 B.C.: Carthaginians under Hannibal deal Romans a stunning defeat at Cumae.

213 B.C.: Emperor Ch'in Shih Huang Ti calls for burning of most books in China.

207 B.C.: End of shortlived Ch'in Dynasty in China; power struggle follows.

206 B.C.: Rebel forces under Hsiang Yü take capital of China.

202 B.C.: Having defeated Hsiang Yü, Liu Pang (Kao Tzu) becomes emperor, establishes Han Dynasty in China.

202 B.C.: Roman forces under Scipio defeat Hannibal and the Carthaginians at Zama.

c. 200 B.C.: Eratosthenes, librarian of Alexandria, makes remarkable accurate measurement of Earth's size.

198 B.C.: Seleucids gain control of Palestine.

197 B.C.: Romans defeat Macedonian forces under Philip V at Cynocephalae; beginning of end of Macedonian rule in Greece.

195 B.C.: Antiochus the Great, at height of his power, arranges marriage of his daughter Cleopatra I to Ptolemy IV of Egypt.

195 B.C.: Hannibal flees Carthage, takes refuge with Antiochus the Great.

191 B.C.: Roman forces defeat Antiochus the Great at Thermopylae.

190 B.C.: Romans under Scipio defeat Seleucid king Antiochus the Great at Magnesia, and add Asia Minor to their territories.

186 B.C.: Mauryan Empire of India collapses.

170s B.C.: Parthians begin half-century of conquests, ultimately replacing Seleucids as dominant power in Iran and southwest Asia.

165 B.C.: Nomadic Yüeh-Chih tribes, driven out of China, arrive in Bactria; later, Kushans emerge as dominant tribe.

c. 150 B.C.: Greco-Bactrians under Menander invade India.

149 B.C.: Romans launch Third Punic War against Carthage.

146 B.C.: Romans complete their conquest of Greece.

146 B.C.: Romans completely destroy Carthage, ending Third Punic War.

133 B.C.: Chinese emperor Han Wu-ti launches four decades of war which greatly expand Chinese territory.

130 B.C.: Wu Ti establishes first civil-service exams in China.

c. 130 B.C.: Kushans begin a century-long series of conquests, ultimately absorbing Greco-Bactrian kingdom.

128 B.C.: Emperor WuTi effectively destroys the power of feudal lords in China.

121 B.C.: Roman reformer Gaius Gracchus commits suicide after some 3,000 of his followers are murdered.

c. 120 B.C.: Chang Chi'en, on a mission for Emperor Wu Ti, makes first Chinese contact with Greek-influenced areas.

108 B.C.: China, under Wu Ti, conquers Korea.

101 B.C.: Marius defeats Cimbri, a northern European tribe.

c. 100 B.C.: End of Olmec civilization in Mesoamerica.

95 B.C.: Tigranes II, who later makes Armenia a great power, assumes throne.

88 B.C.: Social War ends; Rome extends citizenship to non-Roman Italians.

88 B.C.: Sulla, rival of Roman consul Marius, becomes commander of forces against Mithradates the Great of Pontus in Asia Minor.

77 B.C.: Roman general Pompey sent to crush uprising in Spain.

c. 75 B.C.: Julius Caesar distinguishes himself with successful attacks against Cilician pirates, as well as Mithradates of Pontus.

73 B.C.: Slaves under Spartacus revolt in Capua, beginning Gladiatorial War; soon they have an army of 100,000.

71 B.C.: Gladiatorial War ends with defeat of slave army by Crassus.

69 B.C.: Rome begins taking over lands conquered by Tigranes of Armenia; conquest largely complete within three years.

60 B.C.: Julius Caesar, Pompey, and Crassus form First Triumvirate.

55 B.C.: Roman troops under Julius Caesar invade, but do not conquer, Britain; another invasion follows the next year.

51 B.C.: After death of her father, Ptolemy XII, Cleopatra becomes coruler of Egypt with her brother and husband.

49 B.C.: Pompey orders Julius Caesar to return from Rome; Caesar crosses the River Rubicon with his army.

48 B.C.: Cleopatra forced out of power in Egypt by a group loyal to her brother.

48 B.C.: Julius Caesar's forces defeat Pompey at Pharsalus in Greece; Pompey flees to Egypt, where he is assassinated.

48 B.C.: Julius Caesar arrives in Egypt, meets and begins affair with Cleopatra.

47 B.C.: Julius Caesar helps Cleopatra defeat her brother, Ptolemy XIII.

46 B.C.: Cleopatra goes to Rome with Julius Caesar.

44 B.C.: On March 15, a group of conspirators assassinates Julius Caesar in the chambers of the Roman senate.

44 B.C.: Octavian, Mark Antony, and Lepidus form Second Triumvirate.

41 B.C.: Cleopatra and Mark Antony begin political and personal alliance.

37 B.C.: Mark Antony leaves his wife, Octavian's sister, and joins Cleopatra; launches military campaigns in southwest Asia.

37 B.C.: Herod the Great becomes vassal king in Roman-controlled Judea.

36 B.C.: Octavian removes Lepidus from power, begins dealing with Mark Antony.

32 B.C.: Roman senate, at the urging of Octavian, declares war on Cleopatra.

31 B.C.: Roman forces destroy Mark Antony and Cleopatra's fleet at Actium in Greece on September 2; Antony commits suicide.

31 B.C.: Beginning of Octavian's sole control of Rome, end of a century of unrest.

31 B.C.: Beginning of *Pax Romana,* or "Roman Peace," which prevails throughout Roman world for two centuries.

30 B.C.: Suicide of Cleopatra VII; Romans establish control of Egypt.

27 B.C.: Octavian declared Emperor Augustus Caesar by Roman senate; Roman Empire effectively established.

24 B.C.: Romans attempt unsuccessfully to conquer southwestern Arabia.

17 B.C.: Vergil's *Aeneid* published.

c. 6 B.C.: Jesus Christ born.

****

9 A.D.: Wang Mang usurps throne of Han Dynasty in China, establishing Hsin Dynasty.

9 A.D.: Forces of Augustus Caesar defeated by Germans, ending Roman expansion to the north.

14 A.D.: Augustus Caesar dies; his stepson Tiberius becomes emperor, marking official establishment of Roman Empire.

23 A.D.: Han Dynasty regains control of China; beginning of the Later Han Period.

c. 30 A.D.: Jesus Christ dies.

c. 36 A.D.: Saul has vision on road to Damascus which leads him to embrace Christianity; becomes most important apostle.

41 A.D.: Caligula killed by Roman military; Claudius becomes emperor.

43 A.D.: Rome launches last major conquest, in Britain.

47 A.D.: Victorious in Britain, Romans demand that all Britons surrender their weapons.

49 A.D.: Council of Jerusalem, early meeting of Christians attended by the apostle Paul, is held.

c. 50 A.D.: Josephus, Jewish historian whose work is one of the few non-biblical sources regarding Jesus, flourishes.

60 A.D.: After the Romans attack her family, Boadicea, queen of the Iceni people in Britain, leads revolt.

64 A.D.: Rebuilding of Temple in Jerusalem, begun by Herod the Great in 20 B.C., completed.

64 A.D.: Fire sweeps Rome; Nero accused of starting it.

64 A.D.: Nero blames Christians for fire in Rome, beginning first major wave of persecutions.

65 A.D.: After suicide of his advisor, the philosopher Seneca, Nero becomes increasingly uncontrollable.

69 A.D.: Vespasian becomes Roman emperor, begins establishing order throughout empire.

70 A.D.: Future Roman emperor Titus, son of Vespasian, destroys Jerusalem and its temple.

c. 78 A.D.: Kaniska, greatest Kushan ruler, takes throne; later extends Buddhism to China.

79 A.D.: Mount Vesuvius erupts, destroying the city of Pompeii in Italy.

81 A.D.: Death of Titus; his brother, the tyrannical Domitian, becomes Roman emperor.

c. 90 A.D.: John writes Revelation, last book in the Bible.

98 A.D.: Roman historian Tacitus publishes *Germania,* one of the few contemporary accounts of German tribes and Britons.

100 A.D.: The Sakas, a Scythian tribe, take over Kushan lands in what is now Afghanistan.

c. 100 A.D.: Taoism, based on the ideas of Lao-tzu six centuries before, becomes a formal religion in China.

c. 100 A.D.: Establishment of Teotihuacán, greatest city of ancient America.

c. 100 A.D.: Old Silk Road, trade route between East and West, established.

135 A.D.: Roman emperor Hadrian banishes Jews from Jerusalem.

c. 150 A.D.: Nomadic Hsien-Pei tribe of China briefly conquers a large empire.

161 A.D.: Tiber River floods, causing famine in Rome.

161 A.D.: Greek physician Galen goes to Rome; later becomes physician to Marcus Aurelius and other emperors.

165 A.D.: Romans destroy Parthian capital at Ctesiphon, bringing an end to Parthian control over Persia.

175 A.D.: Roman general Avidius Cassius revolts against Marcus Aurelius in Syria, but is assassinated by one of his soldiers.

180 A.D.: Marcus Aurelius, last of the four "good" Roman emperors, dies; he is replaced by his wild son Commodus.

184 A.D.: Yellow Turbans lead revolt against Han Dynasty emperor of China; revolt is crushed five years later by Ts'ao Ts'ao.

192 A.D.: Roman emperor Commodus assassinated; Septimus Severus (r. 192-211), tries unsuccessfully to restore order.

200s A.D.: Diogenes Laertius writes *Lives of the Eminent Philosophers,* primary information source on Greek philosophers.

c. 200 A.D.: Zapotec people establish Monte Albán, first true city in Mesoamerica.

c. 200 A.D.: Anasazi tribe appears in what is now the southwestern United States.

220 A.D.: Later Han Dynasty of China ends.

221 A.D.: Three Kingdoms period in China begins.

c. 226 A.D.: Sassanian dynasty begins in Persia.

235 A.D.: Rome enters period of unrest in which 20 emperors hold the throne in just 49 years.

mid-200s A.D.: Shapur I, Sassanian ruler, takes Syria from Romans.

253 A.D.: Roman recovery begins with the emperor Gallienus, who later brings persecution of Christians to temporary end.

265 A.D.: Three Kingdoms period in China ends.

270 A.D.: Aurelian begins reign as Roman emperor.

270 A.D.: Queen Zenobia of Palmyra launches revolt against Roman Empire, conquers most of Syria and Egypt.

284 A.D.: Aurelian assassinated, Roman army chooses Diocletian as emperor; Diocletian ends period of unrest with series of reforms.

300s A.D.: Buddhism enters China.

300s A.D.: Books of the Bible compiled; some—the so-called Apocryphal Books—are rejected by early Christian bishops.

301 A.D.: Armenia becomes first nation to officially adopt Christianity.

302 A.D.: Diocletian resumes persecution of Christians.

307 A.D.: Constantine, last powerful Roman emperor, begins reign.

313 A.D.: Constantine declares an end to persecution of Christians in Roman Empire.

317 A.D.: Eastern Chin Dynasty established in China.

c. 320 A.D.: Candra Gupta establishes Gupta Empire in India.

325 A.D.: King Ezana of Aksum goes to war against Kush and destroys Meröe.

325 A.D.: Council of Nicaea adopts Nicene Creed, Christian statement of faith; declares Arianism a heresy.

330 A.D.: Constantine renames Greek city of Byzantium; as Constantinople, it becomes eastern capital of Roman Empire.

c. 335 A.D.: Candra Gupta dies; his son Samudra Gupta takes throne, and later conquers most of Indian subcontinent.

c. 335 A.D.: King Ezana converts to Christianity; nation of Aksum embraces the religion.

c. 355 A.D.: Huns appear in eastern Europe.

361 A.D.: Roman emperor Julian begins reign; later tries to reestablish pagan religion.

376 A.D.: Samudra Gupta, ruler of Gupta Empire in India, dies; Candra Gupta II, greatest Gupta ruler, takes throne.

379 A.D.: Theodosius becomes Roman emperor; last to rule a united Roman Empire.

383 A.D.: At Fei Shui, an Eastern Chin force prevents nomads from overrunning all of China.

386 A.D.: Toba nomads invade northern China and establish Toba Wei Dynasty.

394 A.D.: Roman emperor Theodosius I brings an end to ancient Olympic Games.

c. 400 A.D.: End of Kushite kingdom in Africa.

401 A.D.: Visigoth chieftain Alaric, driven out of Eastern Roman Empire, moves westward.

410 A.D.: Visigoths under Alaric sack Rome on August 24, hastening fall of western empire.

420 A.D.: End of Eastern Chin Dynasty in China.

434 A.D.: Huns arrive in what is now Austria; around this time, Attila emerges as their leader.

448 A.D.: Huns, under Attila, move into western Europe.

c. 450 A.D.: Hunas (Huns or Hsiung-Nu) invade Gupta Empire in India.

451 A.D.: Huns under Attila invade Gaul; defeated at Châlons-sur-Marne.

500s A.D.: African kingdom of Aksum establishes control over "incense states" of southern Arabia.

c. 500 A.D.: Japanese adopt Chinese system of writing; beginnings of Japanese history.

c. 500 A.D.: Bantu peoples control most of southern Africa.

c. 540 A.D.: End of Gupta Empire in India.

554 A.D.: End of Toba Wei Dynasty in northern China.

575 A.D.: Sassanid Persians gain control over Arabian peninsula.

581 A.D.: Establishment of Sui Dynasty, and reunification of China.

600s A.D.: Rise of Islam and Arab power.

600s A.D.: Three kingdoms emerge as Korea establishes independence from China.

c. 600 A.D.: Civil-service examinations, pioneered by Emperor Han Wu-ti seven centuries before, formally established in China.

c. 600 A.D.: African kingdom of Aksum declines.

618 A.D.: End of Sui Dynasty, beginning of T'ang Dynasty, in China.

622 A.D.: Mohammed and his followers escape from Mecca (the *Hegira*); beginning of Muslim calendar.

642 A.D.: Founding of Cairo, Egypt.

672 A.D.: Muslims conquer Egypt.

c. 750 A.D.: Decline of Teotihuacán in Mesoamerica.

1300s A.D.: Lighthouse of Alexandria destroyed in earthquake.

1687 A.D.: Parthenon damaged by explosion during war.

1776-88 A.D.: British historian Edward Gibbon publishes *The History of the Decline and Fall of the Roman Empire*.

1798 A.D.: French forces under Napoleon invade Egypt; later French scholars develop modern Egyptology.

1799 A.D.: Rosetta Stone discovered by French troops in Egypt.

1800s A.D.: Gilgamesh Epic of Mesopotamia recovered by scholars.

1800s A.D.: Linguists discover link between Indo-European languages of India, Iran, and Europe.

1813 A.D.: French publication of *Description of Egypt,* first significant modern work about Egyptian civilization.

1821 A.D.: Jean-François Champollion deciphers Rosetta Stone, enabling first translation of Egyptian hieroglyphs.

1860 A.D.: First discovery of colossal stone heads carved by Olmec in Mexico.

1871 A.D.: Heinrich Schliemann begins excavations at Hissarlik in Turkey, leading to discovery of ancient Troy.

1876-78 A.D.: Heinrich Schliemann discovers ruins of Mycenae in Greece.

1894 A.D.: Pierre de Coubertin establishes modern Olympic Games; first Games held in Athens two years later.

Late 1800s A.D.: Archaeologists discover first evidence, outside of the Bible, of Hittite civilization in Asia Minor.

1922 A.D.: British archaeologist Howard Carter discovers tomb of Egyptian pharaoh Tutankhamen.

1947-50s A.D.: Dead Sea scrolls discovered in Palestine.

1952 A.D.: Mycenaean Linear B script deciphered.

1960s A.D.: Archaeologists discover evidence of volcanic eruption on Greek island of Thera c. 1500 B.C.

Research and Activity Ideas

- Pretend you are a pharaoh who has ordered the building of a pyramid, or a Chinese emperor preparing his tomb. What people and items would you want to have with you in the next life? Write a list of these, and explain why each is important.

- Like Hammurabi, Moses, or the Romans who wrote the "Twelve Tables," your job is to create a set of laws to govern a nation. Make a list of things identified as crimes, and the punishment you think would be fair; also make a list of activities you would want to encourage, and how the government could do so. Conduct the group like a Greek democracy: all members of the group have an equal vote, though it is advisable that you first elect a leader to direct the discussion. After creating an initial set of proposed laws, conduct a vote to decide which should become official. Voting should be by secret ballot.

- Just as the ancient peoples had their myths and legends to explain the world, there are myths and legends in modern life. Who are the great heroes and villains of today, and of recent years—for example, political leaders and entertainment figures—and why do you think they are perceived as heroes or villains? How do you think they will be remembered, and what legends have developed or will develop around them? Modern legends often develop from rumors accepted as fact: what rumors have you heard, about things or events of local or national interest, which turned out not to be true? Discuss as a class.

- Choose a civilization covered in this book, and find pictures showing how people dressed in that place and time. Make simple costumes, using materials easily available at home, that resemble the clothing of that ancient civilization. On a given day, all members of the class should come to school in their costumes (or change clothes at school for the event) and conduct class as though it were a gathering of people from different civilizations. Talk to each other "in character," as though you were an Egyptian, for instance, or a Roman. Discuss your beliefs and your world, how you are different and similar—-thus, for instance, if you are a Hindu from India, you believe in reincarnation; or if you are an Israelite, you worship Yahweh.

- Find a map of the Persian "Royal Road," the Old Silk Route in Asia, or the Roman roads (for example in Roy Burrell's *Oxford First Ancient History,* listed in the Bibliography). Compare the length of these roads to interstate highways that run through your area. What problems would travelers on those ancient highways face that people on modern interstates do not?

- Divide into seven groups, each of which will report on one of the Seven Wonders of the World. This may include creating a model, if possible, though models do not need to be detailed. For the Hanging Gardens of Babylon, for instance, one could use houseplants and stacked cardboard boxes. (The Colossus of Rhodes may be depicted with clothing.)

- Look up examples of ancient Sahara rock art in Basil Davidson's *Ancient African Kingdoms,* pp. 43—57 (see bibliography of AFRICA chapter); in the June 1999 *National Geographic* ("Ancient Art of the Sahara" by David Coulson, pp. 98—119); or some other source. Pick out a piece of artwork that interests you, read the caption to learn more about it, and draw your own version.

- Interview a doctor about the Hippocratic Oath. What does it mean to him or her? What are some situations in which he or she has applied the Oath? How do doctors sometimes fail to apply it? Present the results of your interview in class, and discuss as a group.

- Pick a five-page section of text in this series or another appropriate volume. Copy the pages, then read them and highlight all words of more than two syllables. Look these words up in a dictionary and make a list of all those derived from Latin, as well as those derived from Greek. Also include the original Latin or Greek word and its meaning. For example, *section* comes from the Latin *secare,* to cut; *appropriate* from *proprius,* to own; and *volume* from *volumen,* a roll or scroll.

- Conduct an athletic event similar either to a *tlatchli* match, substituting handball, tennis, or volleyball for the Mesoamerican game; or a Greek footrace in the Olympics. Class members should choose whether to be participants or spectators, since both are necessary, but unlike ancient games, girls should be encouraged to take part in competition. If participating in a *tlatchli* game, remember that in Mesoamerican culture, those who lost were sacrificed; therefore players on both sides should later report to the class how they felt while playing. If simulating an Olympic event, class members should be appointed to write an ode to the winner, and to prepare a laurel crown (using small leafy tree branches, for example) for him or her.

- Many ancient peoples were concerned with what happened to a person after they died: the Egyptians and Chinese believed that, with proper preparation, a person would live on the earth; the Hindus believed in reincarnation; the Greeks and Romans believed that most people went to Hades, and a very few good or bad ones went either to the Elysian Fields or Tartarus; and the Christians, of course, accepted the idea of Heaven and Hell. Divide into groups, each of which pretends to hold a certain belief. Explain why your group believes in its explanation of the afterlife.

- Imagine that you are a young person in China, Greece, or Rome, or that you are a member of one of the "barbarian" tribes that threatened those societies. Depending on which group you belong to—-civilized or "barbarian"—-write two pages concerning how you feel about the other group.

Ancient
Civilizations
Almanac

China

8

China is only about 20,000 square miles (51,800 square kilometers) larger than the United States, a difference smaller than the area of San Bernardino County in southern California. It is enough of a difference, however, to make China the world's third-largest nation, in terms of area, surpassed only by Russia and Canada. China and eastern Russia make up the majority of Asia, the world's largest continent. Before the breakup of the Soviet Union in the early 1990s, the two nations shared a long border, but now they adjoin primarily in the Far East, where northern China meets Siberia. To the northeast is the Korean peninsula, the Sea of Japan, and Japan itself. Farther down the coast lies the island of Taiwan, an independent Chinese state; farther still lies Hong Kong, which became part of China in 1997. South of China is a string of nations, from Vietnam in the southeast to India in the southwest. To the west lie a number of Central Asian republics, including Kazakhstan. China's broad expanse encompasses a variety of climatic zones, from the cold north and vast tracts of desert in the west; to plains and mountain areas in the central, western, and northern regions; to lush river basins and tropi-

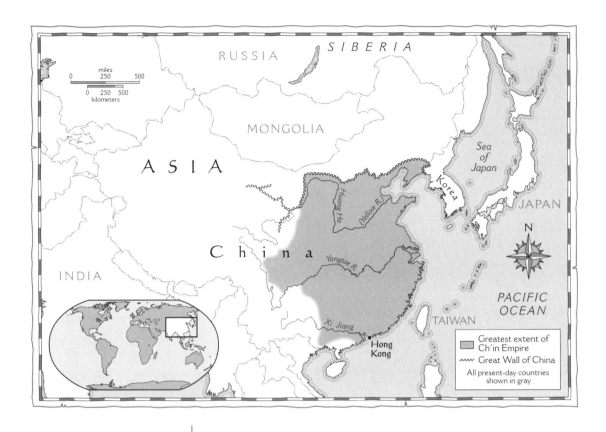

Map of China.
XNR Productions.
The Gale Group.

cal lowlands in the east and south. A number of rivers cut across China from east to west, most notably the Yangtze, the Huang He (or Yellow River), and the Xi Jiang.

Why China is important

As with India, China's population alone would make it worthy of study. It is the most populous nation on earth, with more than a billion people; in fact, two out of every five people on earth live either in China or on the Indian subcontinent. As with India, the reasons to study its ancient history go far beyond the size of its present-day population. China gave the world two of its greatest philosophers, Confucius and Lao-tzu, whose followers developed religions on the basis of their teachings. The numbers of Confucianists and Taoists, however, are dwarfed by the adherents of Chinese folk religions. These religions, which originated in ancient times, are not viewed as a single faith, but if they were, they would have more believers than all faiths except Christianity, Islam, and Hinduism.

Ancient China also gave the world one of its most splendid civilizations, a center of art and learning seldom surpassed by the empires of the West. Its gifts include paper, silk, and a particularly delightful treat: ice cream. The ancient Chinese discovered such advanced notions as crop rotation in agriculture and the octave in music. They also left behind the most impressive physical structure ever created by human beings: the Great Wall of China. Even the pyramids of Egypt look insignificant beside this vast creation, the only man-made object visible from the Moon.

Prehistoric China (c. 7000–1766 B.C.)

People lived in the area of China as far back as half a million years ago. It appears that a *Stone Age* culture developed in parts of northeastern China, as well as in the southeast of China, in about 7000 B.C. The first culture known to archaeologists was the Yang-shao (yahng-SHOW), which flourished in the western part of the country between about c. 3950 and about c. 1700 B.C. Though they were a Stone Age people, the Yang-shao grew wheat and other grains; made relatively advanced tools out of polished stone, as well as *glazed* pottery; and even domesticated animals such as pigs, cattle, and dogs.

To the north was the Lung-shan (loong-SHAHN) culture, which developed between 2000 and 1850 B.C. The Lung-shan appear to have been related to the Yang-shao; but in the northwest part of China, archaeologists have uncovered evidence of an entirely different group. Bodies discovered in the deserts there, where the hot, dry climate preserved them, suggest an invasion by peoples from as far away as the Ukraine. It is not known who these people were, or whether they were related to the Indo-Europeans who invaded Europe, Iran, and India.

Aside from the knowledge gained by archaeologists, there are legends concerning China's origins. These legends recount that Pangu (pahng-OO), creator of the universe, originated Chinese civilization in the region of the Huang He

Words to Know: China

Alchemy: A semiscientific discipline that holds that through the application of certain chemical processes, ordinary metals can be turned into gold.

Ancestor: An earlier person in one's line of parentage, usually more distant in time than a grandparent.

Annals: Historical records.

Bamboo: A type of plant, plentiful in East Asia, that has hollow stems and is useful for making a variety of objects.

Barbarian: A negative term used to describe someone as uncivilized.

Bronze Age: A phase in the development of a civilization characterized by the use of bronze, which is a mixture of copper and tin. The Bronze Age usually is described as following the Stone Age and preceding the Iron Age.

Bureaucracy: A network of officials who run a government.

Character: In written language, a symbol such as a letter of the alphabet or a hieroglyph.

Civil war: A military conflict that occurs when a group of citizens within a nation attempts to break away from the rule of the government.

Concubine: A woman whose role toward a man is like that of a wife's, but without the social and legal status of a wife.

Consort: Wife.

Contemporary: Someone who lives at the same time as another person.

Cowries: Bright shells that come from a type of ocean creature.

Crop rotation: A process of changing crops on a given plot of ground from year to year in order to preserve the soil.

Cuisine: Style of preparing food.

Currency: Money.

Democracy: A form of government in which the people, usually through elected representatives, rule.

Descendant: Someone who is related to an earlier person, or *ancestor.*

Disciple: A close follower of a teacher.

Divination: The study of physical material in order to discover what the future holds.

Eclipse: In astronomy, an event that occurs when one heavenly body blocks another from view.

Eunuch: A man who has been castrated, thus making him incapable of sex or sexual desire.

Feudal system: A form of political and economic organization in which peasants are subject to a noble, who owns most or all of the land that they till.

Glaze: To paint pottery, which is then baked in an extremely hot oven called a kiln.

Hierarchy: A system of classification according to grade or rank.

Ideogram: A written symbol that stands for an idea or name.

Industry: Manufacturing activity; can sometimes be used broadly to describe an entire branch of business, such as "the movie industry."

Industrialization: A process of transforming a country from an agricultural to a manufacturing economy.

Infantry: Foot soldiers.

Inflation: A situation in which too much currency is in use by the population, resulting in a rise in prices.

Iron Age: A phase in the development of a civilization that usually followed the Bronze Age and was characterized by the use of iron tools.

Jade: A greenish gemstone, particularly valued in East Asia, that acquires a high shine when polished.

Mandate: Permission or authority to rule.

Mint: To produce currency.

Monopoly: Total control over something, usually an industry.

Noble: A ruler within a kingdom who has an inherited title and lands but who is less powerful than the king or queen.

Nova: A star that suddenly grows extremely bright before fading.

Novel: An extended, usually book-length, work of fiction.

Octave: A system of eight notes that forms the basis of a musical scale.

Omen: A message from the gods, usually regarding the future.

Opium: A drug derived from poppy plants that is similar to heroin, though it is usually smoked rather than injected.

Peasant: A farmer who works a small plot of land.

Police state: A type of strict and repressive government control that is maintained through a secret police force rather than a public justice system.

Republic: A form of government, led by a president or a prime minister rather than a monarch or a dictator, that is usually but not always democratic in character.

Ritual: A type of religious ceremony that is governed by very specific rules.

Standardize: To bring things, such as units of measure, into a common system by setting standards for them.

Stone Age: A period in the development of a civilization characterized by the use of stone tools; it was usually followed by the Bronze Age.

Totalitarianism: A political system in which the government exerts total, or near-total, control.

Tyrant: An extremely cruel leader.

Usurper: Someone who seizes power.

(hwahng-HAY) or Yellow River in the plains of northern China. There followed the first of many dynasties who gave their names to phases of Chinese history: the Hsia or Xia (SHAH).

The Hsia Dynasty, which supposedly began about 2200 B.C., is so shrouded in myth and mystery that scholars tend to treat it more as a part of legend than of history—much like the Israelites' account of their origins in the Book of Genesis. According to Chinese legends, the Hsia ruled for nearly 450 years, until the rise of a cruel leader named Chieh (CHAY), who oppressed his people so badly that they revolted against him. This ushered in the era of the Shang (SHAHNG), China's first historic dynasty.

The Shang Dynasty (1766–1027 B.C.)

The Shang Dynasty ruled a large area in northern China, about 500 miles square, that included the region of the modern Chinese capital, Beijing (bay-ZHEENG), at its northern edge. The Shang capital was at Anyang (ahn-YAHNG), situated on a plain in the Yellow River Valley, where archaeologists uncovered a vast series of graves that provided a treasure trove of information about Shang society.

Much earlier, in A.D. 281, robbers at another tomb accidentally discovered a series of records that also provided considerable details about the Shang. The king buried in the tomb had died in the 200s B.C., but his grave contained records of the much earlier Shang Dynasty written on strips of *bamboo*. Tied together with ribbons of silk, these strips formed long scrolls on which scribes had written detailed records. To historians, they were more precious than gold; but to the grave robbers, who set fire to a number of the strips, they were a source of light in the dark tomb. Fortunately, they did not burn them all. What remained came to be known as "the Bamboo Annals" (AN-ulz, or historical records.)

Other important historical texts that provide information about the Shang include the *Book of Documents,* composed during the later Chou Dynasty, and the even later Han Dynasty's *Records of the Historian.* From such annals have emerged a picture of a highly organized society with a complex religion. The Shang were masters of warfare, but they also excelled in their creation of jewelry using *jade,* a greenish gemstone that acquires a high shine when polished. They also developed the first known system of writing in China.

Gods, kings, and priests

Shang society, like that of many dynasties that followed it in ancient Chinese history, was highly structured, with a king at the top and below him a set of *nobles.* Lower still were the common people, and below them a class that existed in many ancient societies: slaves. It was a rigidly defined *hierarchy* (HIRE-ahr-kee), with a vast and unbridgeable gulf between the top levels and the bottom. In that sense, it was not so different from the caste system imposed by the Aryans in India at about the same time. Like the Indian caste system, it had a basis in religion.

The Shang worshiped a number of gods, but the supreme deity was Shang Ti (shahng TEE), whose name means "The Lord on High." They believed that Shang Ti determined whether harvests would be good or bad or whether the nation would win or lose in battle. The king was the highest representative of Shang Ti on Earth. His ability to gain favor with the god determined his legitimacy, or right to rule. As long as he was righteous, he enjoyed a *mandate* (MAN-date; permission or authority to rule)—what the Chinese called the "Mandate of Heaven."

This was an idea typical of ancient societies: thus the Egyptian pharaohs were linked with the god Osiris, and Darius I of Persia announced that he ruled only by the grace of Ahura-Mazda. But in China, where the kings of the Shang Dynasty were believed to be direct *descendants* of Shang-Ti, the perceived link between the ruler and the gods was particularly strong. The Mandate of Heaven was a theme that would continue into modern times, as was the idea of communicating with the gods through one's *ancestors.* If the king prayed to the spirits of his ancestors, it was believed, they would in turn speak to the gods on his behalf.

In order to know the will of the gods, and the wisdom of the ancestors' spirits, the Shang used a system of *divination* (div-i-NAY-shun), the study of physical material in order to find *omens,* or messages from the gods concerning the future. Palm-reading is a well-known form of divination. Shang priests performed their divination with the shells of turtles or the bones of cattle or water buffalo. They would polish the outside of the shells or bones, then dig out holes on the inside to make them easier to crack. After this, they applied heat to the underside. As cracks appeared on the top, they would study these cracks much as a palm-reader observes the lines in a person's hand for "omens" concerning his or her future.

A modern president or prime minister governs through the help of advisors who specialize in areas such as foreign affairs or the economy. In a nation such as America in the twentieth century, where public opinion can make or break a leader, the president may also consult people who conduct polls, or surveys, to find out people's opinions. If the president learns that people do not like a certain policy, he may change it. Though modern people think of polls or studies by specialists as "scientific," the idea is not so different from that of ancient divination. In both cases, the ruler depends on people who can interpret signs in order to tell him what he should do.

Those who interpret the signs—though they may not be as well known publicly as the leader—are extremely influential figures. So it was with the priests of Shang China, who also served as scribes. Their ability to read and write the difficult Shang script was almost as important as their powers of divination.

Other forces in Shang society

In addition to the king and the priests, another important force in Shang society consisted of the royal *consorts* (KAHN-sohrtz), or wives. The role of the consorts is particularly interesting, because China, like most societies, did not grant women a particularly high social status; yet consorts were powerful and could even serve as military leaders. One of the more well-known consorts from Shang history was Fu Hao (foo HOW). She was probably one of the more than sixty-four wives of Shang ruler Wu Ting (woo DEENG), but she was especially powerful, shown by the great wealth of objects—including nineteen sacrificed human beings— in her tomb.

Other important figures in palace life included princes and officials. Because political and religious authority in Shang China were virtually inseparable, princes had the authority to perform religious *rituals* (ceremonies), as did consorts. Officials took on a variety of functions, acting as ministers in charge of specific areas of government or overseeing lower officials. The highly organized Shang state already had a well-developed *bureaucracy* (byoo-RAHK-ruh-see), a network of officials and lower-ranking workers who ran the state.

Beyond the areas directly ruled by the king, there were regions controlled by noblemen, or nobles, who exercised power over their areas but who also submitted to the authority of the Shang ruler. The Shang ruler maintained his position of strength with an army that numbered in the tens of thousands. The Shang used *infantry* (IN-fun-tree), or foot soldiers, as well as archers and chariots. A Shang chariot squadron consisted of five horse-drawn wagons, each with a driver, an archer, and a soldier bearing a battle axe. They must have been a frightening sight to enemies.

The Shang were not what one would describe as "a gentle people." Their legal system prescribed punishments that included mutilation or castration, as well as the tattooing of the face and forehead. On the other hand, there is evidence that people who had been convicted of a crime sometimes received a pardon from the king.

Nonetheless, it is clear that the Shang did not place a high emphasis on giving kindness to the poor or the weak. Shang China was a land in which the people tilled the earth with stone tools and lived in cavelike dwellings while the emperor and nobles enjoyed great luxury. In building their palaces, the wealthy and powerful would often command human sacrifices in order to ensure the gods' favor on their houses. These victims did not always come from the lower classes of Shang China, however: often they were prisoners captured in war. It appears that in a single ancestor-worship ceremony, the Shang sacrificed some 3,000 prisoners.

It should be pointed out, however, that while few ancient civilizations other than those in the Americas practiced human sacrifice, Shang China was probably no more harsh a place to live than most parts of the world during the period from c. 1700 to c. 1000 B.C. Not only was the caste system taking effect in India during the same era, it was a time when, according to the Bible, the Egyptians enslaved the Israelites; and when the Israelites, after escaping from Egypt,

A Look into the Chinese Mind

At one time or another, many an American child hears a story to the effect that, if one digs deep enough into the ground, one will come out on the other side of the world—in China, to be precise. Because it is on the other side of the world, the rumor goes, in China people walk upsidedown.

Of course the Chinese walk right-side up like the rest of humanity, but there is a little truth in the myth: to Americans, China is such a different place that it might as well be upside down. Chinese names, in fact, are "backwards" to Westerners: the family name goes first, and the first name, or given name, second. In its written form, the Chinese language is read from right to left, instead of left to right as in English. Chinese books are read from "back" to "front." For the Chinese, what an American would call the back of the book *is* the front.

The Chinese language is extremely difficult for Westerners to learn. In its spoken form it sounds nothing like the more familiar tongues of Europe. If one listens closely enough to someone speaking French, German, or Italian, one will hear plenty of words that have closely related English counterparts, because these languages are all related to English in the Indo-European family. In Chinese, on the other hand, none of the words sound familiar. Westerners often describe the sound of the spoken language as "singsong."

Given the unfamiliarity of Chinese ways to a Westerner, it is worthwhile for a student of Chinese history to understand the different way that the ancient Chinese viewed the world and the historical reasons behind those views. From ancient times, the Chinese considered themselves the "Middle Kingdom," meaning that they were the center of the world. This self-concept prevailed into modern times and helps to explain why China was slow to adapt to the changes brought by Europeans in the 1800s.

It is easy to understand why the Chinese held this view. In contrast to their own highly developed civilization, the nomads at their borders lived in huts and had no written language. Because the civilization of India lay beyond the high mountains of the Himalayas, and

dealt harshly with many of the peoples they conquered in the process of taking the Promised Land. Hammurabi's laws, which took effect in Babylon about the time the Shang Dynasty began, were unusual for even taking into account the rights of the less powerful.

because other ancient states such as Egypt or Babylonia were thousands of miles away, for a long time the Chinese thought that they were the only civilized people on earth.

These facts resulted in two other key aspects of Chinese history. Because China had no neighboring civilizations on a level with their own, Chinese monarchs could not form alliances with other countries by marrying into their royal houses, as for instance Ramses II of Egypt did when he took a Hittite bride. Instead, Chinese kings could only marry daughters of noblemen, and this sometimes created tense interfamily rivalries. Furthermore, unlike empires such as Persia, China seldom attempted to conquer other peoples, because there were no peoples to conquer—at least, no peoples the Chinese considered worth the effort. The focus of China, therefore, was inward rather than outward.

Instead of viewing themselves in contrast to other societies, people in a given era of Chinese history saw themselves in contrast to other times in China. When they looked closely at their history, they saw it not as a straight line—the way Westerners are accustomed to thinking of time—but rather as a series of cycles. A new ruling house would rise in the land, bringing with it prosperity and order. Over time, however, it would lose the "Mandate of Heaven." Its power would fall, resulting in a period of unrest that lasted until a new house arose.

These cycles seemed to last about 250 or 300 years, and this fact too influenced the Chinese view of the world. Whereas modern Americans are accustomed to looking at time in short spans, the Chinese, particularly the ancient Chinese, viewed time in centuries. This perspective resulted in a certain view of the individual and his or her place in the world.

If one looks at time in periods of 200 or 300 years and if one lives in the most populous nation on earth, it is hard to think that one person really matters a great deal in the grand scheme of things. Thus instead of asserting their individual wills (as Americans are certainly accustomed to doing), the Chinese tended to submit to the authority of rulers.

Achievements of Shang China

Shang society may not have been a model of social justice, but its areas of achievement were many and ranged from agriculture to the written word. As one might expect in such a rigidly structured society, even farming was organized according to hierarchy, with the king controlling the best lands, where his overseers put prisoners of war to work.

Crops grown on Shang farms included rice, soybeans, and millet, the latter a type of grain that they used in making everything from cereals to wines. It appears that Shang farmers employed *crop rotation,* an important agricultural advancement. Certain crops are particularly hard on soil, requiring a high amount of nutrients, and the land needs to be given periods of "rest" by growing other, less demanding crops.

Mulberry trees on farms in Shang China yielded a product for which China would become famous: silk. This extremely elegant, smooth fabric appeared in China around 1750 B.C., and after Europeans learned about it more than 2,800 years later, during the Middle Ages, it became a highly prized item in the West. Another plant grown on Chinese farms was hemp (hemp is a tall herb with tough fibers used in ropes and marijuana). The Shang made use of its narcotic qualities in medical treatments, much as cancer patients in twentieth-century America are allowed legal use of marijuana to ease the painful side effects associated with treatments for the disease.

Among the many vegetables grown on the farms of Shang China were cabbages, radishes, turnips, and scallions (green onions). Fruit farms abounded with melons, jujubes (JOO-joo-beez, similar to figs), peaches, apricots, and persimmons. The Shang also cultivated chestnuts and hazelnuts and raised a variety of farm animals.

Cows in Shang China provided a key ingredient in one of the world's favorite desserts, which made its first appearance in China about 2000 B.C.: ice cream. It is ironic that a famous milk product should emerge from China, because Chinese *cuisine* (KWI-zeen) makes little use of milk or by-products such as cheese or butter. In America, people consider it offensive if someone smells like garlic or onions, whereas the Chinese feel the same way about someone who smells like cheese or milk. Yet theirs was one of the first civilizations to practice milking of cows on a regular basis. Ice cream was made by mixing milk with soft rice, and then chilling this mixture in snow from the high mountains.

These many achievements in agriculture and food production helped fuel a healthy economy. Though the Lydians would become the first nation to actually coin money much later, the Shang used *cowries* (KOW-reez), bright shells from a type of ocean creature, as a form of coin.

Of course such an advanced society would hardly be possible without the development of written communication. The Shang had a system of writing that involved not only pictograms and phonograms but *ideograms* (ID-ee-oh-gramz). Whereas pictograms represent an object and phonograms a sound, an ideogram stands for an idea or a name. Examples of ideograms in everyday life include the dollar sign ($) or the percent sign (%), as well as corporate logos such as the "golden arches" of McDonald's or the three-pointed star of Mercedes-Benz.

From the beginning, Chinese writing was far more complex than that of other ancient societies: instead of a few dozen characters, as in the alphabets of Phoenicia and later Greece and Rome, or a few hundred symbols, as in the alphabets of Egypt or Sumer, the Shang used some 2,000 characters. These characters formed the basis for the Chinese written language, which remains in use today.

Another "language" developed by the Chinese of the Shang Dynasty was music. It appears that as early as 2700 B.C., Chinese musicians understood the concept of the *octave* (AHK-tev), a system of eight notes that forms the basis of a musical scale. (Many students of music in the Western world learn an octave through the familiar pattern *do-re-mi-fa-sol-la-ti-do*.)

As with ice cream, there is a certain irony to this fact, because most Chinese music uses scales that give it an unusual, twangy sound to Western ears. This sound results not from the instruments themselves—one could almost as easily play "Chinese-sounding" music on a guitar or violin—but from the choice of notes that make up a given scale. As for Chinese instruments, several of these developed under the Shang Dynasty as well, including flutes, various other reed instruments, and a bronze bell.

The Chou Dynasty (1027–246 B.C.)

According to legend, the last king of the Shang was a wicked ruler who by his cruelty lost the Mandate of Heaven; therefore, as some philosophers came to believe, the people were

7 2 3 0 1 8 9
NUMBER REPRESENTED

The abacus, a Chinese invention, is a tool used for counting. *Corbis-Bettmann. Reproduced by permission.*

justified in rebelling against him. The rebellion came in 1027 B.C., led by a prince named Wu Wang (woo WAHNG; "powerful warrior"). Wu belonged to a group of people from the western part of China called the Chou or Zhou (ZHOH). The Chou gave their name to the next phase of Chinese history.

The Chou Dynasty would last for a little more than 800 years, making it the longest-lasting dynasty in all of Chinese history. In fact, it would maintain power longer than any system in the history of the world, even longer than the Ottoman Empire in Turkey. Plenty of nations have existed for as long, of course, but not under the same system of rule. Compared with the Chou Dynasty, the history of the American political system, which began with the adoption of the Constitution in 1789, has been a short one.

The eight centuries of Chou rule were not a time of peace and stability, however; far from it. In fact, the extremely lengthy Chou period was broken into three segments of about 250 years, each marked by upheaval. Initially the Chou ruled from the capital city of Hao (HOW) along the River Wei (WAY), which feeds into the Yellow River in western China. Thus the period from 1027 to 771 B.C. would be known to historians as the Western Chou phase. In 771 B.C., however, an invasion by nomads from the north forced them to move hundreds of miles eastward to the city of Loyang (loh-YAHNG). As for the nomads, they would continue to pose a threat to China for centuries.

Although the entire period from 771 to the end of Chou rule in 246 B.C. is referred to as the Eastern Chou phase, most of this time fell into two parts, the second of which extended past the end of the Chou Dynasty: the Spring and Autumn Period (722–481 B.C.) and the Warring States Period (453–221 B.C.) The title "Spring and Autumn Period" sounds pleasant, but it was not. In fact the name comes from a set of annals describing the history of the era, which was a time of

Science in Ancient China

Science flourished throughout many phases of ancient Chinese history. The achievements of Chinese scientists covered a number of areas. At least as early as 1700 B.C., China had entered the *Bronze Age.* Archaeologists have found *Iron Age* tools that date back to about 1000 B.C. It appears that by the 400s B.C., the Chinese had passed on to the next step, making steel from iron.

Around 1500 B.C., Chinese astronomers created a calendar that took into account the phases of the Moon and the length of time it took for Earth to revolve around the Sun—that is, a year. They also recorded *eclipses,* as well as a *nova* (NOH-vuh), a star that suddenly grows extremely bright before fading. Their observations of events in space make it possible for historians to be absolutely certain about dates in Chinese history after 840 B.C.

In 613 B.C., the Chinese made the first recorded sighting of what came to be known as Halley's Comet, which passes by Earth approximately every seventy-six years, most recently in 1986. By the 300s B.C., astronomers in China had compiled a chart showing various stars' location and had identified the procession of the seasons. The seasons are determined by Earth's position relative to the Sun.

Some time after 100 B.C., Chinese mathematicians prepared a textbook on math. Around the same time, Chinese technology produced one of their ancient culture's greatest gifts to the world: paper. Not all Chinese experiments in science yielded such practical results, however: from an early time, scientists in China were fascinated with *alchemy* (AL-kim-ee). Alchemy is based on the idea that through chemical processes an ordinary metal such as iron can be changed into precious gold. Of course this is not possible. Nonetheless, the study of alchemy, which continued in Europe throughout the Middle Ages, helped form the basis for the modern science of chemistry.

near-constant warfare. The name of the Warring States Period leaves no doubt as to the constant upheaval that characterized this phase in Chinese history.

The feudal system and a new class structure

Under the Chou, China began to call itself "the Middle Kingdom." The Chinese—though they did not yet call themselves that—saw their country as the center of the world.

Despite their view of their nation as the Middle Kingdom, however, the Chou rulers were strong only during the Western Chou period. The end of that phase came because a king fell in love with one of his *concubines* (KAHNG-kyoo-bynz), and the relatives of his queen formed an alliance with the *"barbarian"* nomads beyond China. From that point on, various nobles competed with the king for power.

By the time of the Chou Dynasty, China had developed an extensive *feudal system* (FYOO-dul) not unlike the one that would prevail in Europe during the Middle Ages. In a feudal system, a nobleman, or feudal lord, owns vast areas of land that are worked by *peasants*. The peasants may own a small portion of the land that they till, but they do so only if the feudal lord allows them to. Much of their harvest goes to the lord, who in turn provides the peasants with protection against outsiders. The feudal lord is in turn subject to the king, turning over part of his wealth in exchange for the stability offered by a central government.

The feudal system implied a set of shared obligations between people lower on the social scale and those higher up. In the Spring and Autumn Period, however, the mutual obligations between the feudal lords and the king broke down, primarily because of the Chou monarchs' weak leadership. The nobles began to fight amongst themselves as well as against the waves of nomads who continually invaded from the north. Meanwhile, the kings spent most of their time in Loyang, the only area where they held real power.

This situation would become much worse during the Warring States Period, which saw the rise of a new class structure to replace the feudal system. The class structure of China was a little different from the one that prevailed in most ancient societies. The Chinese came to be divided into four groups, as the Indians were under the original caste system. However, the Chinese classes were far less rigid than the system of castes—or even the feudal arrangement that they replaced.

At the top of the social ladder were the *shih* (sounds like "she"), composed of nobles, aristocrats or wealthy people, warriors, priests, and scholars. Most ancient societies, by contrast, placed the last two categories in a separate class, just beneath the nobles, aristocrats, and warriors. Another difference from typical class structures was the high status accorded to peasants, or *nung* (NOONG), the next group. Chinese peasants, like their counterparts in other countries, were far from wealthy, but they came to hold much more respect because they tended the farms that fed the rest of the population. Next came *kung* (KOONG), who were tradespeople or artisans (AHR-ti-zuhnz). At the bottom were *shang,* or businesspeople.

The low status of merchants was yet another ironic fact of ancient Chinese history, because in the twentieth century, the Chinese would emerge as some of the most successful businesspeople in Asia. But in ancient China, the *shih* tended to oversee big business, meaning that the *shang* operated only small shops. Business itself was considered a necessary evil, a fact that would place the Chinese at a disadvantage against other cultures in the future.

At the time of its development, however, the Chinese class structure represented a triumph of social progress. It would prevail, largely unchanged, for more than 2,000 years, thanks in part to one of history's most outstanding individuals, the philosopher Confucius.

The age of great philosophers

In all of history, there have been a handful of individuals whose effect on human affairs was so great that it can truly be said the world would be a different place if they had not lived. Jesus Christ was one of those people, as was the Buddha. In fact, many of these central figures in history have been religious teachers or philosophers—not political leaders or conquerors—who, with few exceptions, led quiet lives.

Such was Confucius (551–479 B.C.), a scholar who earned his living as a tutor to young princes. He lived at the same time as Buddha and died not long before another world-changing individual, the Greek philosopher Socrates. He was also a *contemporary* of Lao-tzu (low-DZÜ; c. 500s B.C.) Lao-tzu was also a Chinese philosopher, but beyond that—and the fact that he too apparently led a quiet life—the two men had little in common.

The schools of thought that Confucius and Lao-tzu founded differed greatly, yet during the Spring and Autumn Period, and later the Warring States Period, China enjoyed a

Like Socrates (pictured), Confucius did not produce any known written works.
Corbis-Bettmann. Reproduced by permission.

sort of golden age in philosophy. This happened in spite of, or perhaps even because of, the turmoil that characterized those eras. Such was also true of the golden age in Greek philosophy, which likewise occurred against a backdrop of war and upheaval less than a century later.

Though a religion would later develop around Confucius's philosophy, his was not a spiritual teaching; instead, he taught principles of social harmony. Confucius believed that in order to achieve a stable and happy society, certain things were necessary: respect for one's elders, loyalty to family, and obedience to rulers. He praised the virtue of kings who treated their people kindly and wisely. He taught that education was the key to all improvement.

Like Socrates, Confucius did not produce any known written works, but his ideas are contained in a book called the *Analects* (AN-uh-lektz). Confucius died in disappointment, unaware that his ideas, which received little attention in his lifetime, would later become the basis for Chinese social organization over thousands of years. The success of Confucian thought owes much to his *disciple* Mencius (MIN-see-uhs; c. 370–290 B.C.), who nonetheless differed from his teacher in some significant ways.

Confucius once said, "I believe in the past and love it," but Mencius was not such a great lover of stability and tradition. Mencius taught that people are basically good and created equal—ideas that sound remarkably like those that fueled the American Revolution in 1776 A.D. The American Declaration of Independence states that when a political system becomes too oppressive, the people are justified in revolting against it. This, too, was a principle taught by Mencius, who wrote that it was appropriate for the populace to rise up against a king who had lost the Mandate of Heaven.

In spite of the differences between the two, the ideas of Confucius and Mencius would in time come together as a philosophy that promoted ideas of mutual respect and harmony between people. Confucius's belief in a stable social order would prevail, and along the way, a religion would develop around his ideas. However, Confucianism, which is still practiced by millions of Chinese, is not a "religion" in the traditional sense. It allows followers to worship the gods of their choice. Its primary emphasis is on the Confucian principle of respect for one's elders, including ancestors.

A religion, Taoism (DOW-izm), would develop around the ideas of Lao-tzu. Whereas Confucius had assumed that it was essential for people to be actively engaged in the political life around them, Lao-tzu taught just the opposite. To Lao-tzu, whose name means "Master Lao," true harmony lay within the soul, not in the social order. He believed that it was important to be at one with Nature, and this required pulling back from social affairs in order to live a life of quiet meditation. With regard to government, Lao-tzu taught that it should be small and weak and should leave its citizens alone.

The Chinese believed that the combination of yin and yang produced everything that existed. *Archive Photos. Reproduced by permission.*

Obviously, there was a great deal of difference between Confucianism and Taoism, whose principles are contained in a book, probably not written entirely by Lao-tzu, called the *Tao te Ching* (dow-day-KEENG) or *Way of Virtue*. But the two schools of thought were not at war with one another; instead, the Chinese—particularly students of yet another school, Naturalism—believed that for every force in one direction, it was right and necessary that there should be a force in the opposite direction. On the one side, there was an active, masculine force called *yang*; on the other, an inactive, feminine quality known as *yin*. The combination of yin and yang, it was believed, produced everything that existed. This concept would become central to Chinese thought.

"Invasion Tatare," battle between the Mongols and the Tatars on horseback.
Archive Photos. Reproduced by permission.

As China underwent the Warring States Period, Chinese philosophy entered what was called the "Hundred Schools" era. As its name suggests, many schools of thought flourished during that time—not only the ideas of Mencius and other followers of Confucius, but the early Taoists and many others. Among these was Mo-tzu (moh-DZÜ; c. 479–438 B.C.) Mo-tzu and his followers, known as Moists, urged rulers to treat their subjects kindly and encouraged the people of the warring states to look upon their enemies as their brothers.

In contrast to this gentle view of humankind was the school of thought known as Legalism, which had its origins in the teachings of the Ch'in advisor Shang Yang (fl. 350–338 B.C.; see sidebar). Whereas most of the other prominent schools of thought in China at the time held that humankind was good at heart, the Legalists believed that human nature was essentially bad. That being the case, people needed strong, harsh rulers who would keep them in line. Chief among the

Legalists was Han Fei-tzu (hahn fay-SOO; c. 280–233 B.C.), who wrote that "the ruler alone should possess all power." Soon such a ruler would appear.

The Ch'in Dynasty (221–207 B.C.)

During the Warring States Period, a particularly strong kingdom under the leadership of the Ch'in, or Qin (JIN) arose in the west, in what is now Szechuan (ZESH-wahn) Province. The Ch'in were hard, rugged monarchs, and they treated their people mercilessly. Under their leadership, a huge army of slave laborers dug a canal that joined the Ching and Lo rivers in 246 B.C., thus making possible extensive irrigation. As a result, the area became so lush that its farms outproduced all others.

Shih-huang-ti was the name Prince Cheng ruled under from 221-210 B.C.

The Ch'in rulers were not merely harsh leaders. There was a system to their iron rule, making their state in some ways a forerunner of modern *totalitarianism* [see sidebar]. A quarter-century after the end of the Chou Dynasty, the Ch'in had built up such great power that in 221 B.C., their Prince Cheng declared himself emperor over China. Thus was born the Ch'in Dynasty, which lasted only fourteen years, but which had proportionately the greatest influence on Chinese history of any period before or since. The very name *China,* as a matter of fact, is a variation on "Ch'in."

Prince Cheng took the name Ch'in Shih-huang-ti (shee-HWAHNG-tee) and ruled as such from 221 to 210 B.C. In contrast to the weak rule of the later Chou kings, the Ch'in government was rigidly organized in a hierarchy that began with the emperor and went all the way down to the village level. The term "emperor," in fact, had never been used for a Chinese ruler to this time, but it would remain in use for more than 2,100 years, until A.D. 1912.

Totalitarianism and the Ch'in State

Throughout history, kind and enlightened rulers such as Asoka of the Mauryan Empire have been rare. There have been plenty of cruel leaders, but the vast majority have been more like Nebuchadnezzar II of Babylonia or Darius I of Persia—that is, good in some ways and bad in others.

Modern times are no exception, and in fact perhaps the greatest collection of truly heartless leaders came to power in the twentieth century. These included Adolf Hitler of Nazi Germany (1889–1945), Josef Stalin of Soviet Russia (1879–1953), China's own Mao Zedong (mow zhay-DAWNG; 1893–1976), and Pol Pot (pohl PAHT; 1925–1998) of Cambodia (kam-BOH-dee-uh). The first three together were responsible for the deaths of millions upon millions of people. Although Pol Pot killed "only" about two million in the years 1975 to 1979, the fact that this occurred in a country with just five million citizens makes him, proportionately, the greatest mass murderer in history.

What made these killings possible? To an extent, technology can be blamed:

instead of spears and swords, their armies had tanks and machine guns. But the vast majority of their victims did not die in war; rather, they died in concentration camps, places where political prisoners were held until they died of starvation or overwork or were murdered. What truly fueled the murders committed by Hitler, Stalin, Mao, and Pol Pot were ideas.

Each of these tyrants subscribed to political beliefs—Nazism in Hitler's case and communism in the case of the other three—commonly described as *totalitarianism* (toh-tal-ih-TARE-ee-uhn-izm.) As its name suggests, totalitarianism calls for total control of the country by its leaders. In a totalitarian system, everything from the economy to schooling to even such seemingly innocent activities as sports and the arts must come under state control. In order to maintain that control, totalitarian leaders deal ruthlessly with anyone who opposes their aims, or who *might* oppose them.

In some ways, the Ch'in state that emerged in western China during the 300s B.C. served as an early model for

The empire of the Ch'in was far more unified than the empires of the Persians or Alexander. The emperor destroyed the power of the nobility, uniting the nation under his supreme power. He strengthened the military greatly. He ordered the building of a vast nationwide system of roads and canals to keep his armies supplied. He *standardized* weights and totalitarianism. Unlike earlier kings, the Ch'in rulers had a clearly defined system that was at least as much the product of scholars and philosophers as it was the creation of kings. In grade school terms, one might say that the class bullies had joined forces with the class "brains."

One such "brain" was Shang Yang, who served in the Ch'in court from 350 to 338 B.C. Shang Yang believed that everyone and everything in the country should center around its ruler, who should command his people's total obedience. He helped create a justification for the Ch'in *police state,* writing that the power of the government should be so great that the people would be less afraid of fighting an enemy nation than they would be of falling into the hands of the Ch'in authorities.

It is doubtful that Shang Yang's ideas had any effect on Hitler or Stalin, who had probably never heard of him. But Mao, who modeled himself on ancient Chinese leaders, most certainly had. In China during the 1950s and 1960s, he built a police state that rivaled any that had ever existed. In an attempt to root out all opposition, in 1966 he launched what was called the "Cultural Revolution," sending young soldiers out into the country to deal with anyone who seemed to oppose Communist or "Chinese" ways.

These included not only people who wanted to farm their land without government supervision but also those who wore Western clothes or listened to Western music. Millions died, and millions more had their lives ruined. A few years later in Cambodia, a Southeast Asian country historically influenced by China, Pol Pot modeled his own massacres on those committed by Mao. (The 1988 film *The Last Emperor* and the 1985 picture *The Killing Fields* provide excellent recreations of events in China and Cambodia, respectively.)

As for Shang Yang, he lived to regret the ideas he promoted. He had said that the king should deal harshly with his subjects. So in 338 B.C., the Ch'in ruler did—by executing a trusted court official named Shang Yang.

measures; the *currency,* or money; the written language; and even the size of vehicle axles. But most of all, he put his people to work in slave-labor gangs.

Unlike the Egyptians who built the Great Pyramids, the Chinese who built the Great Wall of China did not do so willingly. The Wall was intended to keep out the nomads to

The Great Wall of China

Of all the objects created by human hands, none is quite so spectacular as the Great Wall of China. For one thing, it is quite simply the largest man-made object on Earth, the only human creation visible from the Moon. It is a monumental achievement, perhaps the best-known symbol of China throughout the world.

Begun under the reign of the emperor Ch'in Shih-huang-ti in 221 B.C., the Wall was built to repel invaders threatening China from the north. Originally it stretched some 1,500 miles (2,414 kilometers), but it was later extended by the Han Dynasty after 200 B.C. Still later, under the Ming Dynasty, which ruled from A.D. 1368 to 1644, further improvements were made.

Because parts of it were later torn down, the Great Wall is not one continuous structure. Nonetheless, it stretches some 2,150 miles (3,460 kilometers) across northern China. Nor is it just a humble stone fence: its height ranges from 20 to 30 feet (6 to 9 meters). It is 12 feet (3.7 meters) across, broad enough for two mounted warriors to pass one another without either having to move to the side. It is made of earth and stone, with a brick exterior, and is dotted with hundreds and hundreds of guard towers.

the north, the Hsiung Nu (shung NOO), relatives of the Huns who would later threaten the Roman Empire. Its location in the cold mountains and deserts of northern China was an inhospitable one. Some 300,000 people worked on the Great Wall, and thousands of them—the exact death toll will probably never be known—died building it.

For all their labors, the Great Wall, built for the purpose of keeping out the "barbarians" from the north, failed to do so; the invaders simply kept coming around it. On the other hand, many of these nomadic tribes—most notably the Huns—kept moving westward, where they would influence the histories of Persia and India as well as Europe. In this way, the building of the Great Wall had an enormous impact not only on Chinese history, but on world history.

Ch'in Shih-huang-ti died in 210 B.C. and was buried in a style as lavish as that of any Egyptian pharaoh. His tomb contained some 6,000 life-size soldiers made of terra-cotta (TARE-uh KAH-tuh), a type of clay. It was as though the soldiers, many of which sat on terra-cotta horses, were ready to go into battle. A vast array of other treasures have been discovered in the tomb, including chariots, weapons, and even items of linen and silk. Discovered in 1974, the tomb is one of the greatest archaeological sites in the world.

During his lifetime, the people had been unhappy with the iron rule of Ch'in Shih-huang-ti, but because of his enormous power, no one had dared to revolt. After his death, however, a power struggle ensued. Finally in 202 B.C., a new leader named Liu Pang (lee-YOO BAHNG) emerged to establish the Han (HAHN) Dynasty.

The Han and Hsin dynasties (207 B.C.–A.D. 220)

The Han would rule China for more than 400 years, with an interruption of fourteen years. The first phase of Han rule, known to historians as the "Former Han," lasted from 207 B.C. to A.D. 9. In the latter year, a *usurper* named Wang Mang (wahng MAHNG) took the throne and established the short-lived Hsin (DZIN) Dynasty. Fourteen years later, in A.D. 23, the Han regained control, ushering in the period known as the Later Han, which lasted until A.D. 220.

Beginning with the Han, the Chinese adopted a custom of naming their emperors posthumously (PAHS-chum-us-lee; that is, after their death.) Thus during his lifetime, Liu Pang never used the name by which he would become known to Chinese historians: Kao-tzu (gow-DZÜ). Kao-tzu (r. 207–195 B.C.) came from a background of extreme poverty and rose to his position through a combination of cleverness and strong will. Probably illiterate, he had little use for scholars. For this reason the followers of Confucius initially played little role in the Han government. He was a popular ruler nonetheless, a breath of fresh air after Ch'in oppression.

Kao-tzu and the emperors who followed him had to negotiate a difficult situation with the noblemen, eager to regain the power taken from them under Ch'in rule. Later, the emperor Wu-ti (woo-DEE; r. 141–87 B.C.) managed to replace the authority of the noblemen with that of officials. The rise of these officials led to the triumph of Confucian scholars, who—because of their education, not to mention their philosophy, with its emphasis on order in the empire—were ideally suited to positions in the Han state. In 130 B.C., Wu-ti established a set of examination questions for civil servants. These would form the basis for a system of civil service exams, formally established in A.D. 600, that would continue to be used for more than a thousand years.

Though Han rule was more gentle than that of the Ch'in Dynasty, Han Wu-ti nonetheless reinforced the idea of government control over the economy. When people began to privately *mint* (produce) copper coins, this created a situation of *inflation* or rising prices. The Han treasury issued notes to buy back these coins and end the inflation. Usually the term "note," when used in an economic sense, refers to paper money, but the Han notes were animal skins; in any case, like paper money today, they were a symbol of the government's economic power, which gave them their value. Han Wu-ti also sought control over *industry* (production and sale of goods) establishing a government *monopoly* (exclusive control), for instance, over the production of salt and iron.

In foreign affairs, Wu-ti was occupied, as were most ancient Chinese emperors, with the problem of the "barbarians," a situation that would lead to additions to the Great Wall. In the 130s B.C., he sent a representative named Chang Chi'en to the west to try to play the Hsiung Nu off against one another. Along the way, the official came in contact with the Yüeh Chih, a nomadic people who had absorbed aspects of Greek civilization from the Greco-Bactrians they had conquered. This was the first Chinese contact with another civilization; formerly, they had believed that there were no civilized peoples beyond their borders.

The Hsin and Later Han (A.D. 9–220)

But the problem of the Hsiung Nu did not go away, and rulers that followed Han Wu-ti failed to deal with them. This mismanagement, combined with economic problems, paved the way for Wang Mang's brief usurpation. A powerful figure in the Han court, Wang Mang took power in A.D. 9, but his "Hsin

Dynasty" would consist of no rulers except himself. As emperor, Wang Mang tried to break the power of wealthy families by forcing them to give up lands to peasants who had none. This proved too much for the noblemen, who had become increasingly unhappy with their loss of power under the Former Han. They aided the Han in overthrowing Wang Mang in A.D. 23.

Kuang-wu (kwahng-WOO; r. A.D. 23–58) became the first ruler of the Later Han, but in this second phase, Han power would never be as great as it had been. The reason was that in replacing Wang Mang, Kuang-wu had been forced to depend on the noblemen. After the Han returned to power, the noblemen expected something in return. Gradually the power of the nobles returned, and along with it the feudal system.

The influence of *eunuchs* (YOU-nukz) within the emperor's court also began to grow. A eunuch is a man who has been castrated, thus making him incapable of having sex. Monarchs in many parts of the ancient world favored eunuchs as palace attendants, for the obvious reason that their wives and concubines would be safe around them. But what they lacked in sexual desire, the eunuchs of the Later Han more than made up for in their desire for power. Many of them became skilled at political intrigue, pitting noblemen and officials against one another and reveling in the squabbles that followed.

The Later Han period also saw the rise of a new religious force: Taoism. Up to this point, most of the Chinese people continued to uphold traditional faiths such as animal worship. Buddhism had yet to appear in China. Though Confucianism had long since taken hold, it did so primarily within the group of scholars who ran much of the government. Taoism, on the other hand, offered a faith for the masses of people. One of the new movement's principal leaders was Chang Tao-ling (chahng dow-LING; c. A.D. 34–156), who helped formalize the ideas of ancient Chinese philosopher Lao-tzu into a religion.

Lao-tzu, who had little use for politics, would probably have been surprised to see the short-lived, semi-independent state established by Chang Tao-ling and his followers on the edge of Szechuan Province. This move would in turn inspire a group called the Yellow Turbans, who in A.D. 184 revolted against the emperor. Actually, they were revolting against the eunuchs, but as the uprising spread to the countryside, it began to gather steam.

The "Barbarians" of Central Asia

The term "Central Asia" describes a loosely defined area which stretches from the Aral Sea in the west to the Gobi Desert in the east, and from the Tibetan Plateau in the south to Lake Baikal in the north. Today this region includes the nations of Kazakhstan and Mongolia, as well as southern Siberia (a part of Russia) and northwest China. In ancient times, it was the homeland of various peoples referred to by the Chinese as "barbarians."

The word *civilization* has a very distinct meaning. To say that a group of people is uncivilized does not imply a value judgment, any more than it is a value judgment to say that a circle is not a square. The word "barbarian," on the other hand, is usually a negative, prejudicial term not unlike "savage." It suggests a person who slaughters men, rapes women, kidnaps children, and generally causes destruction wherever he goes.

The peoples of Central Asia were most certainly uncivilized; on the other hand, not all of them deserved the name "barbarian" that the Chinese gave them. Most probably did, it is true, but some of these nomads absorbed Chinese culture and became civilized. In any case, the Chinese would later refer to Europeans as barbarians also.

Whether they were barbarians or merely uncivilized, the nomads of Central Asia would have an enormous impact on Chinese and world history. These hardy peoples, outstanding horsemen highly skilled at lightning-quick assaults on their enemies, were among the most powerful and feared warriors of the ancient world. Because of their nomadic lifestyle, which continually required fresh pastures for their animals, they were restless and always on the move.

Over time, central Asian tribes migrated in various directions. The Scythians and other groups moved westward into what is now the Ukraine and Caucasus regions in about 1000 B.C.

A military leader named Ts'ao Ts'ao (DZOW-dzow; c. A.D. 150–230) suppressed the revolt in A.D. 189. Nine years later, in A.D. 208, he marched his troops against the Sun family, who were attempting to create a separate state called Wu in a large area south of the Yangtze (YAHNG-zay) River. The boats of the newly proclaimed Sun Dynasty fought him off in a river battle at Ch'i Pi.

Ts'ao Ts'ao effectively assumed leadership of what was left of Han China, though in fact it still had an emperor. In A.D.

The Yüeh-Chih, whose most powerful group became known as the Kushans, pushed into India, Persia, and surrounding areas in the mid-100s B.C. and would greatly influence the history of that region.

Among the groups that most directly affected China were the Hsien Pei and the HsiungNu. The Hsien Pei reached their high point during the troubled days of the Later Han, when they took advantage of unrest in about A.D. 100 to launch an attack on their "barbarian" enemies, the HsiungNu. Under Tang-shi-huai (dahng-shee-HWIE) in about A.D. 150, they conquered a vast area, wider than the modern-day United States. Though the Hsien Pei holdings receded quickly after the death of Tang-shi-huai, this great conquest would serve as a model for Central Asian empires in years to come. Many such empires would rise—and, because of the nomads' small populations and lack of skill and knowledge in ruling, quickly fall—over the next 1,300 years.

As for the HsiungNu, they reasserted their power after the passing of Tang-shi-huai and, by means of intermarriage and migration, extended their reach through space and time. Some moved westward, where they became known as "Huns." Led by Attila in the A.D. 400s, they would, along with various tribes of northern Europe, take part in the destruction of the Roman Empire. Others married Hsien Pei and members of other nations. Out of this line would come the Turkic and Mongol peoples, who greatly affected world history for a period of many centuries beginning in the Middle Ages. Various Turks and Mongols terrorized medieval Europe; conquered Anatolia (modern Turkey); swept through Persia and surrounding lands; established the powerful Mogul Empire in India; and, under Genghis Khan in the 1200s, conquered China.

220, however, the last Han ruler was overthrown. China, already troubled, was about to enter a period of unrest that would last for more than three centuries.

A period of crisis (A.D. 221–420)

The years from A.D. 221 to 265 were known as the time of the Three Kingdoms. To the north, in what had been the power center of the Han, was the kingdom of Wei (WAY), ruled by the son of Ts'ao Ts'ao. South of the Yangtze was the Sun Dynasty's kingdom of Wu; and westward, in Szechuan, was a third kingdom, Shu. This period might be likened to the Civil War in America (1861–1865): both events were very painful times in China's history that would be remembered with a great deal of emotion on both sides. *The Romance of the Three Kingdoms,* a *novel* written more than a thousand years later, provides a fictionalized account that depicts this as a period of romantic heroism.

In A.D. 265, the state of Wei came under the control of the Western Chin Dynasty, which would rule until 316. Within 15 years, the Western Chin had conquered Wu and Shu, bringing all of China back together again. But in 316, the "barbarians"—both the Hsiung Nu and the Hsien Pei (shin-PAY) from Central Asia—invaded the north. This time, the invaders held on to what they had captured, and it would be a long time until China was whole again.

Going back to the time of the Later Han, the weakened emperors of that dynasty had depended on the help of various nomadic tribes in fighting other, less friendly, groups of "barbarians." Often these helpful foreigners, after aiding the Han in battle, would settle in Chinese territory. This of course was not something the Chinese rulers wanted, but they were hardly in a position to refuse. Worse, the "barbarians" who settled in China began to adopt the more civilized ways of the Chinese, which might seem like a good thing, but a more educated enemy—and the nomads were still enemies of the Chinese, whether they helped them or not—is a more dangerous enemy.

In Rome a few years later, the "barbarians" began to adopt civilized Roman ways. The Romans, like the Chinese of the Later Han and the eras that followed, increasingly relied on the warlike tribesmen to help them fight their wars. But whereas the Huns and others would bring down the Roman Empire forever, the invaders did not destroy imperial China for good.

Like the Chou Dynasty long before, the Chin Dynasty had its "Western" phase and its "Eastern" phase. Again like the Chou, the Eastern phase represented a much-weakened empire. The Eastern Chin Dynasty (A.D. 317–420) claimed much of what had formerly been the Wu state of the Sun Dynasty in the

Buddhist temple.
Susan D. Rock. Reproduced by permission.

south and east. The nomads from the north might have conquered the south as well, had a vastly outnumbered Eastern Chin army not held off some 270,000 horsemen in a battle at Fei Shui (fay SHWEE) in A.D. 383. In 386, the Toba, who like the Hsien Pei were Tartars (TAHR-tuhrz) from Central Asia, invaded the north and established their own dynasty, the Toba Wei (A.D. 386–554). Rather than remaining nomads, they settled down and adopted Chinese ways.

In the late A.D. 300s, things began to stabilize somewhat, with the Toba Wei in control of the north and the Eastern Chin holding the south. It was during this time that Buddhism entered China, assuming quite a different form than it had in India. The Chinese adopted what was called Mahayana Buddhism (mah-huh-YAH-nuh; "Great Vehicle"), which held that others could become buddhas by following the teachings of the Buddha. In 399, a Chinese Buddhist named Fa-hsien (fa-SHIN) traveled south to study the religion firsthand in India. The teachings he brought back quickly spread throughout China.

China to the modern day

The country reunified under the Sui Dynasty (SWEE; A.D. 581–618), which further built up the Great Wall. Confucianism and the arts flourished under the T'ang Dynasty (618–907), but after the T'ang came another of the periods of upheaval that dotted China's long history. Later, after three centuries of rule by the Sung Dynasty (SOONG; 960–1279), the thing happened that the ancient Chinese had always feared: nomads from the north known as Mongols (MAHNG-guhlz) conquered all of China.

Instead of destroying the country, however, the Mongols established a Chinese-style dynasty, the Yuan (yoo-WAHN; 1271–1368). It was during this period that the famed Italian traveler Marco Polo (1254–1324) visited the country. As it turned out, the Mongols did not absorb China; rather, China, with its vastly greater numbers and its highly developed civilization, absorbed the Mongols.

Marco Polo, though he came in peace and greatly admired the achievements of the Chinese, served as an indicator of a force that would prove much more dangerous to China than the Mongols: Europe. Reawakening from the long period of darkness and superstition that had enveloped most of their continent during the Middle Ages, Europe was flowering, with advancements in the arts, sciences, and exploration. Europeans made increasing contact with China during the Ming Dynasty (1368–1644). They found there a quaint, exotic culture that still held on to traditions nearly 2,000 years old. While Europe was experiencing rapid change, Ming China held on to Confucian principles that, while they might have been an advancement at the time Confucius formulated them, now represented a throwback to the distant past.

A harsh introduction to the modern world

In 1644, a group of northern Chinese called the Manchus (MAN-chooz) established what would be the last Chinese dynasty. The Manchu, or Ch'ing Dynasty, lasted until 1912 and saw a period of increasing European involvement in China. But the people of the West were no longer content just to visit: they demanded that the Ch'ing leaders open the country up to foreign trade. While contact with the outside certainly had its positive aspects, events such as the Opium War (1839–1842) served only to reinforce the desires of the Chinese to remain closed off to the outside world.

The war resulted from British attempts to sell *opium* (OH-pee-uhm), a powerful drug similar to heroin, in China; understandably, the Ch'ing rulers did not want them to. Britain easily defeated the Chinese, who went into battle like people out of another time (which they were). Whereas the British had the most powerful army in the world, with state-of-the art military technology, the Chinese sailed out to meet them in creaky old warships. On board one Chinese ship was a poet, commissioned by the emperor to write an ode celebrating what would certainly be a Chinese victory.

The Opium War ended with the British gaining control of Hong Kong, an island off the southern coast of China. Though the war was no doubt the most disgraceful act by any foreign power against China, it was far from the only one. Soon France, Germany, and Russia all had forced China into unequal treaties that allowed those countries to trade extensively in the country without having to be subject to its laws.

Chiang Kai-shek (seated in garden). *Archive Photos. Reproduced by permission.*

As though the attacks by enemies from outside were not enough, China was fraught with internal troubles as well. The Tai-ping (dy-PEENG) Rebellion (1850–1864) was one of the bloodiest civil wars of all time, making its name—which means "heavenly peace"—particularly ironic. Nor were Europeans the only foreigners eager to gain control of China. In 1894, the Chinese fought the first of two wars with a new rising power in the East, Japan.

No wonder then that in 1898, the Chinese made one last attempt to throw out the foreigners. The Boxer Rebellion (1898–1900), while it claimed fewer lives than the Tai-ping

Opium is a drug
manufactured from the
dried juice of a poppy plant.
*Photograph by Robert J.
Huffman. Field Mark
Publications. Reproduced
by permission.*

Rebellion, had even more far-reaching consequences. It brought yet another outside force to bear in Chinese affairs. The United States sent in its Marines to help the other nations put down the uprising and spelled the end of China as an independent force.

China in the twentieth century

A revolution in 1911 overthrew the last emperor of China. In 1912 Sun Yat-sen (1866–1925) established a republic that lasted for just four years. Then China once again dissolved into confusion in an era that recalled the Warring States Period. Beginning in 1916, various warlords ruled the land, but in 1927, a combined force defeated them.

This combined force consisted of two opposing groups. On the one side were the Nationalists, led by Chiang Kai-shek (zhuhng kie-SHEK; 1887–1975), a follower of Sun Yat-sen who favored alliances with the West. On the other side were the Communists, led by Mao Zedong (mow zhay-

DAWNG; 1893–1976), who allied themselves with Soviet Russia. Their period of uneasy cooperation ended in 1934, when Chiang turned against Mao, forcing the Communists on the "Long March," a 6,000-mile retreat deep into the countryside.

Meanwhile, Japan had invaded Manchuria in 1931. Though World War II began in Europe in 1939, for the Chinese it started in 1937, when the Japanese launched a full-scale attack on them. The defeat of the Japanese in 1945 did not bring peace, however. There followed a four-year civil war between the Nationalists, who had heavy American backing, and the Communists. The latter emerged triumphant in 1949.

Mao soon involved his country in the Korean War (1950–1953), which pitted the Chinese and North Koreans against South Korea, the United States, and other nations. The war ended in a

Emperor Ch'ien-lung (1711-1799) was a most successful Manchu ruler. He established trade relations with the United States, and eliminated Turk and Mongol threats to China. *Archive Photos. Reproduced by permission.*

stalemate, leaving Korea divided. China, too, was divided, the Nationalists having fled to the island of Taiwan (tie-WAHN), where they established an independent state. Meanwhile, Hong Kong remained in British hands. Over the next decades, it would grow to become an economic powerhouse.

Recognizing that his own nation's economy lagged far behind much of the world, Mao tried to spur it into rapid industrialization through a program he called the "Great Leap Forward" (1958–1960). In his eagerness to transform the Chinese economy overnight, Mao practically wrecked it, bringing about a famine that claimed more than twenty million lives.

Although it called itself the "People's Republic of China," China under the Communists was a totalitarian system that allowed little room for viewpoints that differed from Mao's. In 1957, using words that harkened back to the "Hundred Schools" period, he invited Chinese intellectuals—that is, thinkers and writers—to make their ideas known. "Let a hun-

Elsewhere in East Asia and the Pacific

In ancient times, China was the most notable civilization in the Far East, but the Chinese were far from the only people in the region; nor was China the only settled country. There were peoples and nations all around it, extending far into the Pacific Ocean to the east, and many of these would rise to much greater prominence in the medieval and modern eras.

To the east was the Korean peninsula, which since World War II (1939–1945) has been divided into two countries, but which was one nation for much of its history. A land that traces its origins to c. 3000 B.C, Korea in ancient times was called Choson (chow-SAHN). Linguists are not entirely certain where the Korean language came from, but it may be related to Mongolian, which would suggest that the Koreans and Mongolians are closely related. China conquered Korea in 108 B.C., but in the A.D. 600s Korea emerged as three independent kingdoms.

Still farther to the east is Japan. Though in modern times Japan has been by far the most dynamic force in East Asia, it was late in developing. The Japanese trace their history back to 660 B.C, when the Yamato (yah-MAH-toh) clan established its rule. The true history of Japan did not begin until about A.D. 500, however, when the Japanese adopted the art of writing from the Chinese. Buddhism arrived half a century later, but many of the Japanese held on to their old religion, Shinto (SHIN-toh), a belief system based on the idea that there are divine forces in all living things. Even today, Shinto is at least as prominent in Japanese life as Buddhism is.

Southeast Asia experienced the influence both of China to the north and India to the west. The influence of India can be seen today in the written languages of modern Burma, Thailand, Cambodia, and Laos, which look much like Sanskrit; and in the religion of Buddhism. At one time, Hinduism was a powerful force in Southeast Asia as well, and it remains influential in some parts of the region. Evidence of Indian culture was particularly strong in Funan (foo-NAHN), a kingdom that controlled much of the area by about A.D. 100.

At the same time, China reasserted its claims over Southeast Asia, claims which dated back to the time of the Ch'in Dynasty. But Chinese interests only went so far: they placed two bronze

dred flowers bloom," he announced. "Let a hundred schools contend." Many of these intellectuals took him at his word and began to criticize the government. There followed a series of arrests, imprisonments, and executions.

pillars, somewhere in what is now northern Vietnam, to mark the southern edge of the civilized world. Meanwhile, the Romans far to the west did much the same thing with Hadrian's Wall in Britain. Beyond those markers, the Chinese said, lived demons and savages; in reality, beyond those markers was the coastal kingdom of Champa (CHAHM-puh), in what is now Vietnam.

Off the coast of Southeast Asia are Java, Bali, and other exotic islands that came to be known as the East Indies, or the modern nation of Indonesia. Indonesia is at the far eastern edge of the Indian Ocean, which became, in the first few centuries A.D., an important "pipeline" for trade between East Asia, India, Africa, and Europe. By about A.D. 400, boats were bringing people from the East Indies as far west as Madagascar (mad-uh-GAS-kahr), a large island off the eastern coast of Africa.

On the eastern side of Indonesia is the Pacific Ocean, which contains some 25,000 islands. South of Indonesia is the continent of Australia and surrounding islands, including those that make up the modern nation of New Zealand.

Sometimes these regions are lumped together under the name "Oceania" (OH-shuh-nuh), a fitting title since the area is mostly under water.

About 50,000 years ago, people migrated from Southeast Asia to Australia. These people are referred to as Aborigines (ab-uh-RIJ-uh-neez), meaning "natives," and they controlled the continent until Europeans began arriving in the A.D. 1600s. Though the Aborigines never had anything approaching an organized civilization—for instance, they had no written language—they possessed a highly developed culture. Their mythology was extensive and included tales of how the world was created by their ancestors in a long-gone age they called "the Dreamtime."

In about 1800 B.C., shipbuilders in Indonesia began constructing canoes big enough to cross wide stretches of ocean, and thereafter people began to arrive on the far-flung islands of the Pacific. By about A.D. 400, they had settled as far away as Easter Island, which is only a couple of thousand miles off the coast of South America.

During the 1960s, China broke away from the Soviet Union because Mao felt that its leaders were compromising the rigid principles of the Communist party. From then on, the Chinese Communists charted their own course. Mao's version

Four army tanks drive through Tianamen Square, as one protester stands his ground. In 1989, students in Beijing protested for democratic reforms resulting in a brutal, military suppression. *Reuters/Corbis-Bettmann. Reproduced by permission.*

of Communism was distinctly Chinese, identifying the Communist system with China and Mao with the ancient emperors. In 1966, he launched the Cultural Revolution, an attempt to root out anything that could be defined as anti-Communist or anti-China. A group of armed youths known as the "Red Guards" stormed into cities and towns, slaughtering millions of people and herding millions more into "reeducation camps," where many died from starvation or overwork. Though the worst days of the Cultural Revolution were over in 1969, and it officially came to an end with Mao's death in 1976, few Chinese families were not affected in some way by this great disaster.

As was typical with ancient monarchs, the death of Mao brought about a power struggle. In 1977, an enemy of Mao named Deng Xiaoping (duhng show-PING; 1904–1997) emerged as leader. Deng too sought to make his country's economy competitive with those of other nations, but he did so more carefully. He encouraged trade with the West, a process already begun by Mao. After a long period of hostility toward the United States, in 1972 Mao invited U.S. President Richard Nixon (1913–1994) for a visit, and relations between the two countries improved in the years following.

China increasingly came to compete with the United States and Soviet Union as a superpower. It tested its first nuclear weapon in 1964, and in 1970 China launched its first satellite. With the end of Mao's rule and the improvements that Deng brought to the economy, it became apparent that by the twenty-first century, China would emerge as an economic superpower as well. Its government began to encourage free economic activity, particularly in cities along the southern coast. In the 1990s, China experienced a new and unaccustomed form of upheaval. Everywhere throughout the country, there were new buildings going up, factories and businesses opening, and Western companies investing.

Modern-day Hong Kong. In 1997, after ninety-nine years of British rule, control of Hong Kong reverted back to the Chinese government. *Archive Photos. Reproduced by permission.*

But there was a dark side to the new China as well. In June 1989, a group of students in the capital, Beijing, led protests calling for *democratic* reforms. The students were brutally suppressed by the military, who killed hundreds and jailed hundreds more. In the United States during the 1990s, evidence began to surface regarding Chinese attempts to buy U.S. nuclear secrets and bribe top officials in the federal government. Many Americans criticized their country's increasingly friendly relations with the government of China, which remained Communist while claiming to have adopted a more free economic system.

When a ninety-nine-year treaty with Britain came to an end in 1997, thus returning Hong Kong to Chinese control, the world held its breath; but it soon appeared that China was willing to allow a relatively free political system in Hong Kong. How long it would allow such freedom, and whether the government of China itself would become more harsh or more open, remained unsettled questions. The country's long, long history offered plenty of answers—and no answers at all. At times China could be as stiffly ordered as any nation that ever existed; at other times it could dissolve into the kind of turmoil that few countries have ever survived. Perhaps, many people hoped, in the twenty-first century the "Middle Kingdom" could steer a middle course between the yin and the yang.

For More Information
Books

Burrell, Roy. *Oxford First Ancient History.* New York: Oxford University Press, 1991, pp. 72–73.

Dijkstra, Henk. *History of the Ancient & Medieval World,* Volume 3: *Ancient Cultures.* New York: Marshall Cavendish, 1996, pp. 349–60.

Dué, Andrea, ed. *The Atlas of Human History: Civilizations of Asia: India, China and the Peoples of Southeast Asia and the Indian Ocean.* Text by Renzo Rossi and Martina Veutro. New York: Macmillan Library Reference USA, 1996, pp. 24–32, 44–47.

Ganeri, Anita. *Legacies from Ancient China.* London: Belitha, 1999.

Gross, Susan Hill and Marjorie Wall Bingham. *Women in Traditional China: Ancient Times to Modern Reform.* St. Paul, MN: The Upper Midwest Women's History Center, 1983.

Langley, Myrtle. *Religion.* New York: Knopf, 1996, pp. 24–33.

Liu, Jenny and Chao-Hui. *Ancient China: 2,000 Years of Mysteries and Adventure to Unlock and Discover.* Philadelphia: Running Press Book Publishers, 1996.

Martell, Hazel Mary. *The Kingfisher Book of the Ancient World.* New York: Kingfisher, 1995, pp. 38–51.

Percival, Yonit and Alastair. *The Ancient Far East.* Vero Beach, FL: Rourke Enterprises, 1988.

Rowland-Entwistle, Theodore. *Confucius and Ancient China.* New York: Bookwright Press, 1987.

Shuter, Jane. *The Ancient Chinese.* Des Plaines, IL: Heinemann Interactive Library, 1998.

Teague, Ken. *Growing Up in Ancient China.* Illustrated by Richard Hook. Mahwah, NJ: Troll Associates, 1994.

Williams, Suzanne. *Made in China: Ideas and Inventions from Ancient China.* Illustrations by Andrea Fong. Berkeley, CA: Pacific View Press, 1996.

Web Sites

Alfred Koo Gallery on the Net. http://home1.pacific.net.sg/~alfredko/index. html#shang (May 1, 1999).

"Ancient China: The Chou." http://www.wsu.edu:8080/~dee/ANCCHINA/ CHOU.HTM (April 27, 1999).

"Ancient China: The Shang." http://www.wsu.edu:8080/~dee/ANCCHINA/ SHANG.HTM (May 1, 1999).

"Ancient China: The Yellow River Culture." http://www.wsu.edu:8080/ ~dee/ANCCHINA/YELLOW.HTM (May 1, 1999).

"Chinese History: The Main Dynasties." *The Chinese Odyssey.* http://tqd.advanced.org/10662/normal_dynasty.htm#ancient (May 1, 1999).

"Daily Life in Ancient China." http://members.aol.com/Donnclass/ Chinalife.htmlXIA (May 1, 1999).

"EAWC: Ancient China." *Exploring Ancient World Cultures.* http:// www.eawc.evansville.edu/chpage.htm (May 1, 1999).

Empires Past. http://library.advanced.org/16325/indexot.shtml (May 1, 1999).

"History of China: Table of Contents." http://www-chaos.umd.edu/history/ toc.html (May 1, 1999).

"Welcome to Xiannong Altar." http://china-window.com/beijing/ tour/museum/xiannong/index.html (May 1, 1999).

The Americas

9

For someone in the United States, it is not hard to "find" the Americas: all one has to do is look down at the ground. The Americas, sometimes called the Western Hemisphere or the New World, consist of two continents, North America and South America. The most commonly used division, however, is between North America—that is, the United States and Canada—and Latin America, which comprises the remainder of the New World, including the islands of the Caribbean. The most significant ancient civilizations of the Western Hemisphere developed in Latin America: the Olmec and other groups in what is now Mexico and parts of Central America (referred to by archaeologists as Mesoamerica); and the Chavín and other cultures in the Andes Mountains of South America.

Why the Americas are important

The Americas share certain characteristics with sub-Saharan Africa (covered in the next chapter), characteristics that distinguish these cultures from most others examined in this book. Archaeologists know much less about these cultures

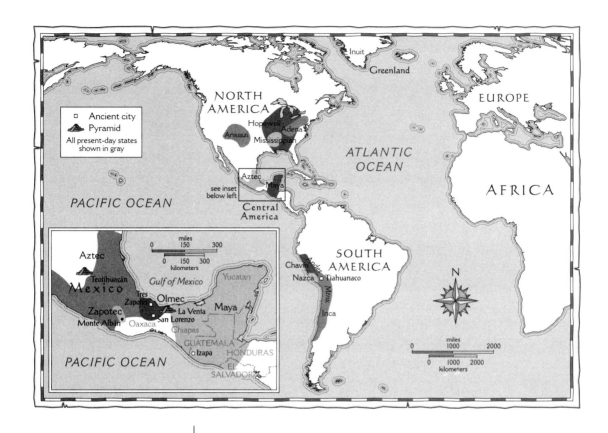

Map of the Americas.
XNR Productions. The Gale Group.

than they do about those of the Middle East, Asia, and Europe. It is virtually impossible to find examples of famous people from ancient America, simply because hardly any individual names have survived in the historical record. The histories of American civilizations, as with those of Africa, are primarily the record of an entire people. Also like African civilizations, those of the New World did not reach their peak in ancient times; rather, they flourished during what is commonly referred to as the Middle Ages. Yet it is important to study ancient America because the great Mayan and Aztec cultures of Mesoamerica developed on a foundation created by the Olmec and the people who established the city of Teotihuacán, just as the splendid Inca Empire of Peru grew from seeds planted by the Chavín.

The peoples of the Americas

The word *Indian,* when used to describe the people living on the American continent at the time Christopher Columbus arrived in A.D. 1492, is based on Columbus's mistaken belief that he had reached India. In order to overcome this error, in the late twentieth century the name "Native American" became more common. However, this name has its own problems, because there is no such thing as a native American. Even the peoples who inhabited the Americas before the arrival of the Europeans were migrants, though they beat the Europeans to the New World by a good 20,000 years or more.

The first Americans came from eastern Siberia, now part of Russia, where even today one will find a hardy native population with facial features much like that of the American "Indian." They began arriving somewhere between 30,000 and 20,000 B.C., during the last Ice Age. With much of North America covered in a sheet of ice two miles thick in places, the seas were lower than they are now. This created a land bridge across what is now the Bering Sea between Alaska and Siberia, and thus like the Israelites crossing the Red Sea, the first Americans simply walked to the new land.

Origins of the "Native Americans"

There is much dispute concerning the approximate date of the first Americans' arrival, how they spread throughout the New World, and the dates of subsequent migrations by groups from Siberia. But it is fairly clear that they could have come only by this northern route, by far the closest approach from the *Old World*—that is, Asia, Africa, and Europe—to the New. It is likewise clear that many of them moved southward. By about 9000 B.C., people lived in the southern tip of South America. They continued to spread throughout the Americas.

Over thousands of years, the first Americans divided into thousands of groups in every part of the New World, yet all these groups shared certain characteristics. This was particularly true of the two most outstanding civilizations of ancient America: the Olmec (OHL-mek) and the Chavín (shah-VEEN).

Olmec, Chavín, and other ancient Americans

There is enormous variety in the lands of North and South America. This variety causes wide differences in the people's ways of life. The Olmec homeland in Mesoamerica (the

Words to Know: The Americas

Basalt: A dark volcanic rock that is dense and heavy.

Ceramic: Relating to a non-metallic material, usually clay, which is baked at a high temperature to make products such as bricks or plates.

Classic (adj.): A term used to describe the highest, best, most memorable, or most significant phase in the history of a civilization or other entity.

Contemporary: Existing or occurring at the same time as someone or something else.

Dictatorship: A system of government in which a ruler or a ruling group holds total or near-total power.

Domesticate: To tame a wild animal.

Drainage system: The use of pipes and sewers to transport waste water from a high-pop-ulation area to a place where it can be disposed of safely.

Elite: The wealthiest and most powerful members of a society, usually a very small group.

Formative: A term describing an early period in the development of something (for example, a civilization), which has a great effect on its later character.

Free enterprise: An economic and political system in which people are allowed to own and operate businesses with a minimum of government interference.

Grid: A network of evenly spaced lines that intersect one another at right angles, as horizontal and vertical lines do.

Irrigation: A method of keeping crops watered, often by redirecting water supplies.

first part is pronounced "meh-so") was a land of steaming rain forests and lush, vegetation-covered mountains. By contrast, the Andes (AN-deez), the high mountains of South America where the Chavín settled, were rocky and dry. Despite these differences in environment, however, the two groups had much in common.

It is a mystery why the Olmec and Chavín, widely separated by distance and apparently ignorant of one another, both constructed pyramids. It is a mystery, too, why pyramid-building seems to have taken place primarily in northeast Africa and in the Americas, areas separated by thousands of miles of ocean. Some people believe that beings from another planet built the pyramids of Egypt, as well as those of the Americas. However, even if one attempts to approach the ques-

Levee: A ridge or dike to confine an area of land that is flooded for irrigation purposes.

Maize: Corn.

Metropolis: A very large and important city.

Middle class: A group in between the rich and the poor, or the rich and the working class.

Mural: A large painting, applied directly to the surface of a wall.

Old World: The Eastern Hemisphere, except Australia, much of which was known to Europeans prior to the 1500s. Sometimes the term refers specifically to Europe.

Pilgrimage: A journey, for religious purposes, to a sacred place or shrine.

Plaza: A large open area or public square, usually but not always in the center of a town.

Pre-Columbian: A term that refers to the time before Columbus (and hence other Europeans) began arriving in the Americas in A.D. 1492.

Racist: A person who believes that race is the primary factor determining peoples' abilities and that one race is superior to others.

Ritual: A type of religious ceremony that is governed by very specific rules.

Shaman: A holy man who, according to believers, is able to enter a state of trance (sometimes induced by powerful drugs) in which he contacts the supernatural world.

Suburb: A city or town on the outskirts of a larger city.

Zenith: Highest point.

tion from the standpoint of a scientist (that is, by studying the facts and attempting to build a theory from them, rather than starting out with a theory and trying to find facts that agree with it), there seem to be no clear answers.

Another curious aspect of ancient American cultures is their relatively low level of technological development in comparison to their achievements as builders. It appears that the Egyptians of the Old Kingdom who built the pyramids had no knowledge of the wheel. When the peoples of America built their own pyramids some 1,500 years later, they also did so without the use of wheels. This is a curious fact, since archaeologists have found wheeled toys at various sites, particularly in Mesoamerica. Why the Olmec did not adapt the wheel to more practical uses is yet another mystery.

The Anasazi cliff dwellings.
Robert J. Huffman. Field Mark Publications. Reproduced by permission.

Furthermore, although the Inca would later *domesticate* the llama (YAH-muh), a relative of the camel that lives in the high Andes, ancient Americans were without beasts of burden. Nor did they possess sophisticated tools. The Chavín became highly accomplished in the art of fashioning objects from gold, but it appears that the Americas did not enter the Bronze Age until about A.D. 1200. Metal was chiefly for decoration, such as gold jewelry; tools, on the other hand, were of stone. Thus, as one contemplates the pyramids of Mesoamerica, it is amazing to consider that they were built by more or less Stone Age peoples.

Both the Olmec and the Chavín civilizations grew out of agricultural systems that began developing in about 3500 B.C. Both served as "parent" civilizations to others that developed around them. Not only did they trade goods with these satellite groups, but they also passed on knowledge and culture to them. Both groups built holy cities, or ceremonial centers, to which worshippers made *pilgrimages.*

Despite the presence of cities, however, the Olmec and Chavín had economies based on agriculture. Each had a central crop as important to their lives as rice was in India and China: corn (or *maize*) in Mesoamerica, and potatoes in the Andes. Like most peoples of ancient times, these early Americans believed that everything had a spiritual significance. Hence agriculture and religion were closely linked, and the power of ancient American gods centered around their ability to bring rain and grow crops.

Finally, the two groups were linked by time. Each fit into the period designated as *Formative* (FOHR-muh-tiv), or Preclassic, by archaeologists. This era lasted from about 1500 B.C. to A.D. 300. The Formative Period included not only the Olmec, Chavín, and their surrounding cultures but the earliest stages of what would become the greatest civilization of *pre-Columbian* America: the Maya. The latter would flourish during the Classic Period, from A.D. 300 to 900, continuing long after "ancient" times. Finally came the Postclassic Period (A.D. 900–1540), dominated by the Aztec in Mesoamerica and the Inca in the Andes. These great cultures of later periods, however, would not have been possible without the Olmec and Chavín who preceded them.

The Olmec (c. 1200–c. 100 B.C.)

Among the achievements of the Olmec were their discoveries in astronomy. Like the Babylonians a little earlier, Olmec astronomers charted the movements of the Sun and Moon and observed how solar and lunar cycles affected the planting and harvesting of crops. Thus they created the first calendar in the New World, based on a 365-day year. They also developed a system of writing as well as a mathematical system based on the numbers one and five, which they represented using dots and dashes.

Though the high point of Olmec civilization began some time between 1200 and 1000 B.C. and lasted until about 100 B.C., its origins go back as far as 2000 B.C. It is possible the Olmec originated on the Pacific coast of what is now Mexico, but they established themselves in the east. Mexico is shaped a bit like a woman's slipper with the toe turned upward: the "toe" is the Yucatan (yoo-kah-TAHN) Peninsula. The place

Who "Discovered" America?

Most children grow up hearing that Christopher Columbus "discovered America," which implies that the explorer found the area that is now the United States. In fact the closest he came was the modern-day Bahamas; John Cabot, who explored the coast of Delaware in 1497, was actually the first European to reach the future United States.

It is much more accurate to say that Columbus discovered the New World. Yet this statement raises a question. There were already as many as 40 million people living in the Western Hemisphere when he arrived. Why do people not say that the first Native Americans, who arrived in the New World thousands of years earlier, "discovered" it?

To some people, it seems downright *racist* to say that Columbus, a white European, discovered the New World, as though the darker-skinned Native Americans did not matter. Yet there is at least some truth to the claim of discovery, because the Europeans, unlike the Native Americans, were in contact with the rest of the civilizations known at the time through writing and face-to-face communication. After Europeans "discovered" the New World, eventually all civilized peoples knew of it.

John Cabot. *UPI/Corbis-Bettmann. Reproduced by permission.*

In fact Columbus was probably not the first European to arrive in the New World. It is quite likely that Vikings from Scandinavia in northern Europe visited in about A.D. 1000. They were certainly white—blond-haired and blue-eyed, even—but they were not civilized, and they did not "discover" the Western Hemisphere. Once again, like the Native Americans, and unlike Columbus and other explorers five centuries later, they did not pass this information on to the rest of humankind.

where the Olmec lived is just to the west of the peninsula, in a large bay along the Gulf of Mexico.

At the height of the Olmec civilization, the area under their control was about 7,000 square miles (18,130 square kilometers), with a population of around 35,000 people. The name *Olmec* means "people of the rubber country," a reference to the fact that they were the first Mesoamerican culture—and perhaps the first in the world—to extract rubber from rubber plants.

Olmec agriculture depended on slash-and-burn techniques as well as the building of river *levees* (LEHV-eez; dikes) to provide irrigation by occasionally flooding their fields with river water. "Slash-and-burn" was exactly what it sounded like. The Olmec would simply cut down all the trees in a part of the rain forest and begin planting crops there. From the standpoint of the environment, it was not a good practice, but slash-and-burn farming was a typical method among many ancient American peoples.

Many of the Olmec dwellings were built into hillsides. Other Indian tribes, like those in the Northwest United States, built longhouses with ornate doorways, like the one in this photo. *Corbis. Reproduced by permisison.*

Three ceremonial centers

The principal Olmec ceremonial centers were San Lorenzo, La Venta, and Tres Zapotes (trays sah-POE-tayz). To visualize these locations, one can imagine the Olmec lands as a big triangle with one point facing downward. The Gulf Coast would be along the top side of the triangle, and San Lorenzo would be at the bottom point. La Venta would be at the right-hand (or eastern) corner, and Tres Zapotes on the left (or western) corner. (These names, by the way, are Spanish, and were therefore not the names the Olmec themselves gave to these places.)

Founded in about 1300 B.C., San Lorenzo was built on a man-made plateau, meaning that human labor flattened out the mountaintop on which it sat. This accomplishment alone implies that the society of the Olmec was advanced. As with projects from the Egyptian pyramids onward, only a very organized nation, and one with a strong central government, can call on its people to undertake such ambitious building projects.

Further evidence of the highly organized Olmec system can be found in the massive public works projects, including *drainage systems,* water storage ponds, and stone pavements, uncovered by archaeologists. San Lorenzo was a city of houses built in the shape of mounds: at one point, there were some 200 of these house-mounds, containing about 1,000 people. But just as *suburbs* surround modern cities, thousands more people—farmers, mostly—lived in surrounding areas.

By 900 B.C., San Lorenzo had declined and was replaced by La Venta. Both cities were built on salt domes, or large deposits of rock salt underneath the earth, but whereas San Lorenzo was primarily a ceremonial center, La Venta apparently also served functions typical of any city, housing tradesmen and people of other professions. In some ways, it was a model for the much more splendid city of Teotihuacán (tay-oh-tee-hwah-KAHN) that would follow it. Thus La Venta was built on a *grid* pattern, as Teotihuacán would later be; and just as Teotihuacán was dominated by the Pyramid of the Sun, La Venta had a main pyramid about 100 feet (30.5 meters) tall.

Olmec stone carving.
Springer/Corbis-Bettmann.
Reproduced by permisison.

After 400 B.C., the focus of Olmec civilization shifted to Tres Zapotes, which lay beyond the Tuxtla (TOOS-lah) Mountains. The Tuxtla were the primary source of *basalt* (BAY-sawlt), a dark volcanic rock from which the Olmec fashioned some of their greatest works, items that have become a symbol of ancient Mexico. These works are colossal stone heads, of which sixteen have been discovered around San Lorenzo and other sites since A.D. 1860. All are generally round in shape, depicting male figures with flat noses and thick lips.

Dating from between 1200 and 900 B.C., the stone heads weigh as much as 30,000 pounds and stand between 5 feet (1.5 meters) and 11 feet (3.4 meters) high. They represent a triumph of the ancient Americans' limited technology. First of all, the heads were carved entirely with stone tools. Even more amazing, somehow the Olmec managed to move them over great distances. Probably they used log rollers to transport the heads through the jungle, then floated them along rivers using rafts.

Olmec religion

It is not known exactly what purpose the heads served. Because of their helmet-like garb, it is possible that they represented players of the *ritual* ball game tlachtli. But it is more likely that they had some religious or political significance, either as representations of divine figures or of kings.

As with many ancient peoples, the Olmec did not make much of a distinction between religion and politics: thus the rulers and the priests were linked. They were the only people who actually lived in ceremonial centers such as Tres Zapotes. The common people inhabited the outlying areas.

Olmec religion placed a high importance on the role of the *shaman* (SHAH-muhn). A shaman is a holy man who, by means of trances—often induced by powerful drugs—was believed to contact the supernatural world. The tradition of the shaman is well known among Native Americans, as it is among their distant cousins in Siberia and Tibet.

Another aspect of Olmec religion calls to mind a tradition more familiar to Westerners: that of the werewolf. The Olmec believed that the shaman had an alterego (a sort of double), a spiritual companion called a *nagual* (nah-WAHL) in the form of an animal. Usually this was a jaguar, a creature considered sacred by the Olmec and the Chavín, both of whom believed it to be the most powerful creature on earth. By becoming one with the nagual, a shaman could enter the spiritual world and manipulate forces on earth, particularly the weather and the success of crops.

The ideas of the nagual and the shaman were not the only aspects of Olmec religion that might seem a little frightening to modern people: the Olmecs had a tradition of human sacrifice. The Jewish scriptures contain an important account of God's demand that Abraham sacrifice his son Isaac, but this was only a test. Except in China under the Shang Dynasty, human sacrifice was virtually unknown among civilizations of the Old World. It was common in the New World, however, particularly in Mesoamerica. Some archaeological evidence indicates that

even infants, as symbols of the renewal of life, may have been sacrificed to the gods in return for a good harvest.

Other Mesoamerican cultures

All around the Olmec were other cultures, the remains of which have been found at archaeological sites throughout Mesoamerica. The most prominent of these, of course, were the Maya. They had developed ceremonial centers of their own as early as 2000 B.C., and by about 300 B.C., they populated parts of what is now Guatemala, Honduras, and El Salvador. The Maya later moved into Mexico, where this greatest of all pre-Columbian civilizations would leave a lasting imprint at the same time Europe was going through the Middle Ages.

In the modern-day Mexican state of Chiapas (chee-AH-puhs), which lies at the southern edge of the country along the Guatemalan border, the majority of the people speak some version of the Mayan language. Chiapas contains an archaeological site at Izapa (ee-ZAH-pah), which may have been a ceremonial center between 1500 and 800 B.C. It is possible that Izapa preserved traditions of the Olmec that later became part of the Mayan culture, including the cult of the rain god.

There were also the Zapotec, who lived in what is now the state of Oaxaca (wah-HAH-kah). The Zapotec adapted the Olmec calendar, using both the 365-day cycle and a 260-day religious calendar. Once every 52 years, the first day of both would match up, and that was a day of celebration for the renewal of the earth. Monte Albán (mahnt ahl-BAHN), the first true city in Mesoamerica, was a Zapotec city. By A.D. 200, it had become a dominant urban center, containing some 30,000 people. It survived until A.D. 800. Yet as great as Monte Alban was, there was another city even greater.

Teotihuacán

Built in about A.D. 100, Teotihuacán was the first true *metropolis* in the Western Hemisphere. Within 500 years, it would grow to become the sixth-largest city in the entire world. Like Rome and Babylon, Teotihuacán would become a symbol and an example to later civilizations; but unlike those splendid urban centers of the Old World, Teotihuacán, whose name means "Place of the Gods," was not at the center of a warlike empire. The Teotihuacános (tay-oh-tee-hwah-KAHN-ohz) were a peaceful people.

Teotihuacán appears to have been a planned city: that is, rather than simply springing up as most cities do, it was designed and laid out. (This was to be the case with another urban center of the New World, Washington, DC, some 1,700 years later.) Covering 8 square miles (21 square kilometers), a vast area for an ancient city, Teotihuacán had a population of between 125,000 and 200,000. Again, this is an astounding figure for its time. Because of sewage and sanitation problems, among other difficulties, ancient cities were seldom larger than small towns in modern times.

Like Rome, Teotihuacán was a meeting place for many cultures. It appears that people from all over Mesoamerica lived in apartment-like buildings. The skyscrapers of Teotihuacán were its pyramids, the most significant of which was

the Pyramid of the Sun. It stood on the city's main street, which the Aztec later dubbed the Avenue of the Dead. Other great temples lined the avenue, which ended at the Pyramid of the Moon.

The people of Teotihuacán worshiped a variety of gods, the most important of which was Quetzalcóatl (ket-zuhl-KWAH-tuhl). Depicted as a serpent with feathers, Quetzalcóatl appears to have been a peaceful god of agriculture. The archaeological evidence shows no record of human sacrifice or warfare at Teotihuacán.

Teotihuacán survived until about A.D. 750, when it began to decline rapidly. Archaeologists have suggested several possible reason for its downfall, including a fire that engulfed much of the city. The fire may in turn have been the result of organized action, either by rebels or outside invaders such as the warlike Toltecs (TOHL-tekz), then on the rise. On the other hand, the end of Teotihuacán may have come because its great

Temple of Quetzalcoatl (close-up of carved zoomorphic stone gods), Aztec culture, Mexico. *Corbis. Reproduced by permission.*

The Ball Game

Modern-day Americans take their sports seriously. North Americans are obsessed with football, as are Latin Americans—though what they (and the rest of the world) call "football" is referred to as "soccer" in the United States. El Salvador and Honduras once even went to war over a disputed soccer match. Ancient Americans took sports at least as seriously. They played a sacred ball game, sometimes called *tlachtli* (t'l-AHK-lee), and sometimes referred to simply as "the ball game."

Though the world's first spectator sporting event may have been in Egypt in the 2600s B.C., a tlachtli court dating back to about 1500 B.C. must surely be the world's oldest sporting facility. Predating the Greek Olympics by more than 700 years, tlachtli, which shares elements with modern tennis, volleyball, and handball, was probably the world's first true sport.

Each team consisted of four or five players, who bounced a small, very hard rubber ball back and forth on a court. Along the sides ran what looked like sloping stone bleachers but in fact were part of the court itself. Balls would bounce at an angle off of the sloping surfaces, making it harder to play. Playing was not that easy in any case, since contestants could use only their hips, thighs, and elbows to move the ball.

The sport required full concentration, especially because the Mesoamerican peoples considered it sacred. Only the elite even got to watch the games, and the penalty for losing was death. A version of tlachtli—minus the human sacrifice, of course!—is still played in parts of Central America.

---

population depleted natural resources and created sanitation problems, which resulted in widespread disease.

The Andes

About 2,500 miles (4,023 kilometers) south of the Olmec lived the people of the Chavín culture, around the border areas of modern Peru and Ecuador. The term "Chavín" refers to Chavín de Huántar (shah-VEEN day WAHN-tahr), a ceremonial center that developed in what is now north-central Peru about 1200 B.C. Like the ceremonial centers of Mesoamerica, Chavín de Huántar was a city of pyramids and platforms, including a large structure dubbed the "Great Pyramid" by archaeologists. The name calls to mind the Great Pyramid of Cheops, but unlike the pyramids of Egypt, those of the Americas were places of worship rather than burial chambers.

Chavín de Huántar was about one and a half miles across and contained a "Great *Plaza*," or open area, in the southeast. To the northwest was the court and temple of the Lanzon, a stone idol representing the supreme deity worshipped at Chavín. Like the Mesoamericans, these people also revered the jaguar; hence there were also the Stairs of the Jaguars leading down to the Great Plaza from the Great Pyramid.

Like other ceremonial centers, Chavín de Huántar had a small resident population (probably no more than 1,000 people)—with thousands more (presumably farmers and laborers to serve the priests and rulers) living in surrounding areas. Between 400 and 300 B.C., however, Chavín de Huántar entered a period of decline. Eventually a less advanced group of people built a village over the site. Yet its memory lived on to inspire the Inca, just as Teotihuacán did the Maya and Aztec.

Other Andean peoples

Numerous other peoples in the Andes were influenced by Chavín culture. Among its *contemporaries* were the Paracas, who lived on the southern coast between 1100 and 200 B.C., and who apparently practiced mummification. Another coastal group were the Moche (MOH-chay) or Mochica (moh-CHEE-kah) people, a nation of warriors who controlled an area about the size of modern Vermont. They flourished between 200 B.C. and A.D. 700, producing fine *ceramics* and some of the most advanced metal objects in ancient America.

Still another coastal people influenced by the Chavín culture were the Nazca. The Nazca flourished between 200 B.C. and A.D. 600. Their most famous works of art are the "Nazca Lines." The lines are representations of spiders, birds, and other creatures, made out of rock formations and grooves cut into the earth. The representations are so large they can be seen only from a great height. Naturally, this fact has long perplexed archaeologists. If the Nazca possessed no flying machines—not even hot-air balloons—why and how did they

The jaguar was revered by the Mesoamerican peoples.
JLM Visuals. Reproduced by permission.

create the designs? There is much dispute over this question, though scientists have shown that it would be possible to create the drawings with the technology available to the Nazca.

Another impressive site near Chavín de Huántar is Tiahuanaco (tee-ah-hwah-NAH-koh), in the Andean highlands of what is now Bolivia. It was to the Andes what Teotihuacán was to Mesoamerica: a great city, much more than a ceremonial center, which served as a focal point for the peoples all around it. Like Teotihuacán, it was the site of impressive achievements in architecture and engineering, including the massive Gateway of the Sun, cut from a single stone. Yet one feature distinguished Tiahuanaco from Teotihuacán or virtually any other major city, then or now.

Whereas Denver, Colorado, boasts of itself as the "Mile-High City," Tiahuanaco had an altitude of 13,125 feet, meaning that it was actually two and a half miles (4 kilometers) high. Though it flourished between 200 B.C. and A.D. 600

(making it contemporary with the Moche and Nazca civilizations, as well as Teotihuacán), Tiahuanaco continued to exert an influence over an area from southern Peru to northern Argentina until about A.D. 1000.

The Americas to the present day

During much of the period between A.D. 500 and 1500, European civilization was at a low point, but in the Americas, those centuries saw the triumph of pre-Columbian civilization. In Mesoamerica, the Maya reached their *zenith,* or highest point, between A.D. 250 and 1000. Teotihuacán flourished from A.D. 300 to 750. The same period saw the rise of civilizations such as the Huari (HWAH-ree) and, after 1200, the Chimu (CHEE-moo) in the Andes. Meanwhile, on the heels of the peaceful Maya came the militaristic Toltecs, also a great civilization, though not as great as the Aztec, who rose to

Elsewhere in the Americas

Though the Olmec of Mesoamerica and the Chavín culture of the Andes were by far the most notable groups in ancient America, they were far from the only ones. The terrain of the Americas is extraordinarily varied, and so were the groups that populated it.

Across thousands of miles to the far north were hardy peoples such as the Inuit (IH-noo-it) of Greenland. These groups lived in houses of ice and survived by hunting walrus, seals, and whales. Thousands of miles to the south, some 1,000 tribal groups lived in the steaming Amazon river basin, a place where it was so hot that people wore little more than loincloths.

Though most Native American peoples were not civilized, their cultures were far from simple. An anthropologist could devote an entire lifetime to studying the layout of family huts in the Amazon, where parts of the dwelling were reserved for males or females, for family or guests, and for various bodily functions. The Inuit and other groups had a complex shamanistic religion, which involved a number of rituals to forge harmony between the natural and the supernatural worlds.

Various cultures thrived in the area of what is now the United States. Peoples in what is now Washington State and other parts of the Pacific Northwest lived well, because the sea provided abundant food. They engaged in *potlatch* ceremonies, in which a member of the community attempted to prove his superior wealth by giving the most away

prominence in about A.D. 1400. This made the Aztec Empire contemporary with that of the Inca in the Andes.

These were brilliant, splendid civilizations, as magnificent as they were in many ways cruel. Many of them practiced human sacrifice, yet they also produced extraordinary triumphs. The Mayans, for instance, used the concept of zero in their number system long before Europeans discovered it. The Inca conquered an enormous empire along the Pacific coast of South America and placed their people under an extraordinarily organized system of rule. The Aztec, like other notable civilizations of ancient America, used complex hieroglyphics for writing. Yet less than forty years after the first Europeans arrived in 1492, the Aztec and Inca, with all their riches and glory, were gone.

to his neighbors. Because the neighbors wanted to prove their own wealth, they usually gave it back.

Throughout an area stretching from the Dakotas to Florida were a variety of groups including the Adena (uh-DEE-nuh), Hopewell, and Mississippian cultures. They built mounds, similar to the tumuli of the Old World, which can be seen today in places such as Crook's Mound in Louisiana and Etowah (EH-toh-wah) in Georgia. They later established the city of Cahokia (cuh-HOH-kee-uh), which flourished in about A.D. 900 near what is now St. Louis, Missouri. It was the largest pre-Columbian city north of Mesoamerica.

The nations in what is now the southwestern United States—the Anasazi (ah-nuh-SAH-zee), Hohokam (hoh-HOH-kahm), and other groups—were some of the most remarkable. The Anasazi, whose name means "old ones," appeared in what is now the Four Corners region (where Arizona, New Mexico, Utah, and Colorado meet) in about A.D. 200. They were most noted for their intricately constructed towns, actually a series of interlocking clay dwellings, which they built against the rock walls of cliffs. Spanish explorers later called these *pueblo* (PWEH-bloh), meaning "town."

By then, however, the Anasazi themselves had disappeared for reasons that are not entirely clear. The name of the Hohokam, who lived in what is now Arizona and developed an elaborate irrigation system, means "disappeared" or "those who have gone."

Ironically, it took the Europeans much longer to conquer the less advanced groups of Native Americans. The United States did not gain full control over the so-called Plains Indians in the West until about 1890. No one ever subdued the peoples of the Amazon river valley in what is now Brazil, many of whom are even today at a Stone Age level of technological development. (They have, however, been threatened ever since Brazil began cutting down the rain forest in the 1960s.)

The Europeans conquered the Inca and Aztec first partly because these groups had the most wealth; also, by being most civilized, they represented the greatest threat. Yet their civilizations had not prepared the Native Americans to defend themselves. They did not possess firearms, nor did they know how to smelt the iron from which firearms were made. They had not ventured out to explore the world around them, which was precisely what the Europeans were doing when they arrived in America. Had the Aztec and Inca been aware of one another, they might have organized an allied force to repel the invaders.

The Europeans had other factors in their favor. There were more of them; they just kept coming and coming. They brought with them diseases such as smallpox, to which Native Americans had never been exposed. Millions of Native Americans died as a result.

By the end of the twentieth century, the majority ethnic groups in North America were British, Irish, and German in origin. Although there were plenty of other groups, Native Americans did not form a sizable part of the population. The reason why was simple: particularly in the United States, the Europeans destroyed the peoples already living there.

Quite a different situation prevailed in Latin America, which takes its name from the development of main languages—Spanish and (in Brazil) Portuguese—from Latin. The *elite* (eh-LEET) in many Latin American countries are almost purely Spanish. Yet many in the population are either Native Americans or a mixture of Spanish and Native American.

Half the population of Peru, for instance, are descendants of the Inca and speak the language of that ancient empire, Quechua (KEH-choo-wah). The spirit of Mesoamerica is alive and vibrant in the *murals* (M'YOOR-uhlz), or large wall paintings, of Mexico as well. And on the site of the old Aztec capital, just 30 miles (48 kilometers) southwest of Teotihuácan, a new metropolis has arisen: Mexico City, home to more than 16.5 million people. In the mid-1990s, it was the world's second-largest city after Tokyo, Japan, and just ahead of two other American cities, Sao Paolo (saw[n] POW-loh) in Brazil and New York in the United States.

For More Information
Books

Dijkstra, Henk, ed. *History of the Ancient & Medieval World,* Volume 11: *Empires of the Ancient World.* New York: Marshall Cavendish, 1996, pp. 1447-88.

Dué, Andrea, ed. *The Atlas of Human History: Civilizations of the Americas: Native American Cultures of North, Central and South America.* Text by Renzo Rossi and Martina Veutro. New York: Macmillan Library Reference USA, 1996.

Leonard, Jonathan Norton. *Ancient America.* Alexandria, VA: Time-Life Books, 1967.

Martell, Hazel Mary. *The Kingfisher Book of the Ancient World.* New York: Kingfisher, 1995, pp. 124-37.

Sattler, Helen Roney. *The Earliest Americans.* Illustrated by Jean Day Zallinger. New York: Clarion Books, 1993.

Waldman, Carl. *Encyclopedia of Native American Tribes.* Illustrations by Molly Braun. New York: Facts on File, 1988.

Web Sites

"Ancient America Time Line." http://www.ilstu.edu/class/hist127/timeline.html (June 1, 1999).

"Ancient Peru: The Inca, Moche, Chimu, Paracas, Nazca and Chachapoya Peoples." *GORP: Great Outdoor Recreation Pages.* http://www.gorp.com/gorp/location/latamer/peru/arc_peru.htm (June 1, 1999).

Latin American Prehistory. http://www.anthro.mankato.msus.edu/LatinAmerica/index.htm (June 1, 1999).

Mesoweb: An Exploration of Mesoamerican Cultures. http://www.mesoweb.com/ (June 1, 1999).

Native American Links. http://www.independence.k12.oh.us/ms/native.html (June 1, 1999).

Pre-Columbian Culture. http://udgftp.cencar.udg.mx/ingles/Precolombian/precointro.html (June 1, 1999).

"Teotihuacán." http://www.du.edu/~blynett/Teotihuacán.html (June 1, 1999).

"Tlachtli: Losers Were Sacrificed." http://www.real-tennis.com/history/tlachtli.html (June 1, 1999).

Africa

10

Africa lies south of Europe and southwest of Asia. Geographically it is about three times the size of the United States, excluding Alaska and Hawaii. At its northeast corner is Egypt, which is connected to the Sinai Peninsula—and hence to the Asian continent by a very narrow strip of land. This is the only spot where Africa touches another continent; otherwise, it is surrounded by water. The Mediterranean Sea separates it from Europe in the north; the Red Sea and Gulf of Aden lie between it and the Arabian Peninsula to the east. Two vast bodies of water—the Indian Ocean on the eastern side, and the even larger Atlantic on the west—surround the remainder of Africa.

Why Africa is important

One of the greatest civilizations of all time, Egypt, was in Africa. Perhaps the only ancient civilizations that can be compared with it are those of Greece and Rome, which were influenced by it. Egypt, of course, has had its own chapter in this series; and Carthage, in North Africa, is also covered elsewhere. The focus of this chapter is entirely on Africa south of the Sahara

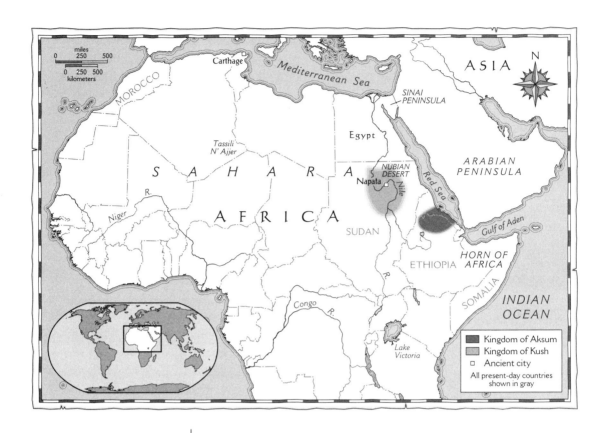

Map of Africa.

XNR Productions.

The Gale Group.

Desert—that is, sub-Saharan Africa—as well as on the desert itself. That desert would have an impact on African history right up to the modern day; so, too, would the African civilizations of ancient times. There was the kingdom of Kush, which developed its own form of writing and briefly ruled Egypt; the kingdom of Aksum, an important trading center; and the Bantu peoples, who developed ironworking and spread it, along with their languages, throughout the southern part of the African continent.

The origins of humankind

Though there is much dispute regarding how humankind began, *paleoanthropologists* (pay-lee-oh-an-throh-PAHL-uh-jistz; scientists who study human origins) generally agree that humanity originated in Africa millions of years ago. The *Paleolithic Age* (pay-lee-oh-LITH-ik), or Old Stone Age, probably began there about 2 million years ago. Eventually human ancestors moved out of Africa to other continents.

Words to Know: Africa

Afrocentrism: A belief that people of African descent should interpret the world from an African perspective.

Apartheid: A system of enforced racial segregation and white supremacy that existed in South Africa from 1948 to the early 1990s.

Cold War: Not really a "war" but an ongoing conflict between the United States and Soviet Union from the end of World War II to the fall of Communism in the early 1990s.

Colonnade: A long series of columns on either side of a walkway. Often, but not always, there is a roof over the columns.

Compound (n.): A number of separate dwellings surrounded by a protective wall.

Condescend: To treat somebody as though they are inferior.

Deify: To turn someone or something into a god.

Depose: To remove from power.

Eurocentrism: The idea that European culture provides the standard by which all others should be judged.

Figurine: A small sculpture, usually a depiction of a person or animal.

Interdependence: A situation in which people rely upon each other.

Neolithic Age: The New Stone Age, c. 10,000–c. 4000 B.C., which began with a dramatic increase in technology and agriculture.

Obelisk: A tall, freestanding column of stone.

Oral tradition: A body of stories and sayings and other cultural information passed down by word of mouth.

Paleoanthropology: The study of human origins.

Paleolithic Age: The Old Stone Age, c. 2,000,000–c. 10,000 B.C.

Racism: The belief that race is the primary factor determining peoples' abilities, and that one race is superior to others.

Regime: Government; usually used as a negative term.

Savanna: Grassland.

Staple: A commodity with widespread or constant appeal.

Stellae: Plural of *stela,* a large stone pillar, usually inscribed with a message commemorating a specific event.

Values: Beliefs about what is good and bad, important and unimportant.

About 10,000 B.C., as the last ice age was ending, the world entered the New Stone Age, or *Neolithic Age* (Nee-oh-LITH-ik). This was a period of dramatic progress in agriculture, toolmaking, and other areas that created the framework for the development of civilization in about 4000 B.C.

Single spreading tree on the golden African savanna.
Corbis. Reproduced by permission.

The Sahara

A continent of extraordinary physical contrasts, Africa has mountains, deserts, tropical rainforests, and, *savanna* (grasslands). Yet except for the savanna and a few other areas, the majority of the African continent offers its inhabitants a meager living at best. This is particularly true of North Africa, which except for a fertile strip along the Mediterranean coast and Nile River, is covered by the Sahara (suh-HAIR-uh) and other deserts.

The Sahara is one of the central facts of life in Africa. It divides the continent as virtually no other physical feature in the world does, and it provides the reason for the great differences between North African and sub-Saharan cultures. Quite simply, Egyptian civilization had little influence on areas from which it was separated by the Sahara. Thus Egypt had much effect on Kush and Aksum in East Africa, but little at all on the Bantu peoples and other groups in southern and western Africa.

By far the world's largest desert, the Sahara today covers some 3.5 million square miles (9.07 thousand square kilometers), an area larger than the continental United States; yet only 780 acres (316 hectares) of it, a little more than one square mile (2.6 square kilometers), is fertile. The rest is mostly stone and dry earth with scattered shrubs. Contrary to the way it is usually presented in movies, only a very small portion of the Sahara consists of sand dunes.

The ancient Saharan cultures (c. 6000–c. 1500 B.C.)

Though the Sahara today is virtually uninhabitable, 8,000 years ago, it was a lush region of rivers and valleys. For thousands of years, it was home to many cultures, some of them quite advanced, to judge from their artwork. Who these peoples were—it appears there were many groups—remains a mystery, though they left behind an extraordinary record in the form of their rock-art paintings and carvings [see sidebar, "The Brilliant Legacy of Saharan Rock Art"].

The rock art, which varies greatly in its representation of human and animal figures, is divided into four historical groups. First is the Hunter period, from about 6000 to about 4000 B.C., depicting a Paleolithic people who survived by hunting the many wild animals then available in the region.

Next was the Herder period, from about 4000 to 1500 B.C. As their name suggests, these people maintained herds of animals and also practiced basic agriculture. Much more civilized than the Hunter people, they produced the most sophisticated Saharan rock art, much of it portraying their herds. In fact, their ability to portray perspective and the movement of the human form was much greater than that of the Egyptians.

As the Sahara began to become drier and drier, however, there were no more herds. Egyptians began bringing in domesticated horses to cross the desert: hence the name of the Horse period (c. 1500–c. 600 B.C.) By about 600 B.C., however, not even horses could survive in the forbidding climate. There was only one creature that could: the hardy, seemingly inexhaustible camel. Thus began the Camel era, which continues to the present day.

Kush (c. 2000 B.C.–c. A.D. 400)

In the southern part of Egypt, and the northern section of the modern nation of Sudan, is the region of Nubia (NOObee-uh). Much of it is covered by the Nubian Desert, but as with Egypt, the Nile River provided a fertile strip of land on which a civilization developed. This was the kingdom of Kush (KÜSH), which existed in various forms for nearly 2,400 years.

The Kushites' language was related to the Semitic tongues of southwest Asia. Yet, from Egyptian tomb paintings, it is clear that they were what modern Americans would call "black"—or, to use a more accurate term, sub-Saharan African. It appears that Semitic peoples migrated across the narrow Red

The Brilliant Legacy of Saharan Rock Art

In about 6000 B.C., what is now the Sahara Desert was a land of fertile green fields, lush valleys alive with all manner of plants and animals, and flowing rivers filled with fish. It was also the home to a series of highly advanced societies whose identity is unknown to historians. In fact, most of what modern people do know about these ancient Saharans comes from the artwork they painted and carved on stone surfaces throughout the desert.

These paintings provide evidence of extensive wildlife in the region, including giraffe, elephants, and cattle. Later scenes show camels. Other pieces illustrate the cultural and political life of the ancient Sahara, including dances, rituals, battles, and the workings of justice. One particularly complex piece portrays judges, police, jailers, and officials, with a man at the center who was apparently found guilty of a crime. Only a highly advanced civilization could have such a formal justice system.

Another painting, obviously from the Herder period, looks as if it were painted in the A.D.1800s—but it is more likely a product of the 1800s B.C. The women in the picture are clearly wealthy and relatively pampered, with complex hairdos. These details indicate that the people of the ancient Sahara had mastered their environment and were well past the point of merely surviving.

After 2000 B.C., the Sahara began to dry up, and the human population almost completely disappeared. If the paintings had been in a tropical rainforest environment, they might have been ruined; as it was, the dry desert air preserved them. Nor did they suffer the fate of Egyptian or Chinese treasures stolen by graverobbers. The Saharan rock art was hard to get to, protected by nests of

Sea to the "Horn of Africa" and intermarried with the peoples living there. Thus even today, the peoples of the Horn, particularly in modern Ethiopia and Somalia (soh-MAHL-ee-uh), have physical features which distinguish them from the peoples living further south.

Regarding the name "Ethiopia," it should be noted that as with Armenia and Macedonia, it refers both to a modern nation and to an ancient region, yet these are not exactly the same. The term *Ethiopian* is derived from a Greek expression meaning "burned skin"—suggesting a dark complexion.

poisonous snakes and miles of forbidding sand dunes.

The world owes a great debt to French explorer Henri Lhote (ahn-REE LAWT), who in 1956 discovered a great collection of rock art at Tassili n'Ajjer (tah-SEEL-ee nah-ZHAYR) deep in the desert. Lhote and his team of artists made it possible for everyone to see the great treasures of the Sahara without going there. Photographing the artwork would not do, especially because many pieces were in dark caves and their colors had faded; therefore he and the others painstakingly copied some 800 works of art, restoring original colors. This was a particularly difficult task given the nature of the environment. Not only was it hard to get to Tassili and other sites, but, in copying the art, members of the team often had to stand on tiptoe or lie on their backs while they worked.

The treasures of the Sahara are more valuable than diamonds. During the late twentieth century, people more interested in money than history (the modern counterparts of the ancient grave robbers) began looting artwork from sites in Morocco. Using crowbars, they removed pictures to sell them in Europe. In response to these and other abuses, the Moroccan Ministry of Cultural Affairs and groups such as the Trust for African Rock Art began working to preserve the treasures of the Sahara.

David Coulson, cofounder of the Trust for African Rock Art, published an article called "Ancient Art of the Sahara," in the June 1999 *National Geographic*. The group also works to preserve prehistoric artwork in other parts of the continent, including South Africa, where the Bushmen left a rich legacy of rock art before they were displaced by the Bantu peoples.

In ancient times, the entire region south of Egypt was often described as "Ethiopia;" indeed, that name was often used to describe all of Africa below Egypt.

Later, the Greek historian Herodotus, describing the multinational force with which the Persians invaded Greek in 480 B.C., noted the presence of both straight-haired "eastern Ethiopians," and curly-haired "western Ethiopians"—the latter dressed in lion skins—among the Persian army. These terms must have referred to Aksumites and Kushites respectively: though neither nation had been conquered by the Persian

Empire, it is possible the Persians recruited "Ethiopian" warriors for their forces.

Early period (c. 2000–716 B.C.)

Whatever their origins, the Kushites were closely linked with Egypt. It appears that contact with the latter began in about 2000 B.C., around the time Kush came into existence. In that first phase of Kushite civilization, its capital was first at Karmah (KAHR-muh), and later at Napata (NAH-puh-tah), a city on the Nile just south of Egypt. The Kushites traded extensively with the Egyptians, but relations were not always friendly. In the 1800s B.C., the pharaoh Senusret III built fortresses to protect against invasion by the Kushites. In the 1500s B.C., an invasion came—only it was Egypt that invaded Kush, not the other way around.

Kush remained an Egyptian colony for hundreds of years, but Egypt began to decline after the end of the New Kingdom in the 1000s B.C. Kush, in turn, was on the rise, particularly under the reign of King Piankhi (pee-AHNG-kee; c. 769–716 B.C.) Piankhi was a fervent believer in the Egyptian god Amon. He may have marched his armies into Egypt and conquered the land, but he seems to have had no interest in staying and building an empire. That job would fall to his brother Shabaka (SHAH-buh-kuh; r. 716 B.C.–695 B.C.)

The Twenty-Fifth Dynasty of Egypt (712–667 B.C.)

In 712 B.C., Shabaka's troops swept into Egypt, and he ordered the execution of the reigning pharaoh. This ended years of Libyan control over Egypt and began the Late Period in ancient Egyptian history. Shabaka established the Twenty-Fifth Dynasty, which lasted for half a century. Like Piankhi, Shabaka embraced the religion of Amon. He assigned his sister Amunirdis I (ah-moo-NEER-dis) an important position as "god's wife of Amon" in the temple at Thebes.

In 698 B.C., Shabaka's nephew Shebitku (SHEH-bit-koo) assumed the Egyptian throne while his brother Taharqa (tuh-HAHR-kuh) apparently ruled over Thebes. If this was indeed the case, it was an arrangement similar to the one between Ashurbanipal of Assyria and his brother Shamash-shum-ukin a few years later. This would be particularly ironic, given the role Ashurbanipal would play in the lives of Shebitku and Taharqa.

The two Kushite brothers appear to have gotten along much better than their Assyrian counterparts. Shebitku favored resistance against the Assyrians, who were on the move in Palestine with an eye toward Egypt. Apparently at his urging, Taharqa's Kushite army aided the Israelites against Assyrian troops under Sennacherib. Also, there seems to have been no struggle for succession: when Shebitku died in 690 B.C., Taharqa took his place. Among the achievements of Taharqa's long reign, which lasted from 690 to 664 B.C., was the building of a *colonnade* (KAHL-uh-nayd), a long hallway of columns, in the temple of Amun at Karnak.

But Taharqa was destined to be the last Kushite pharaoh. After 15 years of peace, his troops fought and defeated an Assyrian army under Esarhaddon in 675 B.C. Four years later, however, the Assyrians returned and overwhelmed Taharqa's forces. He regained control in Egypt for a little longer, but in 667 Ashurbanipal's troops scored a major victory against the Kushites. Taharqa fled to Napata, where he died in 664 B.C.

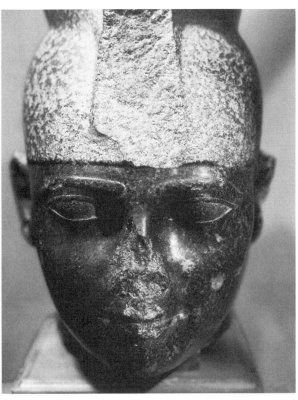

Sculpture of King Taharqa. *Corbis-Bettmann. Reproduced by permission.*

Meröe period (600s B.C.–c. 400 A.D.)

Some time after they were driven out of Egypt, the Kushites abandoned their capital at Napata and moved hundreds of miles upriver—-that is, *southward*—to the city of Meröe (MEHR-oh-wee). Meröe became the Kushite capital some time in the 600s B.C. Thereafter its name was closely associated with that of the Kushite civilization in general. The written language of the Kushites, which developed only after the migration southward, is referred to as Merotic (mehr-AH-tik). Oddly, though the script has been deci-

Ancient Africa: The Debate Rages On

For many centuries, white Europeans (including their descendants in the United States) ignored the achievements of sub-Saharan Africans. This attitude was *Eurocentrism,* the idea that European culture provides the standard by which all others should be judged. Combined with *racism,* Eurocentrism helped justify the slave trade, but even long after slavery ended, many whites continued to take a *condescending* attitude toward Africa.

Obviously, these were ignorant attitudes, and eventually a variety of movements developed in reaction to them. Among these was *Afrocentrism* which, in contrast to Eurocentrism, sought to interpret the world from an African perspective. Afrocentrists placed a great emphasis on the study of African cultures and past civilizations. They pointed out the obvious fact that Egypt was an African civilization, and called attention to its links with Nubia, or Kush.

These were positive and much-needed changes in the character of historical study; but many Afrocentrists went much further. In 1954, for instance, George G. M. James published *Stolen Legacy,* in which he claimed that the ancient Greeks "stole" their civilization from secret societies in Egypt. His "proof" for this extraordinary claim rested primarily on a tradition among the Masons, a group which developed in Europe in the A.D. 1700s. The Masons held that many Greek philosophers such as Aristotle had been influenced by so-called "mystery religions" of Egypt, though the best example of this alleged influence was the fact that Aristotle had written about the concept of the soul—hardly an idea unique to the Egyptians.

Nor was this much of a substantial basis on which to write a history; but in

phered—chiefly by comparing it with hieroglyphic records recording the same events—the language itself has never been translated.

Prior to their development of the Merotic script in about 300 B.C., the Kushites had written in Egyptian hieroglyphs. Egyptian influences were evident in the building of pyramids, which were smaller and much steeper than the pyramids of Egypt. Like the pyramids of Egypt, and unlike those of Mesoamerica, the pyramids of Meröe were built as tombs for kings and queens.

fact James's book was not so much history as it was conspiracy theory—the idea that the world is controlled by a few shadowy figures who pull all the strings. It is difficult to change the minds of people who subscribe to a conspiracy theory, because they interpret every piece of evidence that contradicts them as part of a massive cover-up, and thus as further proof of their position.

Afrocentrists in subsequent years made claims that increasingly went against the record of historical scholarship, and instead of conducting research, they simply looked for "evidence" that agreed with their beliefs. True historical study is scientific in nature: it seeks to discover all possible facts, and from these facts develops a theory about history. It is hard work. Politically or racially motivated "historians"—an extreme example would be the Nazis, with their false explanation of the Indo-European past—have a much easier job. They know in advance what conclusion they intend to reach, and then look for any "facts" (no matter how questionable) to back them up. Anyone who presents other evidence is treated not as a fellow scholar but as an enemy.

Certainly the Egyptians influenced Greece, but to claim that the Greeks "stole" their civilization from anywhere reflects a basic misunderstanding of how civilizations affect one another. In any case, the very idea of viewing cultures in racial terms goes against serious historians' most basic beliefs about how they should study history. Today no one but an absolute quack or racist would claim, for instance, that the achievements of Greece or Rome show the superiority of white people. The glories of the ancient world are human achievements, not racial achievements, and they belong to all people regardless of ethnicity.

The quality of Merotic pottery was outstanding and reflects a standard of craftsmanship equal to that of any ancient civilization. Trade also flourished during the Merotic phase of Kushite history. Not only did the people of Kush trade with the Egyptians along the Nile, they used Red Sea ports to conduct trade with southwest Asian lands. Through Egypt, goods from Kush—including elephants, ostrich feathers, ivory, and various animal hides—reached Greece and Rome; and Greek and Roman products such as jewelry and pottery made their way to Kush.

Mountains of Ethiopia.

Photograph by Cory Langley. Reproduced by permission.

The Kushite civilization reached its peak in the four centuries from 250 B.C. to A.D. 150. By then it had become more and more separate from Egypt, which was conquered in turn by the Greeks and the Romans. Kush began to decline after A.D. 150, however, in part due to the rise of a new Red Sea trading kingdom at Aksum.

Aksum (500 B.C.–A.D. 600)

To a much greater extent than the Kushites, the people of Aksum (sometimes spelled "Axum") were both racially and culturally related to the Semitic peoples who came from the Arabian Peninsula on the other side of the Red Sea. According to tradition, they were associated with the biblical Queen of Sheba, who probably came from southwest Arabia [see sidebar, "Ancient Africa and the Bible"]. Whether or not this is true, it is clear that Aksum had a strong Arabian influence.

Ancient Africa and the Bible

According to tradition, the people of Aksum were associated with the biblical Queen of Sheba and King Solomon of Israel. The Bible suggests that there was a great love affair between the two. Indeed, the biblical Song of Solomon refers to a woman with dark skin.

Another tradition holds that a descendant of Sheba and King Solomon brought the Ark of the Covenant to Aksum. The Ark was a holy relic of the Israelite people, said to contain the stone tablets of the Ten Commandments as given to Moses; and as anyone who has ever seen the movie *Raiders of the Lost Ark* (1981) knows, it was also supposed to possess great spiritual power.

According to a January 27, 1998, report in the *New York Times,* a number of people believe that the Ark, or at least part of it, is in Ethiopia. Reporter James C. McKinley, Jr. wrote that when he asked an Ethiopian deacon where the Ark was, the man "just smiled at what he saw as an absurd question. Everyone in this windswept and dusty land knows that the ark is in a square stone temple beside [an] ancient church, he said."

Regardless of the Ark's whereabouts, it is certain that there has been a strong relationship between Africa and the Bible. Aside from Egypt, which figures prominently in the Israelites' story, the Old Testament frequently mentions Kush (or Cush) as well as the overall region, which writers referred to as Ethiopia.

Judaism took hold in East Africa at an early date, and the New Testament tells a story of an Ethiopian who went to worship in Jerusalem (Acts 8:26-40). The apostle Philip met him and led him to convert to Christianity. Two centuries after these events, King Ezana of Aksum also converted. Thereafter Ethiopia would remain Christian. During the Middle Ages, in fact, a myth spread in Europe concerning a great Ethiopian king named Prester John, who reportedly led a vast Christian empire.

The center of Aksum's cultures was in the Red Sea port of Adulis (ah-DOO-lis), through which it came in contact with, and was influenced by, the Greek culture of Ptolemaic Egypt after the 300s B.C. By the first century A.D., Aksum was on the rise and became an important center for trade with places as far away as China, from which it imported silk, and India. The latter was a source of spices, a particularly important part of life in the time before refrigerators because they slowed down the spoiling of meat.

Moses being blinded by the Ark of the Covenant.
Archive Photos. Reproduced by permission.

Aksum also had a line of strong kings, who also served a religious function. In fact, the kings were considered sacred to the point that the queen mother (i.e., the king's mother) often took over the day-to-day administrative duties. The queen mother went by the title of *Candace* (KAN-des), which is often mistaken for a proper name. It was more like the equivalent of the Roman *Caesar*.

A particularly notable Aksumite monarch was Ezana (AY-zah-nah). In A.D. 325, he went to war against Kush and destroyed its fading capital at Meröe. But around the same time, he came in contact with two young Syrians shipwrecked at Adulis. Through their influence, he converted to Christianity, which became the religion of Ethiopia from then on. Before Ezana, the Aksumites had worshiped a variety of deities not unlike those of the Egyptians. They built *obelisks* (AH-buhl-iskz)—tall, freestanding columns of stone—in honor of gods associated with the Moon, warfare, and other aspects of life.

Aksum's power and wealth grew in succeeding centuries, till much of the region came under the control of its empire. During the A.D. 500s, its authority extended across the Red Sea, to control the so-called "incense states" of western Arabia. These were lush areas on the coast of the Arabian Peninsula—quite different from the desert interior—known for growing spices such as *frankincense* (FRANK-in-sints) and *myrrh* (MUHR).

The Bantu peoples (c.1200 B.C.–c. 500 A.D.)

Around the area of modern-day Nigeria, the Bantu (BAHN-too) peoples had their origins. In some regards, the Bantu do not qualify as a full-fledged civilization the way the Kushites do. They had no written language, nor did they build cities or even stay in one spot. Theirs was a history characterized by migration, as they moved out of their homeland in about 1200 B.C. to spread throughout southern Africa.

In fact, the Bantu were not even a nation or a unified group of people in the way that the Egyptians, Kushites, or Aksumites were. They were simply a group of more or less related peoples, all sub-Saharan African (i.e., "black") in origin. However, as in many other instances, the important distinction is one of language, not race. It was language that gave the Bantu peoples their distinctive character, which has influenced the culture of southern Africa up to the present day. Though they spoke a variety of tongues, they all used the same word for "people": *bantu.*

Whether or not they qualified as a true civilization, the Bantu had a strongly developed culture based on family ties. Families became grouped into clans, and clans into tribes. Loyalty to the extended family—including one's ancestors—was the most important bond in Bantu society. As in China, the ancestors played an important role in Bantu religion, which also *deified* the forces of nature. Though they had a variety of gods, the Bantu also believed in a supreme being above all.

The world of the Bantu peoples was a tightly knit one, in which everyone had a place and everyone belonged. In modern-day southern Africa, where the Bantu peoples settled, this is symbolized by the carefully organized layout of family *compounds,* or enclosed areas with a number of buildings. In the compound, there are specific areas for each family member, as well as areas for the animals and for cooking and other facets of daily life.

No one, it seems, lacked a place in Bantu society. To further strengthen the bonds among people, the Bantu were organized by age and gender groups, for instance, older men often belonged to secret societies. This is not unlike the idea of the Masonic lodge in modern America. For the Bantu, however, the strength of the ties between people meant much more than such ties do to Americans. Whereas Americans are defined partly by their independence, *interdependence* was and is a defining characteristic of Bantu society.

Each society has a certain way that it transmits its *values*: that is, the things that are important to it. In modern America, values are transmitted primarily through the media: TV, movies, radio, magazines, and newspapers. The Bantu, lacking a written language, had a strong *oral tradition*. In other words, they transmitted their values, and indeed much of their cultural heritage, primarily through stories committed to memory by elders.

Music was also an important part of the Bantu oral tradition. At musical performances, everyone present participated. Participation was easy, because every member of the tribe knew the songs—which concerned aspects of daily life as well as the stories of legendary heroes—from early childhood. Greek culture in Homer's time was likewise centered around oral traditions, stories memorized by wandering poets who sang them to listeners, often over a period of days.

Ironworking and agriculture

Another notable quality of the Bantu was their technological advancement in the area of ironworking, a remarkable achievement for a people who had no written language. The Olmec of Mesoamerica, by contrast, did have a written language, yet they never progressed beyond the Bronze Age—and then only in about A.D. 1200. Since the Sahara Desert provided a virtually impenetrable barrier between the Bantu peoples and the Egyptians, it is apparent that they developed their iron-smelting technology entirely on their own.

The same is true of Bantu agriculture: studies by archaeologists and linguists suggest that domestication of plants occurred more or less simultaneously—and indepen-

dently—in several parts of Africa before the Sahara became a desert. By about 1600 B.C., the Bantu peoples had a set of *staple* crops that included rice, yams, and various grains.

As for iron-working, it flourished as early as 1000 B.C. among the Nok (NAWK) people, a Bantu group in what is now Nigeria. The Nok also excelled in textile-weaving, sculpture, and jewelry-making. Based on the large number of high-quality *figurines* (FIG-yoo-reenz), or small sculptures, found at Nok archaeological sites, they must have been wealthy. As with the ancient Saharan culture at its high point, only people well past the point of mere survival could afford to spend so much energy on creating beauty.

The spread of Bantu culture

In their migration southward and eastward into the savanna, which contains the continent's best land, the Bantu displaced a number of native peoples in southern Africa. These

Bantu Languages

Because there are so many different groups of people in Africa, a person needs a *lingua franca* to get around. In northern Africa, Arabic is the common language, whereas in nations that were once colonies of Britain or France, English or French provides a lingua franca. But in much of southern Africa, the common language is native to the African continent.

This common language is Swahili (swah-HEEL-ee), spoken by 49 million people in Kenya, Tanzania, the Congo, and Uganda. Such large numbers for any African language are rare; the average language in Africa has only half a million speakers. But the Bantu language of Swahili provides a common tongue for the mostly Bantu peoples of southern Africa. There are some fifteen other Bantu languages spoken in parts of southern Africa.

included the Pygmies, a group whose average height was under five feet, who were forced into the less desirable rain forest. There were also the Khoisan (koy-SAHN) peoples, speakers of the so-called "click language"—one can hear it spoken in the 1980 movie *The Gods Must Be Crazy,* which humorously contrasts Bushman and Western societies. The Bantu peoples drove the Khoisan-speaking tribes into the much less favorable Kalahari (kahl-ah-HAHR-ee) Desert.

It is doubtful that the Bantu waged war against the native peoples of these areas; they probably did not have to, since they were the more technologically sophisticated group. By about A.D. 500, the ethnic map of southern Africa was more or less complete. The Bantu controlled the best areas. They would continue to do so until the Europeans arrived more than 1,000 years later.

Africa to the end of the Middle Ages

Historians know about several other important ancient African cultures because of their contact with the Phoenicians or the Egyptians. Among the Africans with whom the Phoenicians traded were people living in what is probably now the nation of Senegal (SEHN-uh-gahl) in West Africa.

The western portion of the continent would become the site for a number of important African kingdoms during the period of the Middle Ages in Europe. Among these were Ghana (GAHN-nah), Mali (MAHL-ee), and the Songhai (sawng-HIE) kingdom. Deep in the Sahara arose the kingdom of Kanem-Bornu (KAH-nehm BOHR-noo), which lasted for a thousand years from about A.D. 800 to about A.D. 1800. Notable civilizations in Bantu-speaking lands included the one that developed around the southern African fortress of Zimbabwe (zim-BAHB-way), which flourished from about 1000 to about 1400 A.D.

As with the Americas, African civilization truly came into its own at a time when European civilizations were at a low point. The same was true of the Arab world; in the 600s, Arab armies conquered much of northern Africa, including the area where the Kushite civilization had once been located, in what became the nation of Sudan. In the 1400s, when European civilization experienced a resurgence and Europeans began exploring the rest of the world, the Africans and Native Americans would suffer as a result.

Slavery

Like the Native Americans, the Africans were not united, and this helped make slavery possible. Members of rival tribes would capture and sell their "enemies" to the Europeans, a move that was as foolish as it was greedy. The Europeans did not care about the tribal differences: they would just as soon enslave one African as another. Often those who had sold others into slavery would later be captured and sold themselves.

The slave trade prevailed between the late 1400s and the early 1800s, when Europeans finally woke up to the great crime of slavery. In 1807, England became the first European nation to outlaw the slave trade, and soon afterward it abolished slavery itself. In the southern United States, however, slavery lasted longer because of the agricultural economy of the South. The dependence on agriculture made the American South much less economically advanced than the industrial North, as proved by the victory of the Union in the Civil War (1861–1865).

Colonization

In the 1800s, just as they were protesting the evils of American slavery, the nations of Europe began dividing the continent of Africa into various colonies. By the turn of the century, the only independent nations in Africa were Liberia in the west, founded by freed American slaves; and Ethiopia, site of Aksum and other great civilizations of later times. In

King Hail Selassie appeared in front of the League of Nations and spoke of Italy's attempts to reconquer Ethiopia. *The Library of Congress.*

1890, Italy colonized Eritrea (air-i-TREE-uh), the coastal region where Aksum had been located, though the Ethiopians reclaimed it after defeating the Italians in an 1896 battle.

Colonies changed hands in World War I (1914–1918), but still much of Africa remained under European control. The Italian dictator Benito Mussolini (beh-NEE-toh moo-soh-LEE-nee; 1883–1945) attempted to reconquer Ethiopia and add it to Italian possessions in eastern Africa. The Italians waged a cruel war against the Ethiopians in the 1930s, sending modern fighter planes against soldiers armed with nineteenth-century flintlock rifles. Again, it was a case of superior technology winning over less advanced versions, but the moral high ground belonged to the Ethiopians. King Haile Selassie (HIGH-lee seh-LAH-see; 1892–1975) made a compelling speech before the League of Nations, an organization formed after World War I in order to prevent future wars. Its failure to help Ethiopia provided clear evidence of the League's weaknesses and paved the way for World War II (1939–1945).

Independence

After the war, African nations rapidly became independent. Ethiopia was recognized as a leader among nations and became a founding member of the Organization of African Unity (OAU). Ironically, what brought down Haile Selassie was not the Italian invasion but enemies from within: he was *deposed* and executed by Communist rebels who took over the country in the 1970s.

Ethiopia's problems were just one example of the turmoil that rocked the continent in the decades following independence. There were literally hundreds of civil wars throughout Africa, and the continent was subjected to numerous dictatorships. One of the worst was in the nation of Uganda (oo-GAHN-dah): settled by the Bantu in ancient times and later colonized by Britain, Uganda in the 1970s was ruled by Idi Amin (EE-dee ah-MEEN; c. 1925–), a military officer with the heart of a serial killer.

Much of the planet remained largely ignorant of these problems. As far as most white Europeans and Americans were concerned, Africa's importance had ended as soon as whites left. Though black Africans were still being sold as slaves by the Arab rulers of the Sudan in the 1990s, this excited little moral outrage in the West; in fact, the only African problems that attracted much attention, in fact, were "black-white" conflicts, most notably the controversy over *apartheid* (uh-PAHR-tide) in South Africa.

Under apartheid, a system of dividing people by race, nonwhite South Africans became a permanent underclass. Not only were they forced into lower economic positions than whites, but they could not move around the country freely or use any of the same facilities—for instance, bathrooms—as whites. It was worse than *segregation*, which prevailed in the American South prior to the 1960s. It compared with aspects of the Indian caste system. Ironically, many Indians in South Africa became victims of apartheid as well. Lowest of all were black South Africans, the descendants of the Bantu people who had once claimed the land from the original inhabitants.

Under the leadership of Nelson Mandela (mahn-DEH-lah; 1918–), apartheid was overthrown and the black majority gained control of the country in the early 1990s. Other positive events happened around the same time: with the downfall of the Soviet Union, Communism came to an end in Ethiopia and other African nations as well. Ethnic tension, however, remained high. Unlike the black-white problems in South Africa, these were not conflicts that outsiders could readily

Under Nelson Mandela's leadership, the black majority gained control of South Africa in the 1990s. *Reuters/Corbis-Bettmann. Reproduced by permission.*

A Note on Some of the "For More Information" Sources

Because of the controversies associated with Afrocentrism, the study of African history is more difficult than the study of some other ancient civilizations. In selecting further reading on Africa, care has been taken to avoid works that are clearly not based on historical fact. Still, questionable claims are made in some of the books or Web sites listed below, but these sources are included because they offer valuable information as well.

In researching history, it is always wise to use several sources, including one or two acknowledged authorities on a subject. If one book offers an account of events that differs noticeably from the others, there is a chance its author used unconventional research methods in compiling his or her information. On the other hand, it should be cautioned that just because something differs from the mainstream does not mean it is wrong; it is entirely a question of *why* it differs. Is the work the result of unique research that has yielded new information, as in the case of Heinrich Schliemann's discovery of Troy? Or is the writer simply presenting supposition—something that *might* be true, or something that he or she wishes were true—as fact?

understand. Few could tell the difference between the Hutu (HOO-too) and Tutsi (TOOT-see), two Bantu-speaking groups in Rwanda (ruh-WAHN-duh); but this did not stop the Hutu from massacring half a million Tutsi in 1994.

The Hutu-Tutsi conflict resembled the ethnic problems in the former Yugoslavia during the 1990s; the United States, however, took considerably more interest in the Yugoslav conflict. Sadly, once Africa was no longer a valuable chess piece in the *cold war* between the United States and the Soviet Union, it had little political value. With the wreck that dictatorships had made of African economies, there was little business interest in the continent either. But Mandela's leadership as the first president of the "new" South Africa offered hope for the future. On the ruins of one of the worst European political systems in Africa, many hoped, Mandela and those who followed him might create a model for black Africa in the twenty-first century.

For More Information

Books

Ayo, Yvonne. *Africa.* New York: Knopf, 1995.

Davidson, Basil and the Editors of Time-Life Books. *African Kingdoms.* Alexandria, VA: Time-Life Books, 1978.

Dijkstra, Henk. *History of the Ancient & Medieval World,* Volume 3: *Ancient Cultures.* New York: Marshall Cavendish, 1996, pp. 403-14.

Dijkstra, Henk, ed. *History of the Ancient & Medieval World,* Volume 11: *Empires of the Ancient World.* New York: Marshall Cavendish, 1996, pp. 1543-54.

Dué, Andrea, ed. *The Atlas of Human History: Cradles of Civilization: Ancient Egypt and Early Middle Eastern Civilizations.* Text by Renzo Rossi. New York: Macmillan Library Reference USA, 1996, pp. 56-59.

Dué, Andrea, ed. *The Atlas of Human History: Civilizations of Asia: India, China and the Peoples of Southeast Asia and the Indian Ocean.* Text by Renzo Rossi and Martina Veutro. New York: Macmillan Library Reference USA, 1996, pp. 52-55.

Haskins, James and Kathleen Benson. *African Beginnings.* Paintings by Floyd Cooper. New York: Lothrop, Lee & Shepard Books, 1998.

Martell, Hazel Mary. *The Kingfisher Book of the Ancient World.* New York: Kingfisher, 1995, pp. 114-23.

Motley, Mary Penick. *Africa: Its Empires, Nations and People.* With illustrations by Arthur Roland, Jr. Detroit, MI: Wayne State University Press, 1969.

Vlahos, Olivia. *African Beginnings.* Illustrated by George Ford. New York: Viking Press, 1967.

Web Sites

"Africa in 1000 B.C.E.-600 C.E." http://loki.stockton.edu/~gilmorew/consorti/1cafric.htm (June 8, 1999).

"Africa Timeline." http://www.wwnorton.com/college/history/world-civ/reference/afritime.htm (June 8, 1999).

Ancient Nubia. http://library.advanced.org/22845/ (June 8, 1999).

K-12 Africa Guide. http://www.sas.upenn.edu/African_Studies/Home_Page/AFR_GIDE.html (June 8, 1999).

"Mr. Dorish's Ancient Africa Page." http://www.flinet.com/~rms/sixth/dorish/ 609ancafr.html (June 8, 1999).

Piccione, Peter A. "Excursis IV: Nubia: The Land Upriver." http://www.library.nwu.edu/class/history/B94/B94nubia.html (June 8, 1999).

"Saharan Rock Art." http://www.paleologos.com/saharaan.htm (June 8, 1999).

"Sahara Tassili Frescoes." http://www.paleologos.com/sahang.htm (June 8, 1999).

Greece

11

Greece is a rugged land at the southeastern corner of the European continent, across the Aegean Sea from Asia Minor (modern Turkey) to the east. To the west, on the other side of the Ionian Sea, is Italy. Southward lies the island of Crete. Farther still, in a southeastward direction across the Mediterranean, is Egypt. In observing the map of Greece, three notable facts are clear. First is its location, close to many great centers of ancient civilization; second is its rough coastline, a series of islands, inlets, and peninsulas; and third is its small size. A little more than 50,000 square miles (129,500 square kilometers), it is about as large as the state of Alabama.

Why Greece is important

It is hard to imagine a world without Greece because virtually every aspect of modern life owes something to the ancient Greeks. This is particularly so in Western nations such as the United States, where people enjoy the freedoms associated with democracy, a form of government created in Athens some 2,500 years ago. There are all the benefits of science,

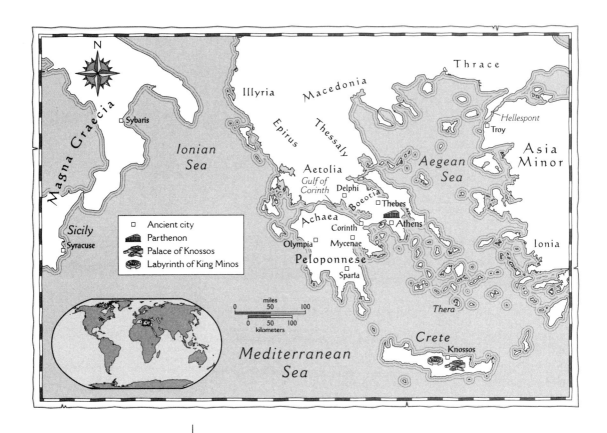

Map of Greece.

XNR Productions.

The Gale Group.

which only emerged as a *discipline* with the Greeks, not to mention the arts, from architecture to theater, which would be completely different without the Greek legacy. Even sports owe a huge debt to Greece, where wrestling, track and field, and a number of other athletic events were born. Finally, there is language itself, which is filled with words derived from Greek—*athletic, architecture, democracy, theater*—and *history*.

Greek geography and history

The study of ancient Greece can be rather confusing because of the tiny geographical size of the country, along with the historical importance of so many spots. Thus it is useful to organize the geographical areas of Greece in one's mind—for instance, by remembering that the focus of Greek history shifted from the south to the north over thousands of years. That history began on the southernmost part of the Greek isles, in Crete (rhymes with "neat"), about 25 miles (40 kilometers) off the Greek mainland. Later on, the city-states of the southern mainland would hold center stage; and in the last phase of Greek history, Macedon (MAS-uh-dahn) in the far north dominated the region.

Greece is shaped like the leg of an eagle or some other great bird. Its "thigh" comes down from Macedon in a southeasterly direction, narrowing to a strip of land that eventually reaches a sort of knee—or rather think of the "joint" as an "elbow," given its angle. Southwest of the "elbow" is an even narrower strip of land, which leads to a giant "claw" at the far southern tip of the Greek mainland. This "claw" is a peninsula called the Peloponnese (peh-luh-puh-NEEZ).

Many of the most important cities of Greek history, including Sparta, Mycenae, and Olympia, were located on the Peloponnese. The upper portion of the Peloponnese, Achaea (uh-KEE-ah), included another important city, Corinth (KOHR-inth). North of Corinth is the Gulf of Corinth, a body of water that forms the western boundary of the "elbow."

The "elbow," bounded by the Aegean Sea (eh-JEE-uhn) on the east, contains the region of Attica (AT-i-kuh). The principal city of Attica was Athens, the birthplace of Western civilization. North of Attica, on the upper part of the eagle's leg, was Boeotia (bee-OH-shuh), a region that contained the city of Thebes. To the northwest of Thebes was the important religious center of Delphi.

The "thigh" included a number of important regions: Aetolia (ee-TOH-lee-ah), Epirus (ee-PIE-ruhs), and Illyris (i-LEER-ee-ah; modern-day Albania) on the western coast; Thessaly (THEH-suh-lee) on the eastern coast; and Macedon at the far north.

Beyond Greece to the northeast, where the nation of Bulgaria is now located, was the area of Thrace (rhymes with "space"). Across a narrow sea passageway called the Hellespont was Asia Minor. Northwestern Asia Minor included the city of Troy. The southwestern coast was the region of Ionia (ie-OHN-ee-uh), which contained a number of important Greek settlements.

Finally, far away to the west, was an area called Magna Graecia (MAG-nuh GREE-shuh), or "Great Greece." These were

Words to Know: Greece

Acropolis: An elevated fortress in Greek cities.

Aqueduct: A long pipe, usually mounted on a high stone wall that slopes gently, used to carry water from the mountains to the lowlands.

Archaic: Old.

Aristocrat: A very wealthy and/or powerful person.

Boycott: To refuse to participate in something as a way of protesting.

Capital: In architecture, the top of a column.

Catharsis: The experience of emotional release that comes from watching a character on stage (or in a movie) undergoing difficult circumstances.

Chaos: Disorder or confusion.

Chastity: The act or state of remaining pure by not engaging in sex.

Constitution: A set of written laws governing a nation.

Democracy: Rule by the people, sometimes directly (direct democracy), but more often through elected officials (representative democracy).

Dialogue: Conversation, usually with a purpose; not small talk.

Dialect: A regional variation on a language.

Discipline (n.): An area of study or endeavor.

Embargo: An act forcing a halt on trade between two countries.

Entablature: In architecture, the decorative band between the capital and the pediment.

Epic: A long poem that recounts the adventures of a legendary hero.

Fluted: In architecture, an adjective for a column marked by grooves.

Fresco: A painting applied directly to a wall.

Frieze: A band of sculptured figures or ornaments.

Geometry: A type of mathematics dealing with various shapes, their properties, and their measurements.

Golden Age: A time of great happiness and prosperity.

Hoplite: A heavily armed foot soldier.

Hubris: Pride and arrogance, which usually leads to misfortune.

Hypotenuse: The long side of a right triangle.

Hypothesis: A statement subject to scientific testing for truth or falsehood.

Labyrinth: Maze.

Laconic: Abrupt to the point of rudeness.

Logic: A system of reasoning, closely related to mathematics, for reaching correct con-

colonies on the Italian peninsula and the island of Sicily south of it, including Sybaris and Syracuse. The term *colony*, in the context of ancient Greece, has a meaning similar to that used clusions about concepts, and for assessing a conclusion that has been reached.

Lyre: A type of harp.

Mortal: Generally, something that does not live forever; specifically, a human being as opposed to a god.

Mosque: A Muslim temple.

Mythology: A collection of stories dealing with the gods and heroes of a specific people.

Ode: A poem honoring someone or something.

Orator: Speaker.

Ostracize: To force someone out of a group.

Pantheon: All the recognized gods in a religion.

Paradox: A situation in which something seems contradictory or opposed to common sense, but is in fact true.

Pediment: The triangular gable end of a roof.

Phalanx: A column of hoplites (heavily armed foot soldiers); the formation was designed for offensive warfare.

Philosophy: A discipline that seeks to reach a general understanding of values and of reality.

Polis: A Greek city-state.

Psychology: The study of the mind and human behavior.

Redistribution: The act of taking wealth from the rich and dividing it up among the poor.

Satire: A type of literary work that makes fun of human follies and vices.

Skepticism: The tendency to approach issues with a questioning attitude rather than accepting things at face value.

Sophist: Somebody who simply wants to argue or who cares more about winning an argument than reaching the truth.

Strait: A narrow water passageway between two areas of land.

Syllogism: A logical formula consisting of a general statement, a specific statement, and a conclusion.

Theorem: A statement of fact in logic or mathematics, derived from other formulas or propositions.

Titan: A giant.

Tyrant: A type of leader in ancient Greece who seized power with popular support. Not the same meaning as the modern word.

Underworld: In mythology, a place of departed souls beneath the earth.

in connection with Phoenicia. The Greek colonies of Italy were important contributors to Greek culture and would play a part in the histories of both Greece and Rome.

The Minoans (c. 2000–c. 1450 B.C.)

At some point during the Neolithic Age, a people called the Minoans (mi-NOH-uhnz) settled on Crete. Historians do not know where the Minoans came from, though it is likely they had their origins in Asia Minor. It is less of a mystery why they were drawn to Crete, which has a sunny, pleasant climate. Its hillsides abound with sweet-smelling flowers. The fertile soil is ideal for planting grains and fruit—most notably grapes and olives. From an early point, wine and olive oil became the most significant products of the area. They remain a major part of Mediterranean cuisine.

In about 2000 B.C., the Minoan civilization underwent a sudden upsurge, entering a *golden age*. For the next five centuries, it would rival the great civilizations of the time: Egypt during the Middle Kingdom and Babylonia around the time of Hammurabi. The Minoans had their own system of writing, which archaeologists refer to as Linear A (LIN-ee-uhr, meaning "like a line"). However, Linear A has never been deciphered; therefore most of what is known about ancient Crete is the result of archaeological finds.

The center of the Minoan culture appears to have been the Palace of Knossos (NAH-suhs), the greatest of some thirty Bronze Age sites uncovered by archaeologists. The evidence of Knossos and three other palaces has led scholars to the conclusion that some time around 1700 B.C., Crete experienced a major earthquake or a series of earthquakes. Afterward, Knossos and the other palaces were rebuilt, this time on a larger scale.

Knossos and other Minoan triumphs

Knossos in particular was a wonder of engineering. Like the magnificent cities of the Indus Valley civilization, it had drainage systems for removing wastewater. *Aqueducts* (AHK-weh-duhktz), long pipes usually mounted on high, sloping stone walls, carried fresh water from a mountain nearly 600 miles (907 kilometers) away. In the bathrooms at Knossos, the royal family enjoyed comforts of a modern home: not only showers, but even flush toilets.

Beyond the palace walls were other feats of Minoan engineering, including bridges and roads made of stone, but perhaps the most famous Minoan structure was one that existed primarily in myth. This was the *labyrinth* (LAB-i-rinth), or maze, of King Minos (MEE-nohs), a legendary figure from whose name "Minoan" is derived. Though the tale of his labyrinth is a myth, it probably had its origins in fact. Visitors were overwhelmed by the size and seemingly endless passageways in the Palace of Knossos. No doubt some traveler came back with fantastic tales of the palace, and from these tales the legend grew.

Around Knossos a city developed. During the *zenith* of Minoan civilization, from about 1700 to 1450 B.C., it held between 40,000 and 80,000 people. In contrast to the cruel King Minos of legend, the real Minoan kings appear to have been fair rulers who worked to build up their land as an economic rather than a military power. Just as the Phoenicians established colonies throughout the Mediterranean, the Minoans founded colonies on the mainland of Greece, Asia Minor, and on islands between. Yet they did not put much effort into building up their military. Again like the Phoenicians, they were more concerned with trade than with warfare.

The Minoans, in fact, were the first great seafaring empire, even before the Phoenicians. They built the best ships of the time, and traded with Egypt and Sumer and with Ugarit in Syria. Because of their naval superiority, they often became "middlemen" for other countries, transporting goods from one place to another and often going into relatively remote parts of the known world. They were also accomplished craftsmen, producing jewelry, pottery, and dyed textiles that spread to the rest of the Mediterranean on Minoan ships.

Theseus fights the Minotaur, half man half beast, inside the labyrinth. *Archive Photos. Reproduced by permission.*

Minoan society and religion

At home, the Minoans enjoyed what was in many ways a much freer society than that of the later Greeks.

Though like most ancient societies, they practiced slavery, slaves were treated quite well in Crete. Women, who even in the Golden Age of Athens were little better than slaves, enjoyed a status more or less equal to men. Judging from Minoan artwork, they wore their hair long and did not cover their breasts. Many were priestesses.

Women's role in the Minoan religion is not surprising, because the Minoans worshiped a female fertility goddess. Though her name is not known, it is clear that she belonged to a type that prevailed throughout the ancient world: Isis in Egypt, Ishtar or Inanna in Mesopotamia, and later the Greco-Roman (GREH-koh) goddess Demeter/Ceres.

Many early religions were dominated by female deities. These "earth goddesses" were usually associated with agriculture and the home. Later ages saw the appearance of male deities, "sky gods" associated with powers of nature—the ocean, thunder, fire—or with other powerful forces such as warfare or the *Underworld*. The Greek *pantheon* (PAN-thee-ahn) would later include a number of male sky gods, most notably Zeus, king of the gods, alongside female earth goddesses such as his wife Hera, goddess of the home.

Minoans also worshiped bulls. One of their more unusual customs, one not fully understood by historians, was bull-leaping. Apparently an acrobat would stand before a charging bull, and at the last moment grab hold of the bull's horns and vault over its back. It is not clear whether this activity was purely religious in nature, like the Olmec ball game, or if it was also a form of entertainment. What is clear is that bull-leaping was extremely dangerous. It is possible, too, that the worship of bulls helped inspire the Minotaur myth.

Religion in ancient Crete seems to have included a number of elements, some of them apparently at odds with one another. On one hand, the Minoans worshiped bulls. On the other hand, they sacrificed bulls and other animals to the earth goddess. The Minoans were in contact with many cultures, however, so these contradictions are perhaps understandable. Another aspect of Minoan religion was the double axe: symbols of an axe with a double head decorate pottery and other items found at Minoan sites, suggesting that it was a sacred object.

The Labyrinth of Minos

According to legend, King Minos of Crete had a vast labyrinth, or maze, underneath his palace. Deep inside the maze lived a fearsome creature, half man and half bull, called a *minotaur* (MIN-oh-tawr). Once a year, Minos would demand that the people of Athens send him seven young men and seven young women to feed to the Minotaur. If the Athenians did not send these young people to be sacrificed, Minos would destroy their city.

Finally a young Athenian named Theseus (THEE-see-uhs), son of the king, went to his father and asked to be sent to Crete with the others. The king reluctantly agreed, with one condition. Normally the ship that carried Minos's victims went under a black sail, in honor of the dead; but if Theseus were successful in his mission, the king said, he should put up a white sail before he sailed into the harbor at Athens. That way his father would know

he was safe and could stop worrying. Theseus agreed and went away with the others to Crete.

When the sacrificial victims were shown to King Minos, his daughter Ariadne (air-ee-AD-nee) was present. She fell in love with Theseus and gave him two gifts to aid him in surviving the labyrinth: a sword and a ball of yarn. He unwound the yarn as he went in. He killed the Minotaur with the sword and, using the yarn, found his way back to the entrance. Theseus escaped the island with Ariadne.

They did not live happily ever after, however. Theseus left Ariadne on an island because one of the gods commanded him to, and even worse, he forgot to replace the black sail with a white one. His father, seeing the ship in the distance, thought Theseus had been killed and jumped off a cliff to his death.

The end of Minoan civilization

It appears that Knossos and the other major centers of Minoan civilization experienced some kind of disaster in about 1450 B.C. As with Teotihuacán in the New World, archaeologists are unsure exactly how Minoan civilization suddenly came to an end, though a number of explanations have been put forward.

Perhaps a tidal wave, the result of a volcanic eruption or earthquake, struck the island and sank part of it. This may in turn have provided the source for the legend of Atlantis, a once-great civilization supposedly submerged beneath the

Atlantic Ocean. The legend received a major boost when no less a thinker than the philosopher Plato wrote about it. In fact "Atlantis" was probably a part of Crete in the Mediterranean. (The lost civilization of the Sahara is like a real-life Atlantis— only it was in the desert, not the ocean.)

In the A.D. 1960s, archaeologists began finding evidence that a great volcano struck the island of Thera (THAIR-uh), between Crete and the Greek mainland, some time around 1500 B.C. Again like Teotihuacán, the natural disaster may have been coupled with political upheaval—perhaps a popular revolt spurred on by the government's inability to deal with the problems, such as homelessness and disruption of normal activities, created by the disaster. It is also quite possible that the earthquake provided an opportunity for invasion by a group who would usher in the next phase of Greek history: the Mycenaeans (mie-suh-NEE-uhnz).

The Mycenaean Age (c. 1650–c. 1100 B.C.)

The Mycenaeans probably came from the Black Sea area starting in about 2800 B.C. Undoubtedly they were part of the Indo-European invasion: their language was an early form of Greek, itself an Indo-European tongue. By 2000 B.C., they had conquered the native peoples of Greece and had settled in the Peloponnese. A warlike people, the Mycenaeans built a Bronze Age civilization that flourished throughout the region beginning in about 1650 B.C.

The Mycenaeans, who had lived in the shadow of the Minoans for a long time, adopted aspects of Minoan civilization. Their language was probably unrelated to that of the Minoans; however, in its written form, they adapted it to the Minoan script, which has been dubbed "Linear B." Linear B was deciphered in A.D. 1952 by an amateur (that is, someone not professionally trained in a field of study) linguist; similarly, an amateur archaeologist would discover the ruins both of Mycenae (mie-SEE-nee), the Mycenaeans' principal city, and of their ancient rival Troy.

Among the findings of amateur archaeologist Heinrich Schliemann (HINE-rik SH'LEE-mahn) were the Shaft Graves, a series of tunnels where Mycenaean royalty had been buried.

The shafts contained enormous wealth in gold jewelry, ornaments, and other objects. Fortunately for the world, this treasure was discovered by a serious historian and not by grave robbers such as those who spoiled the treasures of Egypt and China.

Based on Schliemann's findings, it appears that the Mycenaeans also imitated the Minoans in the building of great palaces. Mycenae was centered around a fortress called an *acropolis* (uh-KRAHP-uh-lis), located on a high spot overlooking the town. This type of elevated fortress would become an important feature of Greek cities in the future. Thanks to Schliemann, scholars have some idea of the Mycenaean original.

The Mycenaean acropolis had a huge main gate and, as with Minoan palaces, had a long series of hallways and passages that ultimately led to the great hall or *megaron* (MEHG-uh-rahn). There the king sat on his throne and oversaw the business of the kingdom. Along the walls were *frescoes* (FRES-kohz), paintings applied directly to a wall, showing various scenes.

Trojan Horse.
Archive Photos. Reproduced by permission.

Also like the Minoans, the Mycenaeans worshiped an earth goddess, but they combined this with worship of sky gods, which formed the basis for the later Olympian religion. The Mycenaeans differed too from the Minoans in their attitude toward foreign affairs. They were at least as interested in waging war as they were in conducting trade. Whereas the Minoans had spread prosperity throughout the region, the Mycenaeans were harsh people who attacked weak cities and formed alliances with strong ones. They did, however, attack at least one strong city: Troy.

The Trojan War

For centuries, people assumed that the Trojan War was completely fictional. The accounts of the war and its after-

The poet Homer.
Archive Photos. Reproduced by permission.

math, set down by the poet Homer in the *Iliad* (IL-ee-ad) and the *Odyssey* (AH-duh-see), are among the central works of Western literature; but nobody took Homer's work seriously as history. Again thanks to Schliemann, the world now knows that Troy was indeed real.

Sometimes referred to as Ilium (IL-ee-uhm)—hence the name *Iliad*—Troy lay along the southern edge of a *strait* called the Hellespont (HEHL-ehs-pahnt). Hellespont, which in modern times is called the Dardanelles (dahr-duh-NELZ), forms part of a long passageway that separates Europe from Asia and joins the Aegean Sea in the west with the Black Sea in the east.

The Trojan War appears to have occurred in about 1200 B.C., but its cause was probably not as romantic as the one Homer gives—the kidnapping of the Spartan queen Helen, the most beautiful woman in the world, by a prince of Troy. More likely it was for military and economic objectives: whoever controlled the Hellespont controlled the entire region, including the lucrative Black Sea trade.

According to Homer, the Trojan War lasted for ten years and resulted in victory for the Mycenaeans. Historians do not know whether this is so, but it is clear that Mycenaean civilization began to decline around the time of the war. Perhaps "winning" the Trojan War cost the Mycenaeans so much in terms of human lives and financial resources that they never recovered.

The Dark Ages (c. 1100–c. 700 B.C.)

History is filled with fascinating chains of events, which are like a string of dominoes falling one by one—only, in the case of historical events, the results are much less predictable. The building of the Great Wall of China in the 200s

B.C., which displaced nomadic tribes from the region, created a series of shock waves felt all to the way to the gates of Rome some 600 years later. What happened in Greece in the 1100s B.C. was similar, though on a much smaller scale.

From the north, in Macedon, came a group of barbarians who moved into Epirus and Thessaly. The Macedonians would later have an enormous impact on Greek history, but at this early stage, their primary effect was to scatter the Dorians (DOHR-ee-uhnz), another barbarian group, from their homeland in about 1140 B.C.

The Dorians in turn swarmed southward, over the strongholds at Mycenae and elsewhere. The Mycenaeans were not the same strong nation that had once taken over from the Minoans. The Dorians, though they may have been uncivilized, had a technological advantage. They had developed iron smelting, and the Mycenaeans, with their Bronze Age weapons, were no match for them. Armed with their superior iron swords, the Dorians swept into the Mycenaean cities, sacking and burning as they went. The Dark Ages had begun.

Greece under Dorian rule

The term "Dark Ages" has often applied to the five centuries after the fall of the Roman Empire in A.D. 476, when civilization all but disappeared from Western Europe. This expression has fallen from favor, however, because it neglects the achievements of that era. Less well known is the use of the same expression to describe the period from about 1100 to about 700 B.C. in Greece. Here again, how-

Heinrich Schliemann

Unlike recognized scholars of his day, Heinrich Schliemann (1822–1890), an amateur archaeologist, took seriously the Greek legends of Mycenae and Troy. He had read about them in a book given to him as a boy, a rare present in his poverty-stricken childhood. Later, as a grown man who had amassed great wealth as a merchant, he set off for Turkey to find the ancient home of the Trojans.

From reading Homer, Schliemann was convinced that the ruins of Troy lay beneath Hissarlik (HIS-uhr-lik) in the western tip of Asia Minor. Needless to say, a lot of people thought he was crazy, but Schliemann and his team began digging and worked tirelessly for years. Eventually they did find Troy, just as Schliemann had expected.

However, they did not find one Troy but *nine*. Lacking bulldozers, ancient peoples did not have any way to remove the ruins of an old building or city, so they usually just piled up dirt and built over them. Thus there were nine different versions of Troy. It appears that the Trojan War took place at the time of the seventh version.

ever, the term "Dark Ages" is deceptive: on the one hand, it was a time when civilization in the area hit a low point; on the other hand, it was during these four centuries that the roots of Greek culture developed.

The Dorians, a tribal society, settled primarily in the southern and eastern Peloponnese. Their rulers took over what was left of the Mycenaeans' fortresses and palaces. Whenever there was a dispute between individuals or families, as there often was, the parties involved would go to their king, who served as a judge.

There was no real sense of justice, however, as there might have been in a society governed by formal laws such as those set forth by Hammurabi or Justinian. Life in Greece under Dorian rule was more like Israel during the time of the judges, when "everyone did as he sought fit." Men walked around armed, just in case there was trouble. The Dorians spoke a *dialect* (DIE-uh-lekt; a regional variation of a language), of Greek. Dorian was distinct from Aeolian (ay-OHL-ee-uhn), spoken in an area running from Thessaly to the edge of the Peloponnese, and from Ionian, spoken by the Mycenaeans and others on the Peloponnese itself. The Dorians did not, however, have a written language. Linear B script died out in the Dark Ages.

Other aspects of life declined as well. The arts, most notably pottery—examples of which have been found by archaeologists in the region—clearly suffered under Dorian rule. Having destroyed the Mycenaeans' cities, the Dorians no longer had access to their trade routes. The once-rich land of Greece became poor as a result. In contrast to the gold of the Mycenaean tombs, Dorian burial sites have yielded little in the way of precious metals and gems. The Dorians buried their dead with offerings of bone, stone, and clay. It is not surprising, then, to discover that the population of the area also dropped rapidly during the Dark Ages, no doubt as a consequence of poverty.

The seeds of a greater flowering

To varying degrees, similar conditions—poverty, ignorance, and lawlessness—would prevail during the other "Dark Ages" that would sweep over Europe some 1,500 years later.

Egypt in Greece

It is probably no mistake that the Greek city of Thebes shares its name with an even older Egyptian city. Indeed, it may have been settled by Phoenician travelers who had been to Egypt. Legend holds that King Cadmus (KAD-muhs), the mythical founder of Thebes, introduced the Phoenician alphabet to the Greeks, who developed their own version of it.

There is even a legend of a sphinx in Thebes. Like the sphinx of Egypt, this one had the body of a lion and the head of a human—a woman and not a pharaoh in the case of the Grecian sphinx. Nor was she merely a statue, but rather a monster that terrorized travelers coming to Thebes. To each she asked a riddle: "What animal is it that in the morning goes on four feet, at noon on two, and in the evening upon three?" Those who could not answer correctly—and no one could—were killed. It took the great hero Oedipus (ED-i-puhs) to solve the riddle, which so angered the Sphinx that she killed herself. His answer? See below.

Certainly there is no question that the Greeks were influenced by older cultures of Africa and the East. Thus Herodotus wrote that "the names of all the gods have been known in Egypt from the beginning of time." An Ionian trading colony was established at Naucratis (NAW-kruh-tis) on the Nile delta in the mid-600s B.C. The colony gave the Greeks exposure not only to the civilization of Egypt (whose Great Pyramids were as old to them as the ancient Greeks are to modern people) but also to the brilliant civilizations of the East, such as Babylon.

The answer to the Riddle of the Sphinx: The creature is man, who in childhood creeps on all fours, as an adult walks on two legs, and in old age walks with the aid of a cane.

But as with that later era, the Dark Ages in Greece carried with them the elements that would lead to a great cultural flowering in centuries to come. Also as in the later Dark Ages, civilization never really died out. A few Mycenaeans held on in the mountainous region of Arcadia (ahr-KAY-dee-uh) in the central Peloponnese, and farther east, in Attica—specifically, in an insignificant village named Athens. Other Mycenaeans traveled farther east, across the Aegean to Asia Minor. There they founded a number of cities in a region they called Ionia, just south of Lydia.

As the name suggests, the people of Ionia spoke the Ionian dialect, as did those of Athens. The Ionian town of Miletus (mi-LEE-tuhs) would become the birthplace of philosophy in the 500s B.C. Much earlier, it would be the place where the Greek religion reached full definition. It would also be in Ionia that the first great writers of the Western world, the poets Homer and Hesiod (HEE-see-uhd), established a literary tradition based on the gods and their deeds.

The foundations of Greek culture and civilization

Though people consider Homer one of the greatest writers of all time, for centuries many believed that he never existed. Rather than a single figure named "Homer," some suggested, the name had been given to a group of poets who together composed the works attributed to him. But just as Schliemann proved the existence of Troy, scholars came to believe that there really was a poet named Homer. They can say only that he lived some time between 900 and 700 B.C.

Most likely Homer was a wandering poet who earned his living by going to towns and presenting his tales—the "movies" of his day. Often he is depicted as blind; certainly he did not rely on reading and writing for his art, but rather memorized his long stories, which he sang over many nights while strumming upon a harp-like instrument called a *lyre* (pronounced just like "liar"). These stories were the *Iliad* and the *Odyssey,* fictional accounts of gods, heroes, and their actions during the Trojan War and afterward. They were the central works of Greek literature, and particularly Greek literature as it concerned the conflict with Troy.

More is known about Hesiod, who flourished in about 800 B.C. His most important works were the *Theogony* (thee-AH-juhn-ee) and *Works and Days*. The *Theogony* tells about the creation of the universe and the origination of the gods. *Works and Days* includes the story of Prometheus. In writing these epic poems, Hesiod, like Homer, was setting down traditions already established, rather than making up new stories.

These traditions were the Greeks' *mythology,* a collection of tales about gods and heroes. Usually mythology is

Herod Atticus Ancient Theatre, Athens, Greece. *AP/Wide World Photos. Reproduced by permission.*

passed down orally. Most Greek myths became a part of literature, either in the works of Homer or Hesiod or in the writings of later Greek poets and dramatists. Eventually they formed the cornerstone of Western literature, along with the Bible. As with the Bible, expressions and stories from the Greek myths are a part of daily life in America and other Western nations. In ancient times, they helped give the Greeks a common culture.

Gods and Titans

According to the Greeks' religion, the world was created out of a state of confusion, symbolized by the god *Chaos* (KAY-ahs), whose name has become part of the English language. From Chaos came Uranus and Gaea, parents of the *Titans* (TIGHT-uhnz). Most likely the gods known as Titans, of whom the most important were Cronos and Rhea, were older deities of the Mycenaean age or before.

Cronos, whose name in Greek means "time" (hence English words such as *chronology* and *chronometer*), was said to devour his own children, just as time ultimately brings to an end anything that has a beginning. No wonder, then, that his children—Zeus, Poseidon, and Hades—revolted against him. The success of their revolt established the twelve Olympians (oh-LIMP-ee-uhnz), so named because the Greeks believed they lived high atop Mount Olympus in Thessaly, as the supreme gods.

Chief among the Olympians was Zeus, their king. His brothers were Poseidon, who ruled the sea, and Hades, lord of the Underworld. Though Zeus had a wife, Hera, he was constantly fathering children through goddesses and *mortals* (MOHR-tuhlz), or humans. The other eight Olympians were all his children, but only two—Ares and Hephaestus—were by Hera. Among Zeus's most famous mortal children was the hero Heracles (HAIR-uh-kleez), more commonly known as Hercules.

The Olympians dealt severely with the Titans, most of whom they confined to Tartarus (TAHR-tuhr-uhs). Tartarus was the lowest region of Hades (HAY-deez), the Greeks' name both for the Underworld and for the god who ruled it. Hades itself was not a place of punishment; rather, it was just a dreary world where the souls of most people went when they died. Exceptionally good people went to the Elysian Fields (ehl-EE-zhuhn), a heavenly place. Exceptionally bad people went to Tartarus, the Greek version of Hell.

Two of the Titans, Atlas and Prometheus (proh-MEETH-ee-uhs), managed to escape Tartarus, only to suffer other terrible fates. The Olympians condemned Atlas to hold the world on his shoulders for all time. Even more complex was the story of Prometheus, who along with his brother Epimetheus (ep-i-MEE-thee-uhs), created man and the other animals out of clay. It was Epimetheus's job to give each animal a special gift: claws to the eagle, a protective shell to the turtle, and so on. But when it came time to provide a gift to man, Epimetheus had nothing left. Therefore Prometheus went up to Olympus, where from the chariot of Apollo—who raced daily across the sky in the form of the Sun—he stole the gift of fire.

The gods dealt with this crime in two ways, first by punishing man for accepting Prometheus's stolen gift. This

they did by sending Pandora (pan-DOHR-uh), the first woman, to live in the home of Epimetheus. Each deity had given her a gift, such as the gift of beauty from Aphrodite and the gift of music from Apollo. But Pandora was also very curious. When she discovered a sealed box in Epimetheus's house, she had to know what it contained. In fact it contained all the things Epimetheus had withheld from man: diseases, bad emotions, and all manner of other evils. When Pandora opened it, she released all its terrible contents into the world. But there was one thing left at the bottom of the box, which would give humanity the strength to deal with all other hardships: hope.

As for Prometheus, the gods punished him by chaining him to a rock atop a mountain in the Caucasus. Every day, an eagle ate his liver, which then grew back at night. He tried to bargain for his release by telling Zeus a secret regarding the goddess Thetis, but it did him no good. Later he was saved by Heracles, who shot the eagle and set Prometheus free. Throughout the ages, Prometheus has remained an inspiring figure to writers, poets, and philosophers. His theft of fire has come to symbolize heroic acts on behalf of humanity. "Promethean" is an adjective for daring originality and creativity.

Greek religion in practice

It is easy to see a relationship between the stories of Pandora and Prometheus and the biblical account of Adam and Eve's sin. Greek mythology even had its own story of a Great Flood, not unlike that of the Sumerians and Israelites. But in fact there were far more differences than similarities between the religion of the Greeks and that of the Israelites.

The account of Adam's and Eve's sin in Genesis is an incredibly complex piece of symbolism that carries with it a whole range of concepts: guilt, sin, redemption, and so on. The Prometheus tales are simple stories to explain why the world is the way it is. As important as they are, they are far from being the foundation of the Greek religion, whereas it is impossible to imagine the Bible without the Eden story and the great drama it set in motion. Prometheus's theft of fire, while it offended the gods, was hardly a sin; in fact, it made the world a much better place, unlike the eating of the apple.

There was simply no concept of sin in the Greek religion. Rather than being good or evil, actions either pleased the gods or displeased them. The Greeks did their best to avoid angering the gods. To worship them, they made offerings at temples. There was no bible other than the myths. To learn the will of the gods, the Greeks went to places such as Delphi (DEL-fie), a city north of the Gulf of Corinth.

At Delphi was a shrine called the Oracle of Delphi (OHR-uh-kuhl), inhabited by a priestess who would, for a fee,

The Garden of Eden.
Archive Photos. Reproduced by permission.

answer any question visitors put to her. As with much else from Greece, the Delphic Oracle has become a part of modern language, often referred to as a symbol of great wisdom. Actually, the term "Delphic Oracle" refers to the shrine itself rather than the priestess, who was called the Pythia (PITH-ee-uh). The words of the Pythia were notoriously vague, much like modern horoscopes, which can be interpreted to mean almost anything one wants them to mean.

Again, the Pythia was not like the prophets of Israel. The prophets would never have dreamed of accepting money for telling the future, which was a holy gift from God. Both the Old and New testaments contain a number of stories concerning the terrible fate of men who did prophesy for money. This idea would have made no sense to the Greeks. However, just as there was no sin, there was no holiness. Certainly if one were looking for a model of righteousness, one would hardly look to Olympus.

Unlike Yahweh or Jehovah, Zeus and the others never claimed to be perfect. No modern soap opera has as many cheating husbands, scheming wives, and all-around dastardly figures as the Court of King Zeus. Whereas Jehovah abided by specific laws that restrained his behavior as well as that of humankind, the Greek gods were bound by no law other than their own desires. They were basically just like humans, only with much more power. This aspect is readily apparent in the Greek "scriptures"—the myths concerning the world's origins and other deeds of the gods, as well as the many stories associated with the Trojan War.

The Troy tale

Of the many stories about the Trojan War (sometimes collectively referred to as the "Troy tale") the most important are Homer's two great works, the *Iliad* and the *Odyssey*. Like the Sumerian *Gilgamesh*, these are *epics,* or long poems recounting the adventures of legendary heroes. A popular misconception about the *Iliad* is that it concerns the entire Trojan War, but in fact it takes place over the space of a few days in the tenth year of the war. Homer's tale does not even recount the most famous story of the war, that of the "Trojan Horse."

The roots of the Trojan conflict began when Zeus fell in love with the sea-goddess Thetis (THEE-tis). He would have married her, but he knew from Prometheus that she was destined to bear a son who would be greater than his father. Therefore he arranged her marriage to a mortal king named Peleus (PEEL-ee-uhs). He invited all the gods and goddesses to the wedding except Eris (AIR-is), the goddess of *strife.*

Spiteful Eris "crashed" the wedding party and presented a golden apple, which she said belonged to the fairest, or most beautiful, of the goddesses. Hera and two of Zeus's daughters, Athena and Aphrodite, each considered themselves the fairest. They demanded that Zeus judge the contest between them. Zeus wisely declined; instead, he sent them to a young prince named Paris, son of King Priam (PRIE-uhm) of Troy. Each of the goddesses tried to bribe Paris to choose her. Paris was most swayed by Aphrodite's gift: if he would choose her, she said, she would give him the most beautiful woman in the world as his wife.

There was just one problem. The most beautiful woman in the world, Queen Helen of Sparta, already had a

The Gods of Greece and Rome

Below is a listing of Greek and Roman goddesses, along with a short description and their relation to Zeus. Note that only deities are mentioned. Most of Zeus's children were the result of his union with one or another mortals, who are not named because they were not important figures in Greek mythology. An asterisk (*) signifies an Olympian.

Greek Name	Roman Name	Description
*Aphrodite (af-roh-DIE-tee)	Venus	Goddess of love; daughter of Zeus
*Apollo	Apollo	God of the sun, poetry, healing, and light; son of Zeus
*Ares (AIR-eez)	Mars	God of war; son of Zeus and Hera
*Artemis (AHR-ti-mis)	Diana	Goddess of hunting and *chastity*; daughter of Zeus
*Athena (ah-THEE-nuh)	Minerva	Goddess of wisdom, crafts, and war; daughter of Zeus
Cronos (KROH-nohs)	Saturn	Ruler over the Titans; father of Zeus
Demeter (di-MEE-tuhr)	Ceres (SAIR-eez)	Goddess of agriculture and fertility; sister of Zeus
*Dionysus (die-oh-NIE-sus)	Bacchus (BAK-us)	God of wine, fertility, and ecstasy; son of Zeus
Eros (AIR-aws)	Cupid	God of love; son of Ares and Aphrodite
Gaea (GEE-yah)	Tellus	Goddess of the Earth; wife of Uranus and mother of Cronos
*Hades (HAY-deez)	Pluto	God of death and the Underworld; brother of Zeus
*Hephaestus (heh-FES-tus)	Vulcan	God of fire; son of Zeus and Hera
*Hera (HAIR-uh)	Juno	Goddess of the Earth; sister and wife of Zeus
*Hermes (HUHR-meez)	Mercury	Messenger of the gods, and god of travel and commerce; son of Zeus
Hestia	Vesta	Goddess of the home; sister of Zeus
Pan	Pan	God of forests, flocks, and shepherds; son of Hermes
Persephone (puhr-SEF-uh-nee)	Proserpina (pruh-SUHR-peh-nuh)	Goddess of grain; daughter of Zeus and Demeter
*Poseidon (poh-SIE-duhn)	Neptune	God of the sea; brother of Zeus
Rhea (REE-uh)	Ops	Goddess of abundance; wife of Cronos and mother of Zeus
Uranus (YOOR-uh-nuhs)	Uranus	God of the heavens; father of Cronos and other Titans
*Zeus (ZOOS)	Jupiter	Ruler of the gods; son of Cronos and Rhea

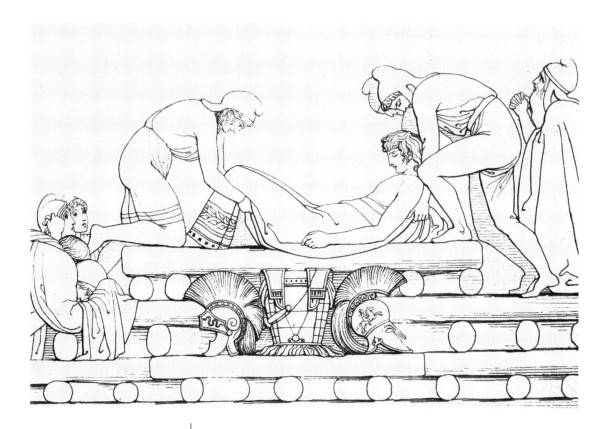

husband, King Menelaus (min-uh-LAY-uhs). Years before, the other kings of great cities had pledged that if anything should happen to her, they would protect her. Paris, with Aphrodite's help, managed to win Helen over and bring her back to Troy. As soon as Menelaus found out that his wife was gone, he called on the other kings to help him.

The two most important of these kings were Agamemnon (ag-uh-MEM-nahn) of Mycenae and Odysseus (oh-DIS-ee-uhs)—sometimes called Ulysses (you-LI-seez)—of Ithaca (ITH-uh-kuh). Agamemnon organized the Greek force that would go to Troy, which consisted of 100,000 soldiers and 1,000 ships. Hence it was said that the beautiful Helen had a "face that launched a thousand ships."

Even more significant was Achilles (uh-KIL-eez), the son of Thetis, who as prophesied was much greater than his father Peleus. At his birth, his mother had held him by his heel and dipped him in the River Styx (sounds like "sticks"), which runs through the Underworld. This made him completely invulnerable to harm, except in one place—on his heel, which had not touched the water. She knew that he would die at Troy, so she tried to hide him from the Odysseus and Agamemnon; but it was Achilles's destiny to be a warrior, so he went with them.

Two other important warriors were Ajax, second only to Achilles in bravery, and, on the Trojan side, Priam's son Hector. Hector is the second most important figure in the *Iliad*, after Achilles. The Trojans, after all, were quite close to the Greeks. The war between the two cities was like a conflict between cousins, not alien societies.

For nine years, the Greeks camped outside Troy and attempted to conquer the city. Though they gained other cities and much treasure, which they divided among themselves, they could not take Troy. The *Iliad* began with a dispute over "treasure," two girls captured by Agamemnon and Achilles. When the gods took mercy on the father of Agamemnon's girl, he was forced to return her. Afterward he helped himself to Achilles's girl. This angered Achilles, who withdrew from battle to sit in his tent and sulk. Meanwhile, Hector was on the move.

Eventually Hector would come close to victory, though by that point it would be clear that he and his family were doomed. The Greek force did not know this, however. Without their greatest warrior, they were at a disadvantage. Therefore Achilles's servant and closest friend, Patroclus (puh-TRAHK-luhs), took his armor and went into battle. The Trojans killed him, thinking he was Achilles.

The killing of Patroclus finally moved Achilles to action. Overcome by grief and anger, he settled his dispute with Agamemnon and went into battle. In the climactic scene of the *Iliad*, Achilles and Hector fought man to man. Achilles thrust his spear through Hector's neck. Still filled with rage, he continued to torture Hector's dead body for days. Finally the gods commanded him to stop. Priam came to retrieve the body of Hector, and Achilles greeted him in peace. The *Iliad* ended with Hector's funeral.

Other myths continued the Trojan War to its close. One told of how Apollo helped Paris fatally wound Achilles by a shooting an arrow at his one vulnerable spot. (Hence the modern expression "Achilles heel.") Other stories recounted the deaths of Paris and Ajax. Then there was the famous tale of the "horse" that ended the war. On Athena's advice, the Greeks pretended they were sailing for home, but in fact sailed only a few miles away, to an island near Troy. There they built a huge wooden horse and concealed their best warriors inside. When the Trojans found the horse, they took it into their city as a sign of the gods' favor. As soon as it was inside the gates of Troy, however, the Greek warriors jumped out and slaughtered many Trojans before the rest of the army arrived through the opened gates and overwhelmed the city.

The end of the Trojan War was not the end of the Troy tale: a number of works, most notably the *Odyssey,* told what happened to the great heroes of the war afterward. The Roman *Aeneid* also took up where the Trojan War left off. Thus the Troy tale provided a foundation for the great national epics of two ancient civilizations.

Archaic Greece (c. 700–c. 500 B.C.)

Already by the latter part of the Dark Ages, Greece was awakening. For the first time, the peoples of the Greek mainland and isles began to see themselves as one culture if not one nation. They called themselves Hellenes (heh-LEENZ). Words such as Hellenistic describe their civilization.

Part of the Greeks' awareness of themselves came from contact with other lands. In about 850 B.C., they began trading with other peoples. This led to an increase both in wealth and knowledge. The following century saw the rise of city-states. By 700 B.C., Hellenistic culture had begun to flower. From that point historians date the Archaic Age (ahr-KAY-ik, meaning old) in Greece.

Among the unifying factors of Greek culture were religious and national myths. Throughout the land, people believed in more or less the same gods; shared the same set of myths concerning the Trojan War, including the *Iliad* and the *Odyssey*; and admired the same mythic heroes, particularly Heracles. There was also a single Greek language, despite the existence of regional dialects.

Finally, just as the Olmec of Mesoamerica had their ceremonial centers, virtually all Greeks held three sites sacred.

At Delphi, there was the Oracle. Off the Aegean coast to the east was the island of Delos (DEE-lohs), legendary birthplace of Apollo and Artemis, which would play a major role in Classical Greece. Thirdly, there was Olympia in the far western Peloponnese, where the peoples of the city-states gathered every four years for a series of contests and religious celebrations called the Olympic Games.

The Olympic Games

First held in 776 B.C., the Olympics were a model for other festivals such as the Pythian Games at Delphi. Most followed a similar structure. The Games included not only athletic contests but artistic ones—poetry and drama competitions, for instance—as well as religious services. As with the ceremonial ball game of the Olmec, the Olympic Games were not so much a form of entertainment as they were a form of worship.

At first, the athletic part of the Games consisted of just one contest, a foot race of about 200 yards. Eventually, however, the Games stretched to five days. The Greeks added more events longer foot races; the pentathlon (pehn-TATH-uh-lahn), which combined five different track and field events such as boxing and wrestling; chariot races; and something called *pankration* (pan-KRAT-ee-ahn), a sort of organized brawl.

A man could get badly hurt in an event such as the pankration. The ancient Games were dangerous in a way that most modern competitions are not: not only was there not much in the way of medical attention, but participants frequently got killed. For this reason, not to mention the fact that men competed in the nude, only married women were allowed to watch the athletic events.

The English word *agony* is derived from a Greek term for an athletic contest. And what did the Olympic athletes receive for all this agony? A wreath or crown of olive leaves. No wonder, then, that at the Battle of Thermopylae, a Persian officer who questioned his Greek prisoners about their Olympic Games remarked in amazement, "What manner of men are these we are fighting? It is not for money they contend, but the glory of achievement."

There was certainly plenty of glory. Great writers such as Euripides (you-RIH-puh-deez) and Pindar (PIN-duhr) composed *odes* to Olympic heroes. The sculptor Praxiteles (prak-SIH-tel-eez) built monuments in their honor. A 40-foot (12.2 meters) tall gold and ivory statue of Zeus, one of the Seven Wonders of the World stood in the temple at Olympia, clear evidence of the great importance the Greeks attached to the place.

Eventually, the Olympic Games became a tool of the wealthy and powerful, as rulers began using them for political purposes. Until then, however, the Olympics helped to bring the various peoples of Greece together in a spirit of ardent competition.

The formation of city-states

The many factors unifying Greece were significant, since there were plenty of other forces pulling it apart. Except for rare periods, Greece would never be a single nation, but rather a collection of city-states, or cities that also functioned as separate nations. The Greeks called a city-state a *polis* (PAH-luhs), from which the English language takes words such as *police* and *politics*. The plural of *polis* was *poleis* (pah-LAYZ).

At one time there were as many as seven hundred poleis in Greece, though only a few assumed real significance. One of these was Thebes (pronounced like "thieves," but with a *b*) in Boeotia, a city much older than most on the Greek mainland. Founded as early as 1500 B.C., Thebes had the same name as an Egyptian city established some five centuries earlier.

On the northeastern corner of the Peloponnese was another important city, Corinth. Founded by the Dorians, it had emerged as an important trading center. Much later, Corinth would figure in the early history of Christianity, with the inclusion of Paul's two letters to the Corinthians among the books of the New Testament.

Then there were two other cities, that stood above the rest in importance. These two were Athens and Sparta, rivals for leadership of the other Greek city-states. In fact, they were not merely rival cities; they were rival ways of life.

The militaristic world of Sparta

Sparta lay on the southeastern Peloponnese, in a region once called Laconica (luh-KAHN-i-kuh). To this day, the word *laconic* describes someone with a clipped, abrupt way of speaking. Likewise the word *spartan,* meaning "without luxury or comfort," is part of the English language as well.

Established by the Dorians in the 800s B.C., Sparta was also called Lacedaemon (lah-seh-DEE-muhn) after its mystical founder. The city was ruled by two kings, descendants of an early monarch; the real power, however, lay in the hands of an *oligarchy,* a small ruling group. Sparta's oligarchy consisted of some thirty men, all over sixty years in age.

Below the oligarchy were the citizens, a term that does not have the same meaning in modern America. Whereas anyone born in the United States is an American citizen, with all the rights and privileges that come with citizenship, in ancient Greece only a select few enjoyed the benefits of citizenship. A better comparison would be America at the time of its founding, when only white men could become citizens. In Sparta, the rules were even more strict: a man had to be a direct descendant of the original Dorian founders of the city. Thus there were never more than 7,000 Spartan citizens at one time.

Besides the tiny group of citizens, there were their families, who enjoyed a relatively high status. Below them was a much larger group of foreigners and other noncitizens. At the bottom was by far the largest class in Spartan society, many times larger than all the others combined: slaves, or *helots* (HEH-luhtz).

Not even citizens of Sparta enjoyed an easy life. Noncitizens ran businesses and held other positions because Spartan citizens had one job only, the central focus of their lives from birth to the age of thirty: war. From 735 to 715 B.C., they fought a long conflict with the neighboring polis of Messenia (meh-SEE-nee-uh). Spartans took so many slaves they were afraid of being overthrown. Such fears on the part of the Indo-Europeans spawned the caste system in India; in Sparta such fears they led to the creation of a militaristic society.

Like the Assyrians, the Spartans were geniuses at the art of war. During the conflict with Messenia, they developed the concept of the *hoplite* (HAHP-light), a heavily armed foot solider, which became the standard for Greek warfare. Hoplites formed a phalanx (FAY-lankz), a column of soldiers usually 8 men deep and as many as 200 men wide. Armed with spears, they surged against an enemy. When the first rank fell, the next group moved in. Warfare in any age is awful, but prior to the twentieth century—when at least decent medical care was available to troops on the field—it was truly horrible. Yet the Spartans were fabled for their bravery, in part because they had spent their whole lives preparing for war.

If a boy were born with any physical problems, he was simply left to die. The ones who survived went to live in barracks at age seven. For the next five years they underwent rigorous physical training. Even the Spartans were Greeks, however, and as such a civilized people: thus from ages twelve to eighteen, boys studied poetry and music. But at eighteen, they submitted to a year of endurance and survival training, much as a member of a modern special operations team such as the Navy SEALS must do.

At the end of this training, the boy had become a hoplite and received a year off. During this time, he married and spent time with his wife, but at the age of twenty, he went off to serve in the army for ten years. Assuming he survived battle, he was free of all obligations at age thirty, when he received a plot of land that would be farmed by helots. At that point, he might become a citizen; then again, he might not, in which case he would not be allowed to participate in political life until he reached the age of sixty.

Few modern people would find the life of a Spartan male attractive. It should be noted, however, that contrary to what one might expect, the life of a woman in Sparta was in some ways better than that of her Athenian counterpart. Spartan girls received physical training along with boys, in order that they might produce stronger babies. Though this might seem like another hardship, it also implies a higher status than that of women in Athens, who lived their lives in shadow, far from the world of men. Also, during the years when their men were away, Spartan women ran the home and all business affairs, assuming a degree of control far beyond that of Athenian women.

The birth of democracy in Athens

Sparta might be considered, along with Ch'in China, an early model of totalitarianism, whereas Athens was the birthplace of *democracy,* or rule by the people. As it first came to prominence during the Dark Ages, Athens followed a path not unlike Sparta's, with rule by an oligarchy descended from the original tribes of Attica. The city grew, however, and by about 700 B.C. dominated all of Attica. Eventually there was not enough food for everyone. The food shortage led to widespread discontent in the mid-600s B.C. This helped to usher in the age of the *tyrants.*

In modern times, "tyrant" refers to an extremely cruel leader. The original tyrants were not necessarily bad rulers. They were usually *aristocrats,* or members of the wealthy class, who managed to get enough popular backing to seize power illegally, as they had done in other city-states. The leaders of Athens were afraid this might happen in their own city. When a would-be tyrant named Cylon (SIE-lahn) very nearly seized power in the 620s B.C., they decided it was time to take steps to prevent such an occurrence.

In 621 B.C., the Athenian oligarchs appointed Draco (DRAY-koh) to create a set of laws to maintain the public order. The code of Draco was an exceptionally harsh one, prescribing death for a whole range of offenses and heavily weighting the legal scales in favor of the oligarchs. Today the word *draconian* (drah-KOHN-ee-uhn) is used to describe extremely severe laws.

Not surprisingly, the draconian code did little to quell popular unrest. In 594 B.C. the oligarchs appointed a truly remarkable individual as *archon* (AHR-kahn), or leading official of Athens: Solon (SOH-luhn; c. 630–c. 560 B.C.) Faced on the one side with the demands on the poor, who threatened a revolt if he did not *redistribute* land, and on the other side with the demands of the aristocrats, who wanted to hold on to their wealth and power, Solon instituted a number of political reforms to hold the Athenian state together.

He reorganized the whole system of government, extended the rights of citizenship, canceled all debts, introduced a legal code to replace Draco's, and took other measures that created the framework for democracy. But Solon's reforms only whetted the desires of the people—particularly the rising middle class—for more. In 561 B.C., his second cousin Peisistratus (pie-SIS-truh-tus), who in 570 had led the Athenians to victory in battle against a nearby polis, seized control of the Acropolis and established himself as tyrant of Athens.

Peisistratus proved to be an enlightened ruler. He introduced many popular reforms, for instance by initiating public projects in order to provide jobs to the poor. But his sons Hippias (HIP-ee-uhs) and Hipparchus (huh-PAHR-kuhs), who ruled jointly after his death in 527 B.C., were tyrants in the modern sense of the word. In 514 B.C., Hipparchus was assassinated, and Hippias became more cruel than ever. Finally, in 510 B.C., the Athenians threw him out.

The oligarchs tried to come back to power, but they faced an unexpected foe in Cleisthenes (KLISE-thuh-neez; c. 570–c. 500 B.C.) A supporter of Solon, he had been banished by Peisistratus, then had returned to power briefly under Hippias and Hipparchus. Cleisthenes established an entirely new system of political organization. Instead of being divided by tribes or classes, the people of Attica would be grouped by geographical region. Within each region, the citizens would vote for officials who would represent them in the Athenian assembly, its governmental body. This was the birth of representative government, as practiced today in the United States and other democratic nations.

Among the powers of the new representative government was the authority to *ostracize* (AHS-truh-size), or send into exile, any official who appeared to be gaining too much power. It was a system that put everyone on an equal basis, and the oligarchs were not happy with it. But the spirit of the times was with Cleisthenes, and in 502 B.C. the Athenians adopted a new *constitution* based on his reforms. The new political system gave the Athenians a vigor they had never felt before. During the two centuries that followed, their city would become the dominant Greek polis.

The arts in Archaic Greece

Throughout Greece, but particularly in Athens, the arts began to flourish in Archaic times. Poetry entered its first flowering with writers such as Sappho (SA-foh; fl. c. 610–c. 580 B.C.) One of the few prominent women of ancient Greece, Sappho lived on the isle of Lesbos (LEZ-bohs) in Asia Minor. Her work concerned jealousy and the pains of love, often for other women. Thus the English word for a homosexual woman became *lesbian,* though some scholars have suggested that Sappho was writing about an ideal kind of love rather than anything explicitly sexual. In any case, homosexuality was quite common in ancient Greece, where men and women lived virtually separate lives.

The Archaic Age saw developments in pottery and its decoration. One of the most frequently seen symbols of ancient Greece is the Grecian vase or urn, which in about 700 B.C. began to feature primarily human or human-looking figures—warriors, maidens, heroes, and gods. "Black-figure" technique, introduced in Corinth, would have widespread importance. Artists using this technique would paint areas of the vase black and then draw figures against the black by making very shallow, narrow cuts. Artists in Athens took on the black-figure technique as their own but later introduced red-figure vase painting. Using the red-figure method, the artist painted around the figure in black and left the figure itself in the red of the clay. Instead of making cuts, artists added details by painting them in.

The depictions of the human figure on the vases of the time were astonishingly accurate, a sign of the degree to which Greek art had developed. Also impressive was sculpture representing the human form, in particular the *kouros* (KOO-rohs; pl. *kouroi*). The kouros was a type of nude, always a young male, depicted with his arms at his side and one foot forward. Kouroi were intended to be viewed from the front. Despite the achievement represented by the kouroi, however, comparison with later sculptures showed just how far Greek artists progressed in the Classical Age. The Archaic Age sculptors had not yet worked out the proportions of the human figure—for instance, the size of the head in relation to the feet.

The Archaic Age marked the first phase of distinctly Greek architecture. The Greeks had built in wood since at least the end of the Mycenaean Age, but in the 600s B.C., they began building in stone. Their temples soon exhibited elements of what would become the recognized Greek style: a row of columns supporting a *pediment* (PED-uh-mehnt), the triangular gable end of a roof. The pediment might often be decorated with a *frieze* (pronounced like "freeze"), a band of sculptured figures or ornaments.

The columns holding up the roof were *fluted,* or marked by grooves. The space between the column and the

pediment—the *capital,* or top of the column, and the *entablature* (ehn-TAB-luh-choor), the decorative band above it—developed distinctive styles. The most simple of these was the Doric order, which developed in the Peloponnese in the 600s B.C. Within half a century, the Ionic order emerged in eastern Greece. Characterized by spiral scrolls (what might be commonly described as "curlicues") on the capital, the Ionic is probably the most recognizable of all Greek styles. Finally, the 500s would see the introduction of the much more elaborate Corinthian order.

The birth of philosophy and science

Though the architecture of Greece is one of its visible legacies, some of the most significant Greek contributions to the modern world cannot be seen: democracy, for instance, and philosophy. The latter word comes from two Greek roots that together mean "love of knowledge." Originally, the term was applied to all forms of study. Even today, when a person completes a doctor's degree, the highest educational level in most disciplines, he or she most often receives a "doctorate of philosophy" degree, which is what the term "PhD" stands for in Latin.

The word *philosophy* is used in many ways, but in its purest sense it means a search for a general understanding of values and of reality. It is interesting to observe that in the century from 600 to 500 B.C., as Western philosophy was come into existence in Greece, Eastern philosophy had its birth with Confucius and Lao-tzu (low-TSOO). However, Eastern and Western approaches to thought are radically different from one another, so much so that they are rarely studied together. The concerns of Confucius and Lao-tzu, after all, were quite different from those of the first Western thinker, who sought to identify the underlying nature of the world.

The conclusion reached by Thales (THAY-leez; 625?–547? B.C.), who lived in the Ionian city of Miletus (muh-LEE-tuhs), was that "everything is water." In other words, Thales thought that the whole world is in a fluid state, like water. Thales had first come to fame for predicting a solar eclipse on May 28, 585 B.C.; later he made several advances in the area of *geometry* (jee-AHM-eh-tree). He was the first true scientist: with his statement about water, he was developing the first hypothesis (hie-PAH-thuh-sis), a Greek word that means a statement subject to scientific testing for truth or falsehood.

Yet he was not talking only about the physical world, as scientists do, but also about what people in a later time would have called the mental or spiritual worlds—the realms of philosophy. In Thales's time, no one had any idea that there was a distinction between those worlds. Indeed, he was the first in a long line of thinkers (a line that has continued to the present day) concerned not only with philosophy, but also with mathematics and/or science.

Another great philosopher-mathematician was Pythagoras (puh-THAG-uh-ruhs; c. 580-c. 500 B.C.) Born in Samos (SAH-mohs), an island off the coast of Asia Minor, he settled at the other end of the Greek world, Crotona (kruh-TOH-nuh) in southern Italy (then called Magna Graecia). He is most famous for the Pythagorean *Theorem* (puh-thag-uh-REE-uhn THEE-uh-ruhm), which states that in a triangle with a right angle (i.e., a 90-degree angle), the square of the length of the hypotenuse (hie-PAHT-eh-noos), or longest side, is equal to the sum of the squares of the other two sides. This was far from his only contribution to thought, however, and though none of his actual writings have survived, the record left by his followers shows that he had far-reaching ideas on everything from music to government.

The lack of surviving writings by Pythagoras is a problem common with many ancient Greek thinkers and writers: only a tiny portion of the plays by Greek dramatists, for instance, survive. Likewise, only fragments remain from Heraclitus (hair-uh-KLY-tuhs; c. 540–c. 480 B.C.) Instead of water, Heraclitus maintained that the world was made of fire—that everything is conflict and change. His most famous statement was: "You cannot step into the same river twice, for other waters are ever flowing on."

Heraclitus has been compared with the Pythia because he was often so hard to understand. Parmenides (pahr-MEHN-eh-deez; born c. 515), who like several others was a scientist as well as a philosopher, was quite the opposite. He came from Elea (E-lee-uh) in southern Italy. Parmenides introduced the use of logic in philosophy. His thoughts survive primarily in two fragmentary poems contrasting "The Way of Opinion" with "The Way of Truth." In the latter poem, a goddess states the central idea of Parmenides' work: "only Being is; not-being cannot be."

In contrast to Heraclitus, Parmenides saw everything as part of a single, harmonious whole called "Being." Because everything was part of everything else, in his view, nothing ever changed. His disciple Zeno of Elea (ZEE-noh; c. 495–c. 430) tried to prove this idea with his famous *paradoxes* (PAIR-uh-dahk-sehz). A paradox occurs when something seems contradictory or opposed to common sense but is in fact correct. Zeno's paradoxes, however, failed to proved that motion is impossible. Instead, they only proved the flexibility of logic and set off whole new debates. Even at this early stage in the history of philosophy, there were many schools of thought. Disagreement about the nature of the world would only widen as time went on.

The Classical Age (c. 500–338 B.C.)

The Classical Age in Greece is one of the most celebrated periods in the history of civilization. There has been no other era quite like it, when so many outstanding figures appeared on the scene at the same time. It was a time when philosophy, literature, sculpture, architecture, politics, and many other fields of human endeavor reached a high point.

No wonder, then, that a period of just 75 years within the approximately 160 years of the Classical Age would come to be known as the Golden Age (479–404 B.C.), the brightest phase of Athens's history. Even shorter was the brilliant Age of Pericles (PAIR-uh-kleez; c. 495–429 B.C.), who led the city for just three decades.

Not only was the Classical Age brief, but it was marked by war from beginning to end. First, there was a war between the city-states and an enemy from outside, a conflict which united all the Greek peoples under Athens's leadership. Then, there was a conflict between Athens and Sparta, the Peloponnesian War (431–404 B.C.), which ended in disaster for Athens. Finally, there was the eruption of a new power from the north, the Macedonians, who would sweep over Greece in 338 B.C.

The Persian Wars (499–449 B.C.)

For years, the kings of Lydia in Asia Minor had had their eyes on the Ionian colonies. Under Croesus in about 550 B.C., the Lydians finally subdued Ionia. Their victory was to be short-lived, however. In 546 B.C., Cyrus the Great of Persia captured all of Lydia and subdued the Ionian city-states.

Problems in Ionia quieted down for half a century, but in 499 B.C. Miletus led the other city-states in a revolt against the Persians. Athens and the offshore city-state of Eretria (eh-REE-tree-uh) sent troops to support the revolt. Darius I, the Persian ruler, responded by burning Eretria in the summer of 490 B.C. Shortly afterward, the Persians sailed to Marathon, a city on the coast of Attica, just 26 miles (41.8 kilometers) from Athens.

Despite the fact that they were outnumbered three to one, the Athenian hoplites defeated the Persians. Before the battle, Miltiades (mil-TIE-uh-deez; c. 554–489 B.C.), the commander of the Greek forces, sent a runner to Sparta, 150 miles

The Olympic Games—Ancient and Modern

In 1894, exactly 1,500 years after the ancient Olympics ended, a French baron named Pierre de Coubertin (koo-buhr-TAN; 1863–1937) resurrected them. Coubertin saw the Olympics as a way to bring the nations of the world together in peace. He presided over the first modern Olympics at Athens in 1896. Except in 1916, 1940, and 1944 (during the two world wars) the Games would be held every four years thereafter, with the addition of Winter Games in 1924. (Starting in 1994, the Winter Games were held in even-numbered non-Olympic years.)

By the 1980s and 1990s, however, the Olympics began to be plagued by a series of problems. On several occasions, nations *boycotted* the Games—that is, they refused to participate as a form of political protest. There were concerns that athletes were cheating by taking drugs to help them perform. Many observers feared that the Games had been taken over by wealthy corporations and powerful politicians. People longed for a simpler time; what most did not know, however, was that the problems of the modern Olympics were not new.

The Spartans initiated the first sports boycott in 420 B.C. By attacking Athens and thus resuming the Peloponnesian War, they broke the Olympic truce. The Olympic truce stated that no city should attack another during the Games. Rather than pay a fine to the temple at Olympia, Sparta kept its athletes at home. A few years later, a tyrant named Dionysius the Elder (die-uh-NISH-uhs; c. 430–367

(241 kilometers) away, with a message that the Athenians needed reinforcements. The runner's name was Phidippides (fi-DIP-uh-deez), and by the time he returned to Marathon, the battle was over. The commander needed someone to carry the message of victory to Athens, which was about to be attacked by Persian ships, so he sent Phidippides. The latter is said to have run at top speed, gasped out the message as soon as he reached Athens, and died. Though this story may be part legend, it certainly marks the origins of the marathon, a 26-mile race that became an Olympic event.

Darius longed to repay the Greeks for Marathon, but he did not live to do so. The job fell to his son Xerxes, who marched a vast army against Greece in 480 B.C. Three key battles followed in the space of about a year.

B.C.) convinced an athlete from another city to compete for his own town of Syracuse. The athlete, Dicon (DIE-kahn), might be considered the first "free agent" in history.

After Dionysius, more and more kings and wealthy men began trying to get a share of the Olympic athletes' glory. Some brought their royal horse teams to the chariot races, where their wealth gave them the advantage. Few had the honesty of Alexander the Great, who competed as an ordinary athlete and tied for first place in a sprint competition. At the other extreme was the Roman emperor Nero, who attended the A.D. 68 Games. Because Rome controlled Greece, Nero could demand any prize he wanted. Therefore he won the chariot race even though he was thrown from his chariot. Between the Olympics and other contests such as the Pythian Games, Nero won more than 1,800 first prizes as an athlete, singer, harpist, and actor.

In A.D. 394, nearly 1,200 years after the Olympics first began, the Roman emperor Theodosius I banned them because, as a Christian, he considered the Games a *pagan* (PAY-guhn) festival. By then, however, the Olympics had long before ceased to hold the importance they once had. The city of Olympia died out. Its stadium and *hippodrome* (HIP-uh-drohm, a place for chariot races) were destroyed; so was the statue of Zeus. Robbers carried off the gold and ivory. After an earthquake in the 600s, a nearby river flowed over the site of the Games, covering all traces of its former glory.

The first battle took place at Thermopylae (thuhr-MAHP-uh-lee), a narrow mountain pass on the coast of Boeotia. The Persians, helped by a Greek traitor, managed to attack the Greeks both from the front and the rear. The Greek commander, Sparta's King Leonidas (lee-oh-NIE-duhs; r. 490?–480 B.C.), recognized the impossibility of the situation. He ordered his entire force of about 7,000 to retreat—except for his 300-odd Spartan hoplites. Some 700 Boeotians chose to remain with them. Together the thousand warriors—Leonidas included—fought to their deaths. Despite the bravery of Leonidas and the others, the Persians won at Thermopylae, but only with a heavy expense in casualties.

Xerxes and the Persian army next marched to Athens, which they found deserted: the residents had been removed to the tiny island of Salamis (SAH-luh-mis) off the western coast of Attica. An angered Xerxes ordered the city burned. But the Greeks had a secret weapon, and it sat waiting for the Persians in the narrow strait that separated Salamis from the mainland. This was a fleet of triremes (TRY-reemz), a highly mobile type of warship with three rows of oarsmen and a bronze battering ram on the front.

The Athenians had built the triremes at the urging of the archon and general Themistocles (thuh-MIS-tuh-kleez; c. 524—c. 460 B.C.), who now posed as a traitor and sent a message to Xerxes, advising him to trap the Greeks in the strait by closing off both ends with his warships. It was a brilliant piece of strategy. By blocking the entrances, the Persians kept themselves from bringing in reinforcements, whereas the light and maneuverable triremes moved back and forth with ease, simply going around the Persians' bulky ships. Xerxes, who had ordered his throne placed in a spot where he could watch his fleet's victory, instead witnessed its defeat. Soon afterward he left Greece, never to return.

In the following year, 479 B.C., an outnumbered Greek force led by Spartan hoplites overwhelmed Xerxes's son-in-law Mardonius (mahr-DOH-nee-uhs) at Plataea (pluh-TEE-uh) on the coast just north of Salamis. A few days later, in a sea battle at Mycale (MI-kuh-lee) just off the Ionian coast, the Greek navy completed the defeat of the Persians.

The Delian League (478–338 B.C.)

In the view of many Greeks, their people had set aside their old differences, joined together as one, and triumphed over the "barbarians." In fact, it was not as simple as that. Although Boeotian hoplites had fought with distinction at Thermopylae, much of Boeotia—united under the leadership of Thebes as the Boeotian League—had sided with the Persians. Likewise Epirus, Thessaly, and other large portions of Greece had either supported Persia or remained neutral.

Still, the victories were impressive, particularly given the odds. The heroes of the Persian Wars seemed the equals of legendary figures from the *Iliad*. The myth of Greek unity was strong enough to build in the Greeks a supreme sense of self-confidence as a people. This was especially true in Athens, which had emerged as a leader of the poleis. The defeat of the Persians ushered in a Golden Age.

Seizing the moment, Athens in 478 B.C. called on the other city-states to join it in a federation of city-states headquartered on the sacred isle of Delos. This was the beginning of the Delian League, which ultimately included most of the city-states that faced the Aegean, from Attica to Thrace to Asia Minor and many islands in between. It was the first time independent states had ever joined in a federation, and in the twentieth century it would become the model for international security alliances such as the United Nations (UN), the North Atlantic Treaty Alliance (NATO), and others.

Under the direction of Aristides (ahr-es-TIE-deez; c. 530–c. 468 B.C.), former archon of Athens, the League members agreed that each state would contribute ships for the defense of Greece or, if they could not afford ships, money for the building of ships in Athens. The members of the League turned from defense to offense, chasing the Persians off the Ionian coast in 468 B.C., destroying the new fleet with which Persia had planned to launch a new offensive in the Aegean. The League was also effective against another threat: pirates. In about 475 B.C., it destroyed the Aegean pirates' stronghold on the island of Scyros (SIGH-rus), thus making the area safe for shipping. Despite its value to all of Greece, the League was not so much an equal partnership of states as it was a vehicle for Athenian domination. Eventually Athens's leading role became painfully clear to other city-states, which were forbidden to withdraw from the League or to quit paying their contributions—money which, as it turned out, was going to Athens to pay for massive building schemes. Athens spent much of the 450s B.C. subduing other Greek states. After signing a peace agreement that formally ended the Persian Wars in 449 B.C., it set out to build an empire.

But Athens was not content to merely control the city-states of Greece; it wanted to control the world. For about a decade, its military forces waged a number of campaigns in far-flung places, from Sicily to Egypt to Phoenicia. Most of these ended in disaster. Certainly the overall policy seemed to follow no rhyme or reason. Had they continued their willy-nilly campaigns, these would have spent the Athenians' energy.

Like a figure in a Greek tragedy, Athens suffered from its own large-scale *hubris,* for which it would ultimately pay in several ways. One of these was a war with Sparta, which had its own Spartan League. Also, the Athenian conquests would inspire Philip of Macedon—who dissolved the League in 338 B.C.—with a vision of a vast Greek empire, as his son Alexander would ultimately create. But in the meantime, Athens would enjoy one of the brightest moments in human history: the Age of Pericles.

The Age of Pericles (460–429 B.C.)

Athens had been destroyed by Persia, and Themistocles had led efforts at rebuilding in the decade that followed the defeat of the Persians. But he was ostracized in 470 B.C., and leadership of Athens fell to others. Then in 460 B.C., Pericles became archon (chief government official), and in the next thirty-one years he would institute so many reforms and direct the construction of so many splendid buildings that the era of his leadership would come to be known as the Age of Pericles or the Periclean Age (pair-uh-KLEE-uhn).

Although Cleisthenes (Pericles's great-uncle, as a matter of fact) had introduced democracy in Athens more than 40 years before, it was far from well established. There was a strong aristocratic party, that would happily have returned to the old days of the oligarchy. Among its leaders was Cimon (SIE-muhn; c. 510–c. 451 B.C.), son of Miltiades and leader of the force that had destroyed the Persian fleet in 467 B.C. When the helots of Sparta attempted a revolt in 465 B.C., Cimon urged the leaders of Athens to support the Spartan aristocracy. In 462 B.C., Athens sent a force to help suppress the revolt.

But just when Cimon was ensuring the stability of the old order in Sparta, something quite different was afoot in Athens. Also in 462 B.C. the city enacted a series of reforms that dramatically increased the power of its citizens over their government. Formerly a representative democracy, Athens became a rare example of a *direct democracy*. Direct democracy is a system in which all citizens are permitted, and indeed expected, to vote on issues before the government. Direct democracy is possible only with a very small, highly informed population, as was the case in Athens.

The democratic reforms were the work of young Pericles, who also extended the rights of citizenship to more men, poor as well as rich. He instituted a number of magnificent building projects financed by the cities of the Delian League, whose gold had been removed to Athens for "safekeeping." Among the projects was one that had originated with the Themistocles, the building of a protective corridor, called the "Long Walls," to connect Athens with its port at Piraeus (pie-REE-uhs) five miles away. Within the city, Pericles oversaw the building of many splendid temples and other public buildings. Perhaps none was as magnificent as one that survives to the present day: the Parthenon (PAHR-thuh-nahn).

The Parthenon sits atop the Acropolis in Athens. Its damaged beauty (it suffered an explosion during a war in A.D. 1687, when it was used as a munitions warehouse) seems to whisper of another time. A temple to Athena, the maiden, or *parthenos,* for whom Athens was named, it was far more than a beautiful building. Even today, architects are mystified by the brilliant design of Ictinus (ik-TIE-nuhs) and Callicrates (kuh-LIK-ruh-teez), the chief architects. They seem to have possessed an incredibly advanced understanding of how humans see objects in space. In a number of places where lines appear straight, they are actually curved, because a truly straight line would have seemed curved. The columns bulge at the center in order to look as though they taper gently from bottom to top.

Historians have less of a clear idea about the interior of the Parthenon. Long before the explosion, the temple was altered in order to make it first a Christian church, which it remained for about a thousand years, and later a Muslim *mosque* (MAHSK). At the center of the temple was a huge statue of Athena, designed by the great sculptor Phidias (FI-dee-uhs; fl. c. 490–430 B.C.) The temple included a number of treasures, among them the throne on which Xerxes had sat as he watched his defeat by the Greeks at Salamis; yet without question the greatest treasure was the statue of Athena itself. Like the Olympian Zeus, another sculpture by Phidias, it was made of gold and ivory. It probably showed Athena with a shield and weapons of war.

Not only is the Parthenon a symbol of the great Periclean Age, its story is also tied with the end of that brilliant time. Pericles' enemies had never gone away, and as a means of getting at him, they accused Phidias of stealing part of the gold intended for the statue. After Phidias disproved these charges, they charged him with carving pictures of himself and Pericles on Athena's shield—something which, if true, would have been a serious offense to the goddess. They managed to make the charges stick. Though Pericles stuck by Phidias, the sculptor was imprisoned.

The attacks of his enemies helped render Pericles less effective in his later days, but he would ultimately become a victim of his own creation. Perhaps the biggest city of its time, Athens's population in the Periclean Age may have been as high as 200,000, of which a quarter were citizens. The rest—women, children, foreigners, and slaves—lived poorly in comparison to the citizens, though they were generally much better off than their counterparts in Sparta and elsewhere.

Despite the great complexity of its civilization, the physical life of Athens was simple. People lived on a diet that consisted of little more than bread, olives, fruit, cheese, fish, and wine. At night they slept on the flat roofs of their houses because the interiors, made of sun-dried brick, was usually hot. There were public baths and steam rooms, and also open-air public toilets. Athens had no plumbing, and people simply threw their waste into the streets, which of course encouraged the spread of disease. In 429 B.C., Athens suffered a plague in which Pericles himself died.

The Peloponnesian War (431–404 B.C.)

Other problems lay on the horizon for Athens. For a long time, a conflict with Sparta had been simmering. As early as 459 B.C., the two had clashed over control of Megara (MEH-guh-rah), an Attic seaport west of Athens. For many years afterwards, there was occasionally fighting between Athens and Sparta. When all-out war finally came, Megara was its immediate cause.

The people of Corcyra (kohr-SIE-ruh), off the northwest coast near Epirus, had always had tense relations with the Corinthians who had colonized their island some 300 years before. When civil war broke out between the oligarchs and democrats of the island, Corinth moved in to suppress the democratic revolt. Quickly the lines were drawn: Athens, as the birthplace of democracy, was determined to spread freedom like a new religious faith, and Corinth and its powerful ally, Sparta,

were just as determined to suppress the threat. Aided by the Athenians, the democrats of Corcyra drove out the Corinthians in 433 B.C. Corinth demanded help from Sparta, and the two sides prepared for war as tensions mounted. Then, in 431 B.C., Athens imposed a trade *embargo* on Megara, by then a member of the Spartan League. In response, Sparta declared war.

Aware that his army was no match for Sparta's, Pericles decided to take a defensive strategy, bringing all the people of Attica inside the fortifications around Athens. Thanks to the Long Walls, the city still had access to the sea, but the Spartans ravaged the countryside, burning olive trees that had taken many years to grow. Even worse, overcrowding helped spawn the Great Plague of 429 B.C. Facing severe criticism for his handling of the war, Pericles led several expeditions against cities on the Peloponnese. The results of these attacks were uneven and in any case were overshadowed by the devastating effects of a 40-day siege against Athens conducted by the Spartans in his absence.

The Peloponesian War.
Archive Photos. Reproduced by permission.

Within a year, Pericles was dead. Though he had not proven an able general, he had been a great leader. The men who succeeded him were far from his equals in ability. On the one side was a group led by Nicias (NIS-ee-uhs), who urged peace with Sparta; on the other was Cleon (KLEE-ahn) and his faction, who wanted to pursue the war with vigor. Cleon won out. At first his policy seemed to succeed. In 425 B.C., Athens defeated Sparta in battle, and Sparta surrendered. In the following year, the Spartans were again on the move under a new leader, Brasidas (BRAS-uh-duhs). The two armies clashed over the Athenian colony Amphipolis (am-FIP-uh-luhs) in Macedon in 422 B.C. This engagement ended in a Spartan victory—and the deaths of both Cleon and Brasidas.

In 421 B.C., Nicias managed to secure what appeared to be a peace agreement, but forces on both sides wanted the war to continue. Among these was Alcibiades (al-suh-BIE-uh-deez; c. 450-404 B.C.), a truly dastardly figure who in 415 B.C. led an ill-advised attack against the Corinthian colony of Syracuse in Sicily. When Alcibiades was accused of mutilating statues of Hermes, leadership of the Athenian force fell to a reluctant Nicias, who perished at Syracuse in 413 B.C.

Alcibiades had meanwhile switched sides. He helped the Spartans in 412 B.C. by inciting an Ionian revolt against Athens, thus effectively destroying the influence of the Delian League. He also encouraged the Spartans to appeal to an old enemy, Persia, for help. Sparta took up the idea, signing a treaty with the Persians, but the Spartans did not trust the traitor Alcibiades, who switched sides yet again. Amazingly, the Athenians put him back in leadership, and he led them to several victories. After a defeat in 407 B.C., however, he was stripped of his general's rank, and three years later, in 404 B.C., was murdered in Phrygia.

By that time, the war was over. In 405 B.C., Lysander (lie-SAN-duhr; d. 395 B.C.), the Spartan naval commander, had formed another alliance with the Persians. Together they defeated Athens at Aegospotami (ee-guh-SPAH-tuh-my) off the coast of Thrace. Athens, once rich and glorious, had been reduced to melting gold temple ornaments to pay for its war effort. Only the memory of their shared struggle in the Persian Wars kept the Spartans from destroying Athens completely. They did destroy the Long Walls, however, and placed the city under Spartan rule, bringing to an end a Golden Age that was all too brief.

The end of Classical Greece (404—338 B.C.)

If the Spartans expected to replace Athens as leaders of Greece, they were to be disappointed. Military authority was no match for the vast influence Athens enjoyed thanks to its extraordinary advancement in a multitude of areas. The Peloponnesian War simply left a power vacuum, which Macedon would fill less than seventy years later.

Historians frequently use words such as "inept" or "clumsy" to describe Sparta's handling of its leadership role. After centuries of isolation from the mainstream of Greek civilization, all the Spartans knew how to do was to maintain what they already had. When they tried to apply to Athens methods that had worked in Sparta, they failed miserably, as in the case of the Thirty Tyrants. This was a group of politicians who, with Spartan backing, seized power in Athens in 404 B.C. They proceeded to settle old scores with the democratic factions, and waged a reign of terror that resulted in many deaths. Within a year, the Athenians had driven out the Thirty Tyrants.

By 395 B.C., Athens had recovered sufficiently to join two old Spartan allies, Corinth and Thebes, in a revolt against Sparta. Though the Spartans managed to defeat the others in the Corinthian War, which ended in 386 B.C., the conflict showed that Spartan rule could only be maintained by constant effort. It also prefigured Sparta's fall. In 371 B.C., the Theban commander Epaminondas (i-pam-i-NAHN-duhs; c. 410–362 B.C.) led his troops to victory over Sparta at Leuctra (LEWK-truh).

Like the Periclean Age, the Spartan Age had lasted about a third of a century; but unlike the Age of Pericles, few mourned its passing. The next one-third century belonged, more or less, to Thebes, though Athens continued to assert its importance through figures such as Demosthenes. In any case, the poleis of Greece proper had sapped their energies in squabbling. The focus was about to shift northward, to Macedon.

Logic: Road Map of the World

Logic is a system of reasoning for reaching correct conclusions about concepts and for assessing a conclusion that has been reached. It is closely related to mathematics. Aristotle developed the ideas of logic considerably, creating a formula called a *syllogism* (SIL-oh-jiz-uhm), which consists of a general statement, a specific statement, and a conclusion. The most famous example is "All men are mortal. Socrates is a man. Therefore, Socrates is mortal."

Like math, logic has nothing to do with anything outside itself. When adding two plus two, it does not matter if the "two" refers to two apples or two hand grenades. Similarly, logic can be applied correctly to untrue statements.

No one illustrated this fact better than Zeno of Elea, though that was not his purpose. Setting out to prove that motion, and therefore change, were impossible, he put forward the four paradoxes of motion.

Each paradox is a little story, each slightly different, and together they make up the first set of brainteasers in history—puzzles that have delighted and irritated children and adults alike.

In one paradox, Zeno referred to an arrow being shot from a bow. At every moment of its flight, it could be said that the arrow was at rest within a space equal to its length. Though it would be some 2,500 years before slow-motion photography, in effect he was asking his listeners to imagine a snapshot of the arrow in flight. If it was at rest in that snapshot, and at every other moment it was supposedly in motion, then when did it actually move?

Another paradox involved the great hero Achilles in a footrace against a tortoise. Because he was so much faster than the tortoise, Achilles allowed it to start near the finish line—a big mistake because, as Zeno set out to prove, Achilles

Great figures of Classical Greece

With all the turmoil that characterized the Classical Age, it may seem odd that the period is considered one of the greatest in history. And yet it was, a time when philosophy and literature flowered alongside science, the arts, and even politics. It was, in fact, the time when history—literally—was born.

Prior to Classical Greece, the writing of history had tended toward one of two extremes. On the one hand, it might could then never pass the tortoise. By the time he got to the point where the tortoise started, it would have moved on to another point, and when he got to that second point, it would have moved on to yet another point, and so on. There would be no point at which Achilles could pass the tortoise.

These and Zeno's other two paradoxes, which were similar in concept, failed to prove that motion was impossible, but they did impress philosophers with the importance of logic itself. Through use of logic, Zeno seemingly created a series of statements that could not possibly be true.

Hidden in his problems, however, was a set of false assumptions, which later became clear to modern philosophers. In each paradox, he treated either space or time as though they were made up of an infinite number of points—for instance, infinite arrow "snapshots." In geometric theory, a line does have an infinite number of points, but the same is not true in the real world. In the real world each "point"—a millionth of a second of time, for instance"—actually has some length. If there were an infinite number of tiny points, each period of time or length of space would be infinite as well. Of course this is not the case.

People usually study logic only in college, and very few people do so then. The irony is that everyone uses logic every day, and plenty of people use it incorrectly. There is no reason to believe that Zeno deliberately misled his listeners, but often people do use logic incorrectly in order to lead others to false conclusions. Everyone should have some knowledge of logical thinking in order to avoid being misled. A person who is not equipped with an understanding of logic is like someone trying to drive a car without knowing how to read road signs.

be a mixture of myth and fact, exciting enough, but not always reliable, as in the Homeric legends or the Old Testament account of the world's creation. On the other hand, it could be a mere series of names or facts, as in other parts of the Old Testament or in the annals of the Shang Dynasty kings.

Herodotus (heh-RAHD-uh-tuhs; c. 484–c. 425 B.C.) is known as the "Father of History" because he was the first writer to deal with historical events in a systematic way. In his history of the Persian Wars and other writings, he managed to

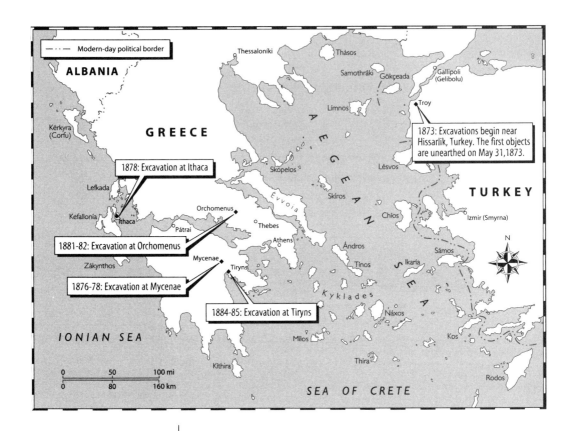

Map of Greece, Turkey, and the Aegean Sea, with important archaeological sites excavated by Heinrich Schliemann marked.

XNR Productions. Gale Research.

present a compelling narrative, or story, while at least trying (not always very hard) to conform to the facts.

Thucydides (thoo-SID-uh-deez; c. 471–401 B.C.) had a much tougher approach to facts, which earned him a reputation as the first critical historian. A critical historian is someone who looks deeply into events rather than simply accepting them at face value. As a commander of a force that went up against Brasidas, he had an eyewitness perspective for the writing of his *History of the Peloponnesian War.*

Xenophon (ZEHN-uh-fahn; c. 431–c. 352 B.C.) had even more military experience, having served in the army of mercenaries hired by Cyrus the Younger to use against his brother Artaxerxes. He wrote a number of works, including *Hellenica,* a history of Greece following the Peloponnesian War, and several books on a remarkable man he had known and admired. That remarkable man was Socrates (SAHK-ruh-teez; c. 470–399 B.C.), who so greatly expanded the reach of philosophy that those before him are often referred to as the pre-Socratic (soh-KRA-tik) philosophers.

Philosophers

By the time of Socrates, philosophy had dwindled from the noble pursuits of earlier thinkers to the childish squabbling of the Sophists (SAH-fistz). The Greek root *sophos* means "clever" or "wise," as in *sophisticated,* and certainly the Sophists were clever. A product of the explosion in knowledge that had come from the work of earlier philosophers like Zeno, they sought to use logic for their own purposes. They went around the land, earning money by teaching young men how to be more effective at speaking and arguing, but there seemed no higher purpose to their pursuits. All they wanted was to get ahead in the world—and to argue. For this reason, the word *sophist* entered the English language as a term for somebody who cares more about winning an argument than they do about the truth.

Socrates stood sophistry on its head, calling on people not to question each other, but to question themselves and the underlying beliefs of their society. He developed what was called the Socratic Method, a *dialogue,* (DIE-uh-lawg) or conversation, between a teacher and student. The teacher asks the student a series of questions to help the student discover the answers himself.

Famous for his command "Know thyself," Socrates also said: "The unexamined life is not worth living." It was the first time that anyone had ever suggested self-examination as a path to wisdom. In a sense Socrates could be called an early prophet of *psychology,* the study of the mind and human behavior—yet another word derived from Greek. Certainly he was the father of Western thought, in that he originated the attitude of *skepticism* (SKEP-ti-siz-uhm) toward one's own society that distinguishes the West from all other civilizations.

It was one thing to question oneself and quite another to question government and society as Socrates did, particularly in Athens just after the humiliating defeat of the Peloponnesian War. In 399 B.C., he was arrested and charged with corrupting young minds and encouraging disbelief in the gods. He refused to beg for mercy and was condemned to death by drinking a cup of poison. Present at his death was his disciple Plato (PLAY-toh; 427–347 B.C.), who was so upset by the execution of Socrates that he left Athens and traveled for many years. Upon his return, he founded a school in a garden called Academus (uh-KAD-uh-mehs); hence its name, and that of thousands of schools since: the Academy.

Not only did Plato apply the Socratic Method in teaching his students, he also immortalized his teacher in numerous works that centered around dialogues between Socrates and others. Socrates himself never wrote anything. In Plato's writings he often appeared as a character, not necessarily the actual historical Socrates. This is the case in Plato's most famous work—indeed, one of the most important books ever written—*The Republic*. In it, Socrates and a number of others, including a leading Sophist of the day, discuss the question "What is justice?"

Much of *The Republic* is Plato's recollection of Socrates' answer, his portrayal in words of an ideal society. In this polis, the mass of people will go on as before. There will be warriors to defend them, as always. But rather than mere kings and nobles as the other class of society, the ruling class will be made up of philosophers—wise men who also serve as kings. Much of Socrates' description concerns how these philosopher-kings, or guardians, should be educated.

Clearly this is not a democracy. Indeed Socrates admits that his ideal state is an aristocracy, except in this case, the aristocrats are rich with wisdom instead of money. *The Republic* has been a source of controversy that continues to this day. Many critics charge that Plato helped father modern totalitarianism. Others hold that this view is unfair because the book should be read in view of the time and place in which it was written, a world of tiny city-states rocked by unceasing conflict. In any case, it appears that Plato was merely presenting a model, not something he thought should or would be established.

Plato was interested in ideals and models. The concerns of his greatest student, Aristotle (air-is-TAHT-uhl; 384–322 B.C.), were quite different. Not only did Aristotle develop logic as a formal study, he essentially established the scientific method as a way of viewing the world. Plato would have started with a general idea and then looked for examples of it. Aristotle did just the opposite. He studied nature and from his observations made conclusions. His conclusions were not always correct, but it was his method that mattered. Aristotle is considered the father of the biological sciences.

Aristotle also increased understanding of cause-and-effect relationships, a theme that would occupy philosophers' attention for centuries. Once upon a time, people had simply made up stories—the myths—to explain the causes of things in nature. Often they assumed that if something happened before something else, it "caused" it to happen. Aristotle started the process of sorting out such confusion. He also wrote extensively about everything from politics to physics to literature to the ultimate nature of reality, a subject to which he gave the name *metaphysics* (MEH-tuh-fiz-ikz), or "beyond physics." Just as Aristotle had a famous teacher, he taught a famous pupil: a young Macedonian prince named Alexander, who would soon rule the world.

Socrates and his pupils.
Archive Photos. Reproduced by permission.

Playwrights

In Classical Greece, the relationship between philosophy and literature became well-established. This was clear in the work of Aristophanes (air-uh-STAHF-uh-neez; c. 450–c. 388 B.C.), an Athenian playwright known for his comedies. A friend of the old order, Aristophanes poked wicked fun at Socrates, Plato, and others who promoted new views of society. Certainly he was a conservative, but he was too hilarious to be a stuffed shirt. Plays such as *The Clouds* and *The Frogs* are still funny today. Only eleven of Aristophanes's forty plays have survived, and the work of the great tragic playwrights has suffered similar devastation. In fact, Aristophanes is the only comic playwright whose work is even known today; at least in the case of tragedy, works by three playwrights have survived to the present.

It should be noted that in the context of ancient Greece, comedy and tragedy did not mean exactly what they do today. Comedy was not necessarily funny, even if the *satire* (SA-tire) of Aristophanes was. Instead, the word comedy meant that at the end of the play, everything ended up well for the main characters. And whereas "tragedy" refers to a terrible misfortune, for Greek playwrights it had a much more specific meaning. As explained by Aristotle in his *Poetics,* a tragedy was a play about a great hero with a "tragic flaw," usually pride or *hubris* (H'YOO-bris), that destines him for great suffering. The plot of the tragedy most often focuses on a great misfortune that befalls the hero, and it usually ends with him choosing to go down fighting rather than merely submit to fate.

The first great tragedian (tra-jeh-DEE-uhn) was Aeschylus (ES-kuh-luhs; 525–426 B.C.) Aeschylus won the first prize in tragedy thirteen times at an annual festival in Athens, where playwrights presented trilogies, or sets of three plays. His *Oresteia* (ohr-es-TIE-yuh) is the only such trilogy that has survived. The first play of the *Oresteia* centers on what happens to King Agamemnon after he returns from the Trojan War. In part because of his own tragic flaws, he is murdered by his cheating wife and her lover. The second play focuses on the revenge taken by his son Orestes (oh-REHS-teez). The third finds Orestes coming to terms with his murder of his mother.

Perhaps the most tragic figure in all of Greek drama was the central character in *Oedipus the King* by Sophocles (SAHF-uh-kleez; c. 496–406 B.C.) Without intending to, Oedipus fulfills a prophecy that he will kill his father and marry his mother. When he realizes what he has done, he pokes out his own eyes.

These are horrid events, to be sure, but as noted by Aristotle, himself a great admirer of Sophocles, watching a tragedy such as *Oedipus* gave the audience an opportunity for *catharsis* (kuh-THAHR-sis), or purification through art. Instead of having to go through things themselves, an audience could watch an actor on stage and thus get relief from their own pent-up emotions. Aristotle was not the only one to find deep psychological meaning in Sophocles' play. Sigmund Freud (FROID; 1856–1939), the father of modern psychology, believed that young men have a subconscious desire to replace their fathers as Oedipus did—symbolically, at least—as a way of establishing their own independence.

Also penetrating was the psychological approach of Euripides (yoo-RIP-uh-deez; c. 484–406 B.C.), whose works included the *Medea* (meh-DEE-uh) and *The Trojan Women*. In the latter play is a heartrending speech by Andromache (an-DRAH-muh-kee), wife of Hector, who is forced to give up her infant son to be killed by the Greeks: "Thou little thing that curlest in my arms," she tells the baby, "What sweet scents cling all around thy neck! Beloved, can it be all nothing ... all the weary nights wherethrough I watched upon thy sickness, till I grew wasted with watching? Kiss me. This one last time; not ever again." These were words to break the heart of any parent. Euripides concluded her speech with a suggestion that, following the example of Socrates, he took a highly critical view of his own society: "O, ye have found an anguish that outstrips all tortures of the East, ye gentle Greeks!"

Sophocles and Euripides also took part in, and several times won, the drama competition in Athens. Apparently the competition was part of a festival in honor of the god Dionysus. Over time the plays developed a specific form. Usually there were a few central characters, along with a large group of people called a chorus, who provided a sort of voice-over narration to the play.

Other artists and scientists

There was a religious character to much of the poetry that flourished during the Classical Age. Among the finest poets of the era was Pindar (PIN-duhr; c. 522–c. 438 B.C.), whose most famous works were his *odes* to the victors in the Olympic Games. He was but the most prominent of many, and there were at least a dozen important poets in his time.

As with Pindar, among the most noted works of the sculptor Praxiteles (prak-SIT-uh-leez; fl. 370–330 B.C.) were those he created in honor of Olympic heroes. He sculpted the statues at two of the Seven Wonders of the Ancient World, the Mausoleum of Halicarnassus and the Temple of Artemis at Ephesus. Then of course there was Phidias, the other most notable sculptor of his day, not to mention the architects who, along with him, were responsible for the magnificent Parthenon.

Leucippus and Democritus developed the idea that all nature is made up of tiny particles called atoms. Twenty-four centuries later, humankind would witness the terrible power of the atomic bomb. *Archive Photos/American Stock. Reproduced by permission.*

Nor was Classical Greece weak in the area of the sciences, which were then in their birthing years. Aside from the investigations of Aristotle, there was the work of Leucippus (loo-SIP-uhs; 400s B.C.) and his student Democritus (deh-MAHK-ri-tus; c. 460–c. 370 B.C.) Leucippus established and Democritus developed an idea that was about twenty-four centuries ahead of its time: that all of nature is made up of tiny pieces called atoms. In the twentieth century A.D., scientists such as Albert Einstein (1879–1955) would look deeply into the atom and there find a source of marvelous and terrible power.

Yet another piece of Classical Greece that is as fresh today as it was then is the Hippocratic (hip-oh-KRAT-ik) Oath. The latter is named after the scientist and physician Hippocrates (hi-PAHK-ruh-teez; c. 460–c. 370 B.C.), who developed an oath sworn by graduating medical students through the ages. For instance, one of the pledges in the Hippocratic Oath is "I will give no deadly medicine to any one if asked nor suggest any such counsel."

Modern people might find one of Hippocrates' other ideas—that all diseases are caused by four different bodily fluids, or "humors"—less impressive. The idea of the humors would plague medicine through the end of the Middle Ages, leading to such dangerous practices as removing "excess" blood, which happened to be one of the humors. But when Hippocrates came up with the idea, it was a massive step forward. For the first time, instead of looking for the roots of disease in divine causes (i.e., the gods), Hippocrates looked for the cause in chemicals. Today doctors know that indeed chemical imbalances often are the cause of illness.

The Orators

The Greeks made an art of public speaking, or oratory (OHR-uh-tohr-ee), in the Golden Age and thereafter. As with most other arts, it flourished in Athens, where it formed an important part in the development of democracy. In order to make informed decisions regarding the issues of the day, the people needed to hear informed opinions on many sides. Thus the Greeks placed a premium on speaking ability, an art taught by the Sophists, among others.

Just because the Athenian government was democratic did not mean that it was nice. Modern Americans wring their hands over disagreements in Congress, but in fact the behavior of U.S. politicians is downright civil compared with that of their Athenian counterparts. In Athens, if a speaker bored his listeners, they would boo him and shout him down.

The first important Greek orator was Antiphon (AN-tuh-fahn; c. 480–411 B.C.), who also wrote speeches for lawyers and others participating in murder cases. Lysias (LIS-ee-uhs; c. 445–c. 380 B.C.) is best remembered for his opposition to the Thirty Tyrants installed by Sparta after it gained control of Athens in 401 B.C.. Isocrates (ie-SAHK-ruh-teez; 436–338 B.C.) founded a school where he taught many of the leading orators of the next generation, including Lycurgus (lie-KUHR-guhs; c. 390–324 B.C.) Then there was Lycurgus's associate, Demosthenes.

When Demosthenes was a young man, few people would have picked him to be a future orator. He was physically weak, and his voice was soft, but he was smart. He could have had a good career writing speeches for someone else to deliver. Yet he dreamed of holding audiences spellbound, so he worked on his voice by speaking to the crashing waves on the shore, trying to be heard over them. He put pebbles in his mouth to make speaking still harder. He would often run up and down hills—still speaking with pebbles in his mouth—to strengthen his body. In the end, he became the greatest orator of ancient Greece, and one of the greatest speakers of all time.

Greece under Macedonian rule (338–146 B.C.)

In the early 330s B.C., Greece began to experience rumblings from the north from a people beyond its borders who considered themselves heirs to the Grecian heritage, even if the Greeks themselves did not consider them entirely Greek. They seemed to have come out of another time, a world quite removed from the refinements of Athens—a world more like the Greece of myth, when heroes such as Achilles walked the earth.

They were the Macedonians, a hard, warlike nation who, along with the much softer Lydians, considered themselves the descendants of Heracles. They absorbed the culture of Greece. Unlike the Spartans, they recognized that their focus on warfare and survival brought with it certain limitations. They were more like the Persians in their respect and admiration for the cultures of gentler lands they conquered.

The Macedonians had their origins in the distant past, so far back that myth explained them as descending from a son of Zeus called Macedon. (Similarly, the Bible describes the African Kushites as having come from a grandson of Noah named Cush.) They were goatherders, a tribal people whose animals grazed on the slopes of Mount Olympus. In time they became so cut off from the rest of Greece that their dialect could hardly be understood.

The Macedonians' true history began with Perdiccas (puhr-DIK-uhs), a Greek who came north and took the throne in about 650 B.C., establishing a dynasty that would rule Macedon for more than three centuries. In 510 B.C., his descendant Amyntas I (uh-MIN-tuhs) expanded the kingdom greatly by making an alliance with the Persians. The Persians were on the move in the area, of course, building their empire and soon coming to blows with the Greeks.

Alexander I (r. c. 495–452 B.C.) used Persian help to further strengthen his nation's power; but unbeknownst to the Persian emperor Xerxes, he was supporting the Greeks fighting the Persian Wars. After the defeat of the Persians in 479 B.C., he helped himself to lands between Macedon and Thrace, but his dream of a Macedonian empire seemed to die with him. Not only were the Greeks of the Golden Age too strong an opponent, but the various tribes of Macedon did not always follow their rulers, and the kings after Alexander were weak. Then in 359 B.C., a king powerful enough to fulfill Alexander's dream took the throne.

The Reign of Philip II (359–336 B.C.)

Philip II (382–336 B.C.) reorganized Macedon, consolidating his power in the court and transporting people from various regions of the country to other parts. It was a strategy employed by the Assyrians to prevent local groups from challenging the central authority. In Philip's case it gave him a free hand to extend his control far beyond Macedon's borders.

Philip had invented a new weapon called the pike, a spear some sixteen feet long—a good nine or ten feet longer than the spears of Greek hoplites. Armed with pikes, his army was the most powerful in the region. Between 354 and 339 B.C., he conquered an empire that stretched across the Balkan Peninsula (BAWL-kuhn) in the southeastern corner of Europe. From Illyria in the west to the Danube River (dan-YOOB) in the east, Philip, having broken the power of the Scythians over the Black Sea region, was king. Then he turned his eyes southward, toward the true prize: Greece.

Philip did not consider himself an outsider conquering a foreign land but a fellow Greek bringing the Greeks together. Therefore he went into Greece, not to make war, but to bring peace (at least, from his perspective). Having gained an alliance with Thessaly, he defeated a huge Greek army and put an end to a war in 346 B.C. that pitted various Greek leagues against one another for control of Delphi. As president of the Pythian Games, an important symbolic position, he called on Athens to join other city-states in what he called the Greek League.

Regardless of how Philip viewed himself, Athenians saw him as a barbarian. Leading the attacks against him was Demosthenes (deh-MAHS-thuh-neez; 384–322 B.C.), a famed statesman and orator (OHR-uh-tuhr). Beginning in 351 B.C., Demosthenes made a series of brilliant speeches in which he warned against the Macedonians and their king. In one of these speeches, called the "Philippics," he said of Philip, "Observe, Athenians, the height to which this fellow's insolence has soared: ... he blusters and talks big ... he is always taking in more, everywhere casting his net round us, while we sit idle and do nothing."

Demosthenes urged the Athenians to join Thebes and other city-states in opposing Philip. The two forces met in battle at Charonea (kare-uh-NEE-uh) in 338 B.C. The Greeks were no match for Philip's army, and Charonea marked the end of Greece as an independent force. Soon all the city-states joined the Greek League. Philip prepared to fulfill his ultimate dream of leading a combined Macedonian and Greek force eastward, where they would conquer the Persian Empire. He did not live to see it, however. In 336 B.C., when he was only forty-four years old, Philip was killed by an assassin. Now the crown passed to his son, who would become the greatest conqueror in history.

The Age of Alexander (336–323 B.C.)

When he assumed the throne of Macedon, Alexander (356–323 B.C.) was only 20 years old. Within two years, he would embark on a campaign of conquest that would make him ruler, by the age of 30, over almost the entire world as the Greeks knew it. His empire stretched from the Peloponnese to the Indus River and from the mountains of the Hindu Kush to the Cataracts of the Nile. Except for parts of India and Africa, as well as China and of course the Americas, all the civilizations up to that time would come either under direct Macedonian rule or into alliance with Macedon. No leader had ever conquered so much land in so short a time, and no leader would ever do so again.

In those years of conquest from 334 to 326 B.C., Alexander's empire seemed to promise a newer, brighter age when the nations of the world could join as one, not under Macedonian rule, but in a joint effort which would bring all people together as equals. The Alexandrian Empire made no distinction, or at least little distinction, between racial and ethnic groups: instead, it promoted men on the basis of their ability. In each land he conquered, Alexander and his soldiers took wives and fathered children, not as a way of further subduing the people, but as a way of literally and symbolically uniting themselves with them.

After nearly two years spent consolidating his power in Greece, Alexander marched his troops across the Hellespont in 334 B.C. The first of his army to touch Asian soil, he drove his spear into the ground as a symbol of conquest. He believed himself a descendant of Achilles on his mother's side, so he made one of the only detours of the long journey ahead, visiting Troy. Further on, he stopped in Gordian, capital of the Phrygians, where he cut the fabled Gordian knot. Then it was on to conquest.

After taking all of Asia Minor, in 333 and 332 B.C., the armies of Alexander occupied Syria, Phoenicia, and Palestine.

Alexander's armies next conquered the most ancient of the world's lands, one of which the Greeks were in awe: Egypt. There he founded the city of Alexandria. Then he made a big loop into the desert before leaving Africa and marching deeper into Asia. By 331 B.C., Alexander had taken Assyria and reached Babylon. The next major stop was Persepolis, the capital of the Persian Empire, which he took in 330 B.C. With the Persian Empire gone, he ruled the world.

Alexander truly seemed to be as interested in freeing nations as in controlling them. He gave the Armenians their independence. He also expanded his multiracial policies. From the beginning, Alexander's armies had recruited local troops, but with the full conquest of Persia, this enlistment began in earnest. It was his goal to leave Persia in the control of Persians trained in the Greek language and Greek culture. In addition, he left behind some seventy new towns named Alexandria. This began the spread of Hellenistic culture throughout western Asia.

Over the course of almost six years, from 330 to 324 B.C., Alexander's armies made a giant loop through what is now Iran, Afghanistan, and Pakistan. If Alexander had had his way, they would have kept on going. In July of 326 B.C., however, just after they crossed the Beas River, his troops refused to continue. It had been eight years since they had seen their families, and even if they turned west immediately, it would be many more years before they reached Greek soil again. Reluctantly, Alexander agreed to turn around and head for home.

He sent one group back by sea, commanding them to explore the coastline as they went, and another by a northerly route. He took a third group through southern Iran, on a miserable desert journey in which the entire army very nearly lost its way. Finally, in the spring of 323 B.C., they returned to Babylon. There Alexander began planning yet another conquest: Arabia. But he took ill from a fever, which was not helped by his recently adopted habit of heavy drinking, not to mention the wearying hardships of the desert journey. Unable to move or speak, he took to his bed, where all his commanders filed by in solemn tribute to the great man who had led them. On June 13, 323 B.C., he died. He was not yet 33 years old.

The Hellenistic Age (323–146 B.C.)

In the aftermath of Alexander's death, his generals quarreled over the spoils of his conquests. None of them were remotely Alexander's equal in vision; they were merely soldiers, with no ambition to reshape the world. Seleucus (suh-LOO-suhs; c. 356–281 B.C.) gained control over Persia and Mesopotamia, where an empire under his name would rule for many years. Ptolemy (TAHL-uh-mee; c. 365–c. 283 B.C.) established a dynasty of even longer standing in Egypt. He and his descendants ruled from 323 until 30 B.C.

As for who would rule Macedon and Greece, that was a much thornier question. Alexander's successors fought one another over the European homeland. Seleucus and Ptolemy, along with several others, tried to keep Antigonus (an-TIG-uh-nuhs; 382–301 B.C.) from taking over Macedon. Control passed through several hands, with both Seleucus and Antigonus losing their lives in battles over the Macedonian throne.

In 279 B.C., a new and terrifying force appeared in southeastern Europe: the barbaric Celts or Gauls. Antigonus Gonatas (GAHN-uh-tuhs; c. 319–239 B.C.), grandson of Antigonus, drove out the Gauls and established a Macedonian dynasty that would last until 167 B.C. He controlled much of Greece through puppet rulers and struggled constantly with Pyrrhus (PEER-uhs; 319–272 B.C.), the king of Epirus, for leadership over the region. Then, in 229 B.C., Rome established a military base in Illyria.

Philip V of Macedon (238–179 B.C.) tried to resist the spread of Roman rule. The conflict between the two powers came to a head in 197 B.C. at Cynocephalae (si-nuh-SEH-fuh-lee) in Thessaly. The troops of Philip, like those of his namesake Philip II, fought using the pike. Military technology had moved on, and the Roman units, with their better swords and armor, devastated Philip's army. Yet he managed to escape with a few troops, and in the years that followed, he built up his forces.

Philip left his son Perseus (PUHR-sus; c. 212–c. 165 B.C.) an army of 40,000 men. Still, they were no match for the Romans, who in one battle in 168 B.C. killed some 20,000 Macedonians. They captured Perseus and marched him to Rome, where he died. In 150 B.C. Andriscus (an-DRIS-kuhs), who claimed to be Perseus's son, tried to lead a revolt against Rome. But the Romans crushed the uprising and in 148 B.C. annexed Macedon. Two years later, they added Greece to their empire.

The spread of Hellenistic culture

The period between Alexander's death and the absorption of Greece into the Roman Empire is called the Hellenistic Age. During those two centuries, as Greece itself crumbled, Greek culture spread throughout the Mediterranean and Middle East. It did not come just from Greece, but from a place where the two greatest Mediterranean civilizations met: Alexandria.

That great Egyptian city boasted not only the Pharos Lighthouse, one of the Seven Wonders of the World, but by far the world's greatest library. Ashurbanipal of Syria had founded the first true library three centuries earlier, but Alexandria's, with some 700,000 "books" (actually, scrolls), dwarfed all that had preceded it. No wonder, then, that Alexandria became a center of Hellenistic literature, with a new school of writers who perfected various forms of poetry.

Alexandria was the home of Euclid (YOO-klid; fl. c. 300 B.C.), who established such a thorough system of geometry that he is considered the father of the discipline; it would be more than 2,000 years before mathematicians would be able to improve on his ideas. Also in Alexandria were two of the leading anatomists (that is, scientists who study the human body) of the age: the surgeon Herophilus (huh-RAHF-uh-luhs; c. 335–c. 280 B.C.) and the physician Erasistratus (uhr-uh-SIS-truh-tuhs; fl. c. 250 B.C.), both of whom founded schools of anatomy in the city.

Of course, science also flourished in Greece, where one of the greatest inventors of all time, Archimedes (ahr-kuh-MEED-eez; c. 287–212 B.C.), developed such essential creations as the lever and the pulley. The astronomer Hipparchus (huh-PAHR-kuhs; fl. 146–127 B.C.) discovered a number of key ideas, including the procession of the equinoxes, whereby seasons change according to Earth's position relative to the Sun. Compiler of the first star list, he developed the use of latitude and longitude as ways of finding a position on Earth. He also fathered the mathematical discipline of trigonometry. Pytheas (PITH-ee-uhs; fl. 300

The sculpture, Venus de Milo, was created in the Hellenic Age.
AP/Wide World Photos. Reproduced by permission.

B.C.) was both a scientist and an explorer. He developed the first theories about the tides and their relation to the Moon, and he traveled to the western edge of the known world, around Spain and up toward Britain. He explored much of the Britain on foot.

As Pytheas was venturing into the far West, Hellenism spread eastward. Its greatest political stronghold would be in the Greco-Bactrian kingdom north of India and Persia, which would also be the first semi-Western society known to the Chinese. In India, Chandragupta Maurya observed the example of Alexander and went on to conquer a vast empire that would rule for two centuries.

The influence of Hellenism can be seen in the region of Gandhara (guhn-DAHR-uh), on the borders of modern-day Pakistan and Afghanistan. The sculpture of Gandhara bore the imprint of a culture thousands of miles away. Early images of the Buddha, for instance, were modeled on statues of Apollo. It was clear that sculpture had come a long way from the kouroi of Archaic times, which were meant to be viewed only from the front. Figures of the Hellenistic Age were usually represented with their bodies turned, so that the viewer was forced to walk around each statue in order to fully see it. Two of the world's most famous sculptures, the *Venus de Milo* and *Winged Victory,* date from this era.

Increasingly ornate Greek styles of architecture, reflecting the Corinthian order, spread throughout the East as well. Palmyra in Syria, for instance, looked like a city from Classical Greece, only the style of its buildings was much more flowery than that of Athens in the Golden Age. Such buildings provided concrete evidence of the Greeks' impact, which they made almost wholly without the use of the sword. Long after Alexander and his troops departed, a little of Greece remained in the East, where it would become woven into the fabric of local culture.

Greece and Rome

In the Middle Ages, when civilization all but disappeared from Europe, the Arab world would preserve Greek culture and philosophy, particularly that of Aristotle. Farther west, the Byzantine Empire (BIZ-uhn-teen), which grew out of the Roman Empire's eastern branch in Greece, would maintain a very formal, strict, and static version of civilized learning while Western Europe faded into darkness.

Just as it is impossible to imagine the world without Greece, so it is impossible to fully appreciate the Hellenic impact on civilization without seeing its influence on the last great society of the ancient world: Rome. As Greece was dying out, preparing to pass the torch to the Romans, two new schools of philosophy arose in Athens, Stoicism (STOH-ih-siz-uhm) and Epicureanism (ehp-ih-K'YOOR-ee-uh-niz-uhm). Between them, these two views of the world reflected what was to come for Rome.

The Stoics placed a premium on dignity, bravery, and self-control. So, too, did the early Romans. Indeed, one of their rulers would rank among the greatest Stoic philosophers. The Epicureans originally taught enjoyment of life's simple joys, but in time this became corrupted. The word epicurean in modern usage means someone who lives for pleasure. Nothing could better describe the later Romans who helped bring about the fall of their empire and the end of civilization in Western Europe for many years.

But before it could fall, Rome had to rise. In its time Rome became a more splendid empire than any that preceded it. Its realm was larger than Alexander's, and it held it for much longer. During that time, the Romans—the greatest Hellenistic kingdom of all—deepened and widened the influence of the Greeks. Thanks to Rome, Greece would never die.

For More Information
Books

Barber, Richard W. *A Companion to World Mythology*. Illustrated by Pauline Baynes. New York: Delacorte Press, 1979.

Bardi, Piero. *The Atlas of the Classical World: Ancient Greece and Ancient Rome*. Illustrations by Matteo Chesi, et al. New York: Peter Bedrick Books, 1997, pp. 8-33.

Bowra, C. M. *Classical Greece*. New York: Time-Life Books, 1965.

Brumbaugh, Robert S. *The Philosophers of Greece*. Albany, NY: State University of New York Press, 1981.

Bulfinch, Thomas. *Bulfinch's Mythology of Greece and Rome with Eastern and Norse Legends*. New York: Collier Books, 1967.

Burrell, Roy. *Oxford First Ancient History*. New York: Oxford University Press, 1991, pp. 96-205.

Chelepi, Chris. *Growing Up in Ancient Greece*. Illustrated by Chris Molan. Mahwah, NJ: Troll Associates, 1994.

Harris, Nathaniel. *Alexander the Great and the Greeks*. Illustrated by Gerry Wood. New York: Bookwright Press, 1986.

Lyle, Garry. *Let's Visit Greece*. Bridgeport, CT: Burke, 1985.

Martell, Hazel Mary. *The Kingfisher Book of the Ancient World*. New York: Kingfisher, 1995, pp. 62-75.

Nardo, Don. *Life in Ancient Greece*. San Diego, CA: Lucent Books, 1996.

Priestley, J. B. *The Wonderful World of the Theatre*. Garden City, NY: Doubleday, 1969.

Rutland, Jonathan. *An Ancient Greek Town*. Edited by Adrian Sington, illustrations by Bill Stallion, et al. London: Kingfisher Books, 1986.

Tallow, Peter. *The Olympics*. New York: Bookwright Press, 1988.

Warren, Peter. *The Aegean Civilizations: From Ancient Crete to Mycenae*. Oxford, England: Phaidon, 1989.

Web Sites

"The Ancient City of Athens." http://www.indiana.edu/~kglowack/athens/ (June 16, 1999).

"Ancient/Classical European History." http://www.execpc.com/~dboals/class.html (June 16, 1999).

"Ancient Greece." *Exploring Ancient World Cultures*. http://eawc.evansville.edu/grpage.htm (June 16, 1999).

"The Ancient Olympics." http://olympics.tufts.edu/ (June 23, 1999).

"Bulfinch's Mythology." http://www.webcom.com/shownet/medea/bulfinch/welcome.html (June 21, 1999).

"The Classic Page." *Tufts Hellenic Society*. http://www.tufts.edu/org/hellenic/classic.html (June 23, 1999).

"For the Love of Ancient Greece." http://library.advanced.org/12441/ (June 23, 1999).

"Slavery in Ancient Greece." http://www-adm.pdx.edu/user/sinq/greekciv/sport/kirsten.html (June 23, 1999).

"Trojan War." http://webhome.crk.umn.edu/~sneet/WestCiv/TrojanWar.htm (June 21, 1999).

Rome

12

Rome is known as "the Eternal City," a fitting title for a city more than 2,500 years old. It is located almost exactly midway of the boot-shaped Italian peninsula, on its western shore. To the ancient world, it was not merely the capital of a great empire: it *was* the empire. There was the capital city of Rome, which over time continued to conquer regions around it, gradually increasing the population of Roman citizens. People outside of the capital city of Rome, yet in the Roman Empire, enjoyed the rights of Roman citizenship as well.

Why Rome is important

From Roman numerals [see sidebar, "Roman Numerals"] to "toga parties," from the calendar to the names of the planets to a multitude of daily expressions, the influence of Rome is everywhere. Rome left the modern world a vast legacy, symbolized by the word *legacy* itself, which is Latin for bequest, a gift handed down. In fact, *symbolize* and more than half the words in the English language come from the Roman language, Latin. The system of laws of the United States has its

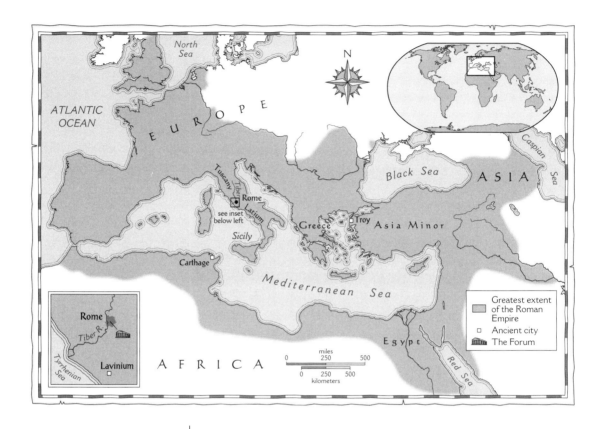

Map of ancient Rome.
XNR Productions. The Gale Group.

roots in ancient Rome, a fact reinforced by the Roman- and Greek-influenced architecture that dominates the official buildings of the U.S. capital in Washington, DC. The English alphabet is based on the Roman alphabet, which in turn was derived from the Greek. In fact the legacies of Greece and Rome are so intertwined that people often speak of them together, using the term "Greco-Roman." The Greco-Roman heritage, along with the religious tradition of Israel, is the foundation of Western culture.

Early Rome (753–507 B.C.)

The Romans traditionally dated the founding of their city at 753 B.C. A number of legends are told of its founding. In fact, the area around Rome may have been occupied as much as a century earlier. The legends themselves have little basis in history. Still, they formed a compelling national myth akin to the Greeks' Troy tale, which is their basis.

Words to Know: Rome

Anthropomorphic: In the image of human beings.

Catapult: A device for slinging large objects, such as boulders, a great length.

Chastity: The act or state of remaining pure by not engaging in sex.

Checks and balances: Built-in safeguards to protect a government from the possibility of one person or group of people gaining too much power.

Conscript (n.): Someone who is drafted into military service.

Constitution: A set of written laws governing a nation.

Dictator: A ruler who holds absolute, or complete, power.

Faction: A political group.

Guerrilla warfare: Warfare by unconventional methods, often involving surprise attacks.

Legal precedent: When a previous legal case has established a certain ruling, that ruling can then be applied to a later case.

Magistrate: An official entrusted with administration of laws.

Middle class: A group in between the rich and the poor or the rich and the working class.

Millennium: A thousand years.

Pagan (n.): Someone who worships many gods, usually deities associated with Nature.

Peasant: A farmer who works a small plot of land.

Plague: Used in a specific sense to describe an epidemic disease that kills a great number of people.

Province: A political unit, like a state, that is part of a larger country or empire.

Republic: A form of government, led by a president or a prime minister rather than by a monarch or a dictator, that is usually but not always democratic in character.

Romanization: The spread of Roman culture and civilization.

Sack (verb): To destroy; usually used in reference to a city.

Satire: A type of literary work that makes fun of human follies and vices.

Standing army: A full-time, professional army.

Toga: A type of loose outer robe worn in ancient Rome.

Veto: The power of one part of a government to prevent another part from taking a particular action.

The story of Aeneas (uh-NEE-uhs), in fact, seems to have arisen among Greek colonists living in southern Italy and Sicily. According to the legend, Aeneas was a Trojan prince who organized a group of escapees from the defeated city and set sail for Italy to establish a new Troy across the seas. Along the way, however, he had a series of trials and tribulations not unlike those of Odysseus in Homer's *Odyssey.*

After a wind blew his ship off course, he wound up on the shores of northern Africa, where he met the founder of Rome's future rival, Carthage (kahr-THEJ). The founder of Carthage was not a man but a woman, Dido (DEE-doh). Dido was queen of Tyre as well as Carthage, a reflection of her people's Phoenician origins. She fell deeply in love with Aeneas. When the gods commanded him to sail onward, he left her behind, whereupon she committed suicide.

After another series of adventures, Aeneas arrived in Latium (la-TEE-uhm). Latium was the ancient name for a region in western Italy, southeast of Rome. Historically, it was inhabited by a group of people called the Latins, or Latini (la-TEE-nee). It appears that the Latins, who were primarily cattle-farmers, came down the Italian peninsula along with other Indo-European tribes some time before 1000 B.C. They passed by the swamps of the Italian countryside until they came to an area of seven rolling hills south of the Tiber River (TIE-buhr). There they began building simple clay huts covered in thatch. Thus began one of the most glorious cities on earth.

The saga of Aeneas went on to tell of an alliance between Latium and another group of people known to have inhabited the region in early centuries: the Etruscans (eh-TRUHS-kuhns). This combined force went up against Aeneas, who had formed an alliance of his own with a group of Greek colonists living on the seven hills of Rome. In fact the Greek colonies were well south of Rome. This part of the legend served to identify the Romans with the Greeks, as the people of Rome would continue to do throughout their history.

Having defeated Turnus, king of Latium, Aeneas married the Latin princess Lavinia and founded a city called Lavinium in her honor. Generations later, the legends recount, another Latin princess named Rhea Silvia (REE-uh) gave birth to twin sons fathered by the war-god Mars. As punishment for violating her pledge of *chastity,* she was forced to abandon the twins, Romulus (RAHM-yoo-luhs) and Remus (REE-muhs), on the banks of the flooding Tiber.

But a she-wolf found them there, and she nursed them until a shepherd found the boys and raised them. In time, Romulus and Remus built a city on the seven hills. Eventually the two brothers clashed. Romulus survived and went on to give the city its name. The legend of Romulus emerged long after Rome did and was used to explain the city's name—along with its symbol, that of a wolf. The wolf symbol would prove a fitting emblem for what became the strongest, fiercest nation in the region. In time the Romans would triumph over the dominant power in Italy, the Etruscans.

The Etruscans

The origins of the Etruscans are a mystery [see sidebar, "The Shadowy Origins of the Etruscans"], though it appears likely they settled on the northwest portion of the Italian peninsula some time between 1200 and 1100 B.C. Part of this region is today called Tuscany (TUHS-kuh-nee), its name a reference to its Etruscan past and its ancient name of Etruria (eh-TROO-ree-uh). There were already people living there, a group known as the Villanovans (vil-uh-NOH-vuhns), who eventually emerged as an Iron Age culture before being absorbed in the Etruscan population.

From an early time, the Etruscans developed links with Greece, from whom they adopted the alphabet that would become Rome's as well. They also adopted gods closely related to those of the Greeks, gods the Romans themselves would adopt. It should be noted, however, that the earliest Romans did not worship *anthropomorphic* (an-throh-poh-MOHR-fik) deities—that is, gods who looked like human beings. Like the Jews, they did not believe the gods could be depicted, but eventually they accepted the Greeks' image of their deities. The distinctions between Greek and Roman mythology would blur so much that the Romans' gods became more or less exact equivalents of the Greeks'.

The Etruscans also took on Hellenic forms of city organization, electing *magistrates* (MAH-jis-trayhtz) to run their cities from about 550 B.C. onward. There were plenty of distinctly Etruscan aspects to their culture as well, however, and

Tomb of the Reliefs.
Corbis-Bettmann. Reproduced by permission.

these too were passed on to the Romans. One of the Roman symbols of authority came from the Etruscans, the *fasces* (fa-SHEEZ), a bundle of sticks with an axe head protruding. Later the fasces would become an emblem of absolute authority displayed by Roman magistrates.

Engineering and architecture were another important Etruscan legacy. Given the local problems with swamps, which bred mosquitoes and with them disease, removal of water was a serious issue in central Italy. The soil of southern Etruria made the digging of tunnels easy. The Etruscans developed an elaborate network of channels for removing excess water. Among their developments was the Cloaca Maxima (kloh-AY-kuh MAK-sih-muh), which drained the site that became the Forum at the center of Rome. The Etruscans also developed an architectural style that influenced the building of temples in Rome for years to come. In their artwork, particularly their vases, they revealed a degree of refinement far beyond that of their crude neighbors in Rome.

Legendary kings of Rome

The Etruscans reached their high point in the 500s B.C. Meanwhile, Rome itself was growing, with a population composed of native Latins, Etruscans, and Sabines (SAY-bynz). The latter were another group of people in central Italy, about whom the Romans later developed a legend.

Supposedly in the years after Romulus, Rome had far more men than women. Many of the men were cutthroats and murderers. Few women wanted to live in such a place. In order to get themselves wives, the Romans tricked the neighboring Sabine men into leaving their towns. Then the Romans charged in, raping and kidnapping the Sabine women. Naturally, the Sabine men were furious when they learned what had happened. Only the Sabine women—many of whom, willing or not, now had Roman husbands—were able to stop the two sides from going to war. They proposed an agreement whereby Rome would be ruled by alternating Latin and Sabine kings.

This legend, which is certainly revealing in its portrayal of the early Romans as savage brutes, probably contains some truth. It is quite likely that the Latins shared leadership of Rome with the Sabines, though with the interwoven layers of myth and fact that make up the city's history prior to the founding of the republic, it is hard to tell. Beginning with Romulus, who supposedly reigned from 753 to 718 B.C., there were seven legendary kings of Rome. Romulus was followed by a Sabine, then a Latin, then the Sabine ruler Ancus Marcius (ANG-kuhs MAHR-shuhs), who allegedly reigned from 639 to 616 B.C.

The latter date saw the rise of Tarquinius Priscus (tahr-KWIN-ee-uhs PRIS-kuhs), whose reign supposedly lasted from 616 to 578 B.C. He allegedly waged war against a combined force of Sabines, Etruscans, and Latins, which would indicate that the people of Rome were beginning to see themselves as an entity distinct from their neighbors.

The other three legendary kings after Tarquinius Priscus were all Etruscan. The last of these was Tarquinius Superbus (soo-PUHR-buhs), son of the earlier Tarquinius, who reputedly took the throne in 534 B.C. Legend holds that he was a proud, cruel king with an unruly son, Tarquinius Sextus. The latter is said to have raped Lucretia (loo-KREE-shuh), the beautiful and virtuous wife of a Roman. Lucretia was so overcome

The Shadowy Origins of the Etruscans

Among the most interesting aspects of the Etruscans are their mysterious origins. Language, the most reliable method for tracing the migrations of peoples in prehistoric times, offers no clue. The linguistic evidence makes it clear that the Etruscans were *not* part of the Indo-European migration.

Herodotus wrote that the Etruscans came from Lydia. This seems to be correct, though it does not solve the riddle of their background because they do not appear to have been related to the Lydians either.

The idea of an Etruscan migration from Asia Minor, however, does offer two interesting points to ponder. First, such a migration seems to fit with the Aeneas legend and may have been its source. It is more likely, though, that such a migration would have taken place across land, rather than by sea. Second, the probable date of the Etruscans' move from Asia Minor to the Italian peninsula—some time between 1200 and 1100 B.C.—fits well with a pattern of upheaval at about the same time. The Dorians overwhelmed the Mycenaeans after 1200 B.C., an invasion that resulted from movements of population in the north of Greece. Of even greater significance was the appearance, in about 1200 B.C., of the mysterious "Sea Peoples" who destroyed the Hittites, ransacked the port of Ugarit, and menaced Egypt. Could the migrations of the Sea Peoples have ultimately led to those of the Dorians and the Etruscans?

by shame that she killed herself. This act led to a revolt that overthrew Tarquinius.

As always with early Rome, it is difficult to sort out legend from fact, though it is certain that the Etruscans began a slow, steady decline. Two years after the removal of Tarquinius (the date is not entirely certain, though traditionally it has been identified as 507 B.C.), the triumphant Romans founded the Roman Republic, which was to last for more than 400 years.

The early Republic (507–264 B.C.)

It is interesting to note that the date of Tarquinius's expulsion in 509 B.C. very nearly coincides with that of Hippias's overthrow in Athens. In place of tyranny, the Athenians created a democracy, whereas the Romans instituted a republican form of government. Together, these two systems formed a model for free peoples, or for people longing to be free, up to the present day. In modern times it is rather difficult to tell the difference between the two systems.

Both democracy and republicanism involved elected leaders rather than hereditary kings. At its beginnings, most power was in the hands of the wealthiest Roman landowners, known as *patricians* (puh-TRISH-uhnz). Citizenship in Rome, however, was not as exclusive as in Sparta or even Athens, a fact that no doubt helped lead to Rome's expansion.

Each year, the citizens elected two patricians as *consul* (KAHN-suhl), an office with responsibilities similar to that of the Athenian archon. But whereas the archons started out with a great deal of power that gradually declined with the establishment of democracy, the Romans from the beginning instituted a system of *checks and balances* to prevent consuls from gaining too much power. Not only did the consuls have to be elected every year, but one consul could overrule another by means of a *veto* (VEE-toh; Latin for "I forbid").

Another part of the checks and balances were the various elected assemblies, the most important of which was the senate. Obviously, the Roman senate is the model for the U.S. Senate. Similarly, the government of the United States is built around a system of checks and balances not unlike those in Rome. For a long time, however, there was nothing to check the power of the 300-odd patricians who made up the senate. The patricians controlled public funds—thus giving it *de facto* [see sidebar, "Latin Expressions and Abbrieviations from Everyday Life"] authority over the consuls—and reserved the right to elect a *dictator* or absolute ruler in times of crisis. This system gave no representation to another group in Roman society: the *plebeians* (pleh-BEE-uhnz).

In modern English, the word "plebeian" usually refers to someone who is unsophisticated. The plebeians of Rome, however, were the vast majority of people, a group that included the *middle class* as well as the poor and *working class*. The plebeians became outraged that they were treated as second-class citizens. The patricians, fearing an uprising, allowed the creation of several important institutions.

There already existed a plebeian assembly—in fact, two of them. One was a tribal assembly and the other a body representing the military. Together they supposedly gave all the citizens of Rome a voice in the government. Only in 494 B.C., however, did the collective plebeian assembly gain real power through the creation of a new office. This was the position of tribune, who exercised veto power over the senate's decisions and thus saw to it that the plebeians were not overruled by the patricians.

An important theme that emerged in the early history of Rome was the *rule of law*. Rule of law meant a "government of laws and not of men." Again, Americans can thank the plebeians, whose outrage at their unjust treatment by the Roman legal system led to the establishment of the "Twelve Tables" in 451 B.C. Up to that time, there was no written law. Judges made decisions based on the laws of the senate, as well as *legal precedent* or the previous rulings of judges. Since the plebeians were not allowed to know about the proceedings of the senate, this meant that they could be charged and punished for violations of laws that they did not even know existed. The Twelve Tables provided a clearly defined legal code, which gave citizens protection against the whims of judges.

A pattern of warfare (400s B.C.)

As Rome's government developed, so did its pride and strength, though it was certainly still quite vulnerable to attack. Meanwhile, the influence of the Etruscans faded. They had taken parts of southern Italy, but the Carthaginians (kahr-thuh-JIN-ee-uhnz) put an end to Etruscan dreams of empire in a battle at Cumae (KYOO-mee) in 474 B.C. The Etruscans began to withdraw to Etruria. Etruscan power began to ebb even further.

Eventually the decline of its neighbor would benefit Rome. During the 300s and 200s B.C., Rome would absorb most of the Etruscan cities, but the immediate effect of the Etruscan decline on Rome was negative. No longer did it find itself between the wealthy Etruscan civilization to the north and the equally wealthy Greek civilization in Magna Graecia and Sicily to the south. As Etruria went into an economic downturn, the decline affected Rome as well.

To compensate for these problems, Rome, in what would become a characteristic response, turned to conquest. Actually, at this point it was as much a matter of survival as anything else, with a variety of Latin tribes threatening the city from all around. In 496 B.C., Rome fought a battle with several of its neighbors and won, in large part thanks to the Romans' adoption of Greek military tactics such as the use of the hoplite and the phalanx.

Rome also set a pattern for its future international relations by establishing a treaty with the Latins, which laid out mutual obligations for the preservation of peace. But in another move that established Roman practice for centuries to come, Rome proved quite willing to violate the treaty when it suited it to do so.

Thus in 396 B.C., after a battle of some ten years, Rome broke its promise not to annex new territory when it conquered the Etruscan city of Veii (VEE-yigh). The conquest of Veii added greatly to Roman wealth and helped Rome past its economic troubles. However, just as it was establishing its power on the Italian peninsula, Rome experienced an invasion by a new and terrifying force from the north.

Celtic invasion (390 B.C.)

The invaders were the Celts (KELTZ), referred to by the Romans as Gauls (GAWLZ). These people had been living north of what became Greece and Rome since the end of the last ice age. Archaeologists know little about these earliest Europeans. Some of them settled in the British Isles. There they built a variety of stone monuments and other structures, the most notable of which is Stonehenge.

The Celts came with the Indo-European invasion and occupied the heart of Europe, from what is now Hungary to modern-day France. In Roman times this region was known as Gaul. From Gaul, groups of Celts spread throughout the continent after about 1000 B.C. Some went to the islands of Britain and Ireland, where their language survives to the present day. Others spread in all directions. In about 500 B.C., one group moved southward, over the high mountains called the Alps, and into Italy. About a century later, in 390 B.C., they arrived in Rome.

It was the first time Rome had come in contact with the tribal peoples beyond its borders. It would certainly not be the last such contact. In its latter days, Rome would be threatened by a variety of outsiders who would take part in its downfall. The Romans lumped all these groups together as barbarians. Actually, the Celts were fairly civilized. They had a number of settlements throughout central Europe. They developed a relatively organized society divided into four groups: nobles, warriors, wise men, and farmers.

But the Celts in Italy were obviously on the move. The "warrior" class was most prominent among them. There is a legend that the Celts who marched into Rome in 390 B.C. came upon a group of aged senators sitting in a row on the Forum, or city center. It was also the location of the government center, or Capitol. Allegedly one of the Celts reached out in curiosity to touch the beard of a senator, who reacted with anger. The Celt then slew the senator, while his comrades dealt with the others.

It is also said that the Celts stormed the Capitol for seven months, and that they demanded 1,000 pounds in gold before they left Rome. They probably did not burn the city down completely, as legend holds; but it is clear that they *sacked* Rome. Whatever the truth, it appears that the Celtic invasion was a turning point for the Romans: after that, they determined that they would develop their power so that nothing of the kind ever happened again.

Expansion of the Republic (390–264 B.C.)

As the invaders departed, the patricians attempted to seize power again. What happened instead was an expansion of power among the plebeians, who in 367 B.C. gained the right to run for consul. Ironically, this would prove to be a victory for the patricians' long-term interests. The extension of greater rights among the plebeians helped give rise to a group of wealthy plebeians who increasingly saw themselves as aristocrats rather than as men of the people.

In 338 B.C., the same year Philip II of Macedon won control of Greece, Rome scored a decisive victory over its Latin neighbors. These were the same neighbors with whom Rome had earlier signed a treaty of mutual obligation. Now the Romans turned their eyes to southern Italy, a region called Campania (kahm-PAHN-yah), which until quite recently had been firmly in the hands of the Greeks. A number of factors had changed that, not the least of which was the turmoil following the Macedonian conquest of Greece itself. Furthermore, the dominant Greek leader in southern Italy, the tyrant Dionysius the Elder (c. 430–367 B.C.) of Syracuse, was dead. But another group had also taken note of the Greeks' declining power in the south.

The Samnites were ethnically related to the Romans and Latins. They had helped themselves to the cities of Cumae and Capua (KAP-yoo-uh) in Campania before the Romans went to war with them in 343 B.C. It was no easy victory for Rome, however, because the Samnites fought with what in modern times would be called *guerilla warfare*. (Guerilla is pronounced like "gorilla.") Using hit-and-run maneuvers, they fought the Romans off during three wars between 343 and 290 B.C.

Philip II of Macedon won control of Greece in 338 B.C. *Library of Congress.*

It was a somewhat desperate time for Rome, which saw a number of humiliations at the hands of the Samnites. In order to strengthen the republic, it extended further political power to the poorer plebeians. By 287 B.C., plebeians held the true power in the legislature. Likewise, for its final victory in the war against the Samnites, Rome had to win the allegiance of the peoples in surrounding areas.

Most of these neighboring peoples were Greek. Now that the Romans dominated much of southern and central Italy, they recognized that the Greeks farther south were among their two most formidable opponents for control of the entire country. In 280 B.C., the Greek colonists in the city of Tarentum (tah-REHN-tuhm) in southeastern Italy called upon King Pyrrhus of Epirus (319–272 B.C.) to aid them in battle

Democracies and Republics

Democracy started in Athens, and the republican form of government emerged in Rome at about the same time. Usually the terms "democracy" and "republic" are used almost interchangeably, but they are not the same.

The United States has a republican form of government with a democratic electoral system. Every U.S. citizen has a vote and, by voting, is able to take part in choosing the people who will (in theory, at least) represent their interests in the federal government. Technically, however, in presidential elections, the real voting power rests in the hands of the electoral college, a very small group of representatives who cast votes for a presidential candidate.

Usually the vote of the electoral college is a reflection of the popular vote, but there can be conflict—and when there is, the electoral vote decides the contest. In the 1888 presidential elections, Benjamin Harrison defeated Grover Cleveland, even though Cleveland had more popular votes. The outcome of the Harrison-Cleveland election has troubled many people. If the electoral college can choose a president against the will of the people, then America is not really a democracy, is it?

In fact, America is *not* a democracy in the truest sense of the word. In other words, the government does not simply act on the will of the people at all times. The people make their will known by voting for representatives, not by voting on specific issues.

One of the principle contributions to freedom made by the Romans was their system of checks and balances, a setup in which no one person or area of government could gain too much power. They also introduced the idea of the rule of law, rather than rule by the people.

against Rome. Pyrrhus did defeat the Romans in several battles. He did so at such a terrible cost of his men's lives that his name has remained to this day as a watchword for success that comes at too great a price: a "Pyrrhic victory."

By 275 B.C., the Romans had defeated Pyrrhus. The Romans had thus all but eliminated the Greek challenge to their dominance of southern Italy. In any case, Greece was on a downward spiral, having only recently endured a Celtic invasion of its own. Now the Romans had to face their other principal foe, fighting a series of wars that would stretch across

Rome did not live up to its ideals: jockeying for power, first by Sulla and later by many others, paved the way for the dictatorship of Julius Caesar and the imperial system established by Caesar's nephew Octavian. And certainly the United States has often failed to live up to the ideal expressed by a number of U.S. Supreme Court justices, who have described the American system as "a government of laws and not of men." What that means is that in some instances, no matter what people *feel,* the government is supposed to do what is right.

The Civil Rights Movement of the 1960s is an interesting example of how democratic and republican modes of government work together in the American system. For a century following the passage of laws forbidding racial discrimination, the federal government had failed or refused to enforce those laws in the southern United States. It took a popular movement, led by the Rev. Martin Luther King (1929–1968) and others, to force the government to uphold the laws it already had on the books, and to create new laws ensuring an end to segregation.

The Civil Rights Movement was certainly the "voice of the people"—but only a small minority of the people, made up mostly of African Americans and some whites. The white majority in the South, on the other hand, actively opposed racial integration; and the white majority of the nation as a whole was not much more sympathetic. In other words, if America really were a democracy—that is, a nation ruled by the majority—it would have taken much longer than it did to extend full civil rights to all African Americans. Fortunately for America, however, the rule of law took over.

more than a century. These wars would end with Roman dominance over most of the Mediterranean.

The Punic Wars and other conquests (264–146 B.C.)

Carthage, on the northeastern coast of what is now Tunisia in North Africa, had been established by the Phoenicians some time after 800 B.C.. Hence the name *Punic,* an adjectival form of the Romans' word for "Phoenician." Though the

Ruins of Carthage. Remains of Punic Gate. *Sandro Vannini/Corbis. Reproduced by permission.*

Carthaginians maintained aspects of Phoenician culture, including worship of the Phoenician god Baal, they had long before begun developing on their own. Baal became Moloch (MAHL-ahk), for instance, and the Carthaginians' city became at least as great as the Phoenicia's own Tyre.

Like Tyre, Carthage had natural defenses. It was almost an island jutting out into the Mediterranean, with two large inlets on either side. Rocky cliffs protected it on the west, and the city itself had three layers of walls around it. Particularly impressive was its harbor, into which the Carthaginians built a set of structures to aid in its defense. These structures made it impossible for invaders to see how many warships the Carthaginians had. The center of the protected harbor featured a command post where naval officers could oversee the city's defense.

About a million people lived in Carthage at its height, making it an almost unbelievably huge city by ancient standards. It expanded, adding colonies throughout North Africa, the Iberian Peninsula (where Spain and Portugal are now located), and the island of Sicily off the southern coast of Italy. During the 400s B.C., the Carthaginians had emerged as the dominant sea power in the western Mediterranean. As Rome cleared Italy of all opposition, it became apparent that the two nations were headed for a struggle over control of the region.

The First and Second Punic Wars (264–202 B.C.)

The struggle finally came in the form of the First Punic War (264–241 B.C.) The first war was fought primarily over Sicily, where Carthage had established a stronghold. The Romans recognized the Carthaginians' advantage over them as a naval force, but they had the good fortune to capture a Carthaginian warship. With the help of Greek naval architects, they made 100 such ships in just 60 days.

This was the first example of a technique that would help Rome win many a war in the future: the borrowing (or, more properly, stealing) of technology from enemies. The Romans made an ingenious adaptation of the Carthaginians' ships, however, by installing movable bridges on them. These bridges made it easy, when two opposing ships were in close combat, for soldiers to board the enemy's ship. In this way, the Romans could put their best foot forward militarily, since their greatest strength was their army rather than their navy.

With the end of the war in 241 B.C., Rome controlled not only Sicily, but two large islands to the west, Corsica (KOHR-si-kuh) and Sardinia (sahr-DIN-ee-uh). It was the beginning of Rome's overseas empire, which it further extended—perhaps without fully meaning to—in 229 B.C. After tolerating years of attacks on its shipping by pirates from Illyria, Rome established a military base there. The Romans would use this base as a launch pad for the conquest of Greece over the coming years. Meanwhile, Carthage in 218 B.C. launched an attack against the Romans that began the Second Punic War (218–201 B.C.)

Hannibal (247–183 B.C.), the young general responsible for the attack, was one of history's most brilliant military minds. Sailing across the Mediterranean, he first struck the Romans in a Spanish city that had allied itself with Rome.

Then, taking a vast army (estimates range from 20,000 to 100,000 men), he marched north. Hannibal had in mind an unusual strategy. Instead of crossing the sea to attack from the west, where the Romans could easily have defeated him, he would march his army northward and eastward. With him he had a weapon the Romans had not faced before: war elephants. These sturdy, powerful animals, frightening in appearance, were like living tanks. Though many of them died crossing the Alps, they were still a powerful force in the battles to come.

The crossing of the Alps itself was a heroic, legendary feat. For a long time after he marched into Italy, Hannibal faced Roman generals who were far from his equal. Without any supplies aside from what they could obtain from the countryside, the Carthaginians managed to wage war in a hostile land for nearly fifteen years. They captured several Italian cities and dealt Rome one of the most severe blows in its history when they defeated an army at Cannae (CAN-ee) in southeastern Italy in 216 B.C. Hannibal's armies very nearly took Rome itself in 211 B.C., but the Romans launched a brilliant attack of their own, led by Scipio (SIP-ee-oh; 236-c. 183 B.C.)

Scipio applied the strategy of attacking Hannibal not where he was—in Italy—but where he was not. The first place was Spain, where in 206 B.C., Scipio defeated a Carthaginian force. Then he began launching attacks close to Carthage itself, forcing Hannibal to return to his home in 203 B.C. In the following year, Scipio scored a major victory over Hannibal in the town of Zama, southwest of Carthage.

Growth by conquest (202–146 B.C.)

For centuries, the Romans' behavior had resembled that of an old farmers' saying: "I don't want much; just the land that borders on mine." Fearing conquest by others, they had conquered neighboring lands until they spread beyond Italy. With their two victories over Carthage, their lands grew considerably, including the Spanish coastal area conquered by Scipio.

Hannibal had meanwhile formed an alliance with Philip V of Macedon, who had become understandably worried about the Roman presence in Illyria. This alliance gave the Romans an excuse to step up the ongoing conflict with Philip, which dated back to the early years of the Second Punic War.

In 197 B.C., Rome defeated Philip at Cynocephalae (SIy-no-SEF-a-lay), setting the stage for final victory over the last great power in Greece.

After Alexander the Great died, his empire had been divided into three parts: the Macedonian and Greek homeland, the Seleucid Empire of western Asia, and the lands under the control of the Ptolemies in Egypt. The rulers of each had squabbled between themselves, and thus Philip had made common cause with the Seleucid king Antiochus III (an-tee-AHK-uhs; 242-187 B.C.) against the Ptolemies. Now, with the removal of Philip from the picture, Antiochus made several important moves. First, he married his daughter to Ptolemy V of Egypt. Named Cleopatra, she was the first in a line of queens with that name, the seventh of which would play an important role in Roman history. He also joined forces with Hannibal, who had fled to Syria. Finally, he invaded Thrace, an act that the Romans correctly interpreted as part of a larger plan to gain ground in Europe.

By 190 B.C. the Romans, again under Scipio, defeated Antiochus in battle at Magnesia (mag-NEEZ-ee-uh) in Asia Minor. This victory gave the Romans a new province: the former home of the Lydians on the western third of Asia Minor. It also brought about the end of Hannibal, who committed suicide rather than be captured by the Roman armies.

Rome was not finished with Carthage, however. Even as Roman power grew, Carthage remained a rallying cry, an object of hatred to inspire all Romans. The politician Cato (KAY-toh; 234–149 B.C.), an outstanding writer and orator, called for a return to the simpler values of the early republic. In the case of Carthage, though, he demanded that Rome show no mercy. He ended every speech with the words "Carthage must be destroyed." In 149 B.C., the year he died, the senate fulfilled his wishes by declaring war on Carthage.

The causes were trumped up, but the devastation of Carthage itself was terrifyingly real. After a prolonged siege, the Romans burned the city in 146 B.C., reducing it to a heap of rubble and ashes. These they plowed into the ground, along with salt to ensure that nothing would grow there. A century later, Julius Caesar would establish a new colony on the site of the old city, but the Carthaginians themselves were gone: the Romans had sold them into slavery. To this day, the expression

The catapult (an invention of Archimedes), gave the Roman army the advantage over enemies. *The Granger Collection, New York. Reproduced by permission.*

"a Carthaginian peace" refers to a cruel or unfair treaty imposed on a conquered people.

The power and the glory

With their many wars, it is not surprising that the Romans emerged as the most militaristic people of the ancient world, other than the Assyrians and the Spartans. It became common, in fact typical, for a military leader to hold political power and vice versa (a Latin expression; see sidebar, "Latin Expressions and Abbreviations from Everyday Life"). In the years leading up to and following the establishment of the empire in 14 B.C., both the government and the military attracted around themselves an aura of power and glory that filled the Romans with pride and their foes with awe and terror.

The armies themselves became one of the most impressive aspects of Roman life. Soldiers wore armor not unlike that of the Grecian hoplite, though their uniforms took on distinctly Roman characteristics. Likewise they improved on the Greeks' phalanx, making use of rectangular shields, which they would place side by side and sometimes end to end, thus forming an impenetrable wall. Armies were formed into legions, which consisted of anywhere from 3,000 to 6,000 men. Before long, the Roman legions were the most well-trained and well-equipped fighting force in the world. Using huge *catapults* (an invention of Archimedes) and other forms of "borrowed" military technology, the legions could conquer virtually any city.

When they marched into Rome following a new conquest, the legions received the Roman equivalent of a ticker-tape parade: a triumphal procession. Down the wide streets of Rome, lined with cheering crowds, would come a procession led by standard-bearers. The standards were long staffs. Atop the standards were symbols around which soldiers rallied in battle. Among these symbols were the first flags, though unlike modern flags they hung downward rather than flying in the breeze. Also prominently displayed were other emblems that stood for Rome: the wolf, the fasces, the war eagle, and the initials SPQR (*senatus populus que Romanus,* "the senate and people of Rome.")

Next came a giant statue of Jupiter carried on a *litter.* Then came the spoils of war—treasure removed from the conquered lands. There were pipers and horn players to provide music for the procession and white bulls to be sacrificed on the altar to the gods. Among the procession were thousands of prisoners, including the rulers of the defeated people, who were subjected to special humiliation. This was the fate, for instance, of Perseus, the last Macedonian king. At the center of the parade was the triumphant general himself, hero of the procession, whose place of honor was enhanced by the presence of senators and magistrates on foot behind him. Last were the legions marching in ranks, thousands upon thousands of soldiers.

It was a stirring sight, and it emphasized the power of the Roman Republic. Running through the whole political and military system, from the war eagles on the standards to the majestic white *togas* of the senators, hemmed with a bright red stripe, was a brilliant sense of style. The Romans seemed to understand that it was just as important to appear powerful as it was to be powerful, an idea that would heavily influence nations right up to the time of Nazi Germany.

Downfall of the Republic (146–60 B.C.)

The Romans had always been hard, proud people, but in the Rome that emerged from the wars with Carthage and other nations, life took on a coarseness it had lacked before. Certainly other empires—and Rome was an empire, even if it would not use the word until A.D. 14—had been at least as cruel as Rome. Other empires, however, had not started with the high ideals of the early Romans. As a consequence their morals did not suffer as Rome's did.

One of the principal causes for alarm was the growing gap between rich and poor. During the wars, Rome maintained the largest *standing army,* in proportion to the male population,

Roman Numerals

The Romans had their own number system, quite unlike the so-called Arabic numerals used throughout the world today. The symbols included:

I=1

V=5

X=10

L=50

C=100

D=500

M=1,000

All other numbers were created by combinations of these; for example, the numbers from 1 to 10 were: I, II, III, IV, V, VI, VII, VIII, IX, and X.

Roman numerals survive for a few uses, among them the titles of rulers: thus Ptolemy XIV was the fourteenth Ptolemy. They are also used to date the year of a movie's release. What follows are a few highly recommended movies about Rome, along with their release dates:

Ben-Hur: MDCCCCLIX (1959)

The Fall of the Roman Empire: MDCCCCLXIV (1964)

Quo Vadis: MDCCCCLI (1951)

The Robe: MDCCCCLIII (1953)

Spartacus: MDCCCCLX (1960)

of any nation in history. The *conscripts* (KAHN-scriptz), or draftees, typically came from the poorer classes. These young men were no longer available to tend farms in the countryside. This, along with the destruction of farms by Hannibal's troops, helped lead to the end of *peasant* landholders as a class.

In plenty of poor areas, young men who managed to survive the wars simply chose to seek their fortunes in the glamorous city of Rome rather than to scratch out a living in the country. Once they got to the city, they found it filled with other young men just like them. Without enough jobs to go around, the poor began increasingly to depend on the government for support. This pattern would become much worse in the later empire, when the state tried to keep its poor happy by offering them "bread and circuses"—that is, a combination of cheap entertainment and what modern people would call welfare.

All of this had tragic results. The decline of peasant land holdings led to a growth in power among the aristocracy, who were able to build huge estates with the fields the peasants gave up cheaply. This new aristocracy consisted primarily of "plebeian patricians"—that is, people who had money, even if they lacked a distinguished background. They, of course, would not work these giant estates: for that they needed slaves.

The economies of both Greece and Rome depended on slavery. Rome was so much bigger, though, that slavery there assumed a scale unequaled in history, including in the United States prior to the Civil War (1861–1865). With every military conquest, Rome added to its "wealth" by enslaving the conquered peoples. Deep beneath the surface splendor of Roman society, the bitterness of the slaves was growing. In time they would have their moment, but first other dissatisfied groups would make their voices heard in Roman affairs.

Aside from the peasant landholders who were losing their land, the many people living on the Italian peninsula, though subject to the laws of Rome, did not enjoy any of the benefits that went with Roman citizenship. These issues came to the forefront under a pair of plebeian tribunes, two brothers named Tiberius (tie-BEER-ee-uhs; 163–133 B.C.) and Gaius Gracchus (GIE-yuhs GRAK-uhs; 153–121 B.C.) Both offered reforms: Tiberius called for limits on the amount of land one citizen could own. Gaius proposed extension of Roman citizenship to Latins.

Not only did the Gracchus brothers fail in their efforts at reform, they paid with their lives. A mob killed Tiberius, along with some 300 of his followers. Twelve years later, after Gaius saw more than 3,000 of his own *faction* murdered, he committed suicide. These two deaths set an ominous pattern for the use of violence to settle political disputes.

External conflicts (120s–101 B.C.)

While the land problems went largely unsolved, the near-constant wars continued. In 121 B.C., Rome added southern Gaul to its holdings. In 112 B.C., it marched against the kingdom of Numidia (noo-MID-ee-uh), located in what is now Algeria. Numidia, once an ally of Carthage, had allied itself with Rome, which had an interest in Numidia's political stability. Therefore, when the Numidian prince Jugurtha (joo-GUHR-thuh; c. 160–104 B.C.) murdered his brothers and began making civil war with his cousins, Roman troops marched in.

Jugurtha was brought to Rome, where he was able to bribe his way out of trouble. "In Rome," he said, "all things are for sale." In the end, Roman troops returned to Numidia, where with the help of Mauretania (maw-reh-TAY-nee-uh), a kingdom that included parts of what is now Morocco and Algeria, they removed Jugurtha from power. Numidia would become a Roman province in 44 B.C., as would Mauretania in 25 B.C.

Marius (MAHR-ee-uhs; c. 157–86 B.C.), who led the Numidian campaign, also led a series of attacks on two barbarian tribes, the Teutons (TOO-t'nz) and the Cimbri (KIM-bree). Both tribes came from the north of Europe. Both groups looked quite different from the dark-haired and olive-skinned Italians. Eyewitness observers noted their blond hair—so blond, in fact, that the children's hair appeared white.

The Cimbri would fade from memory after Marius's victory over them in 101 B.C. Not so with the Teutons, whom he had defeated in the previous year. They, along with the Cimbri, were part of a much larger group from what is now called Scandinavia. The Romans called them by a Latin word that means "related": *Germanus*. Thanks to Marius, they retreated, leaving in their wake massive devastation. But they would be back.

Social war and civil war (101–79 B.C.)

On the strength of his war record, Marius soon became an important figure in Roman politics, and he was able to push through a series of military reforms. For a long time, property ownership had been a requirement for service in the army. With the widespread loss of property among the peasantry, the ranks of men eligible for service had diminished greatly. As consul in 107 B.C., Marius removed the property requirement, which led to a massive increase in enlistment. The Roman army, already vast, grew yet more, which created an ominous trend. Soldiers became more loyal to their commanders than they were to the republic. Up to that time, the army had been under the full command of the civilian government, as the

U.S. Army is today. Following Marius's reforms, the army gradually began to emerge as a separate power.

In the 90s B.C., a senator named Drusus (DROO-suhs), whose family had been allied with the Gracchus brothers, again proposed reforms extending citizenship to non-Roman Italians. His assassination in 91 B.C. touched off the Social War (91–88 B.C.) between Italians and Romans. This war ended with the extension of Roman citizenship to all Italians. As for the land problem, the government began offering war veterans estates outside of Italy itself, which would lead to the increasing *Romanization* of the *provinces*.

Rome was headed for an even more serious internal war, a clash between the *populares* (pahp-yoo-LARE-ehz), of which Marius was the leader, and the *nobiles* (noh-BEE-lehz), led by Sulla (SUHL-uh; 137–78 B.C.) As their names imply, these two groups were a later version of the plebeians and patricians, only the populares had considerably more power and wealth than their plebeian ancestors. A sign of how times had changed was the fact that Sulla had served on Marius's staff in the wars with Jugurtha and the Germans; now he was anxious to ensure that his class retained its power. In 88 B.C., he obtained a position that he intended to use for his own purposes: leader of the campaign against Mithradates the Great (mith-ruh-DAY-teez; r. 120-63 B.C.) of Pontus (PAHN-tuhs).

Pontus, a country in eastern Asia Minor, had existed for several centuries. In the preceding two decades Mithradates had been adding to its territories considerably. Once he began threatening Greece, Rome declared war. But just as Sulla was on his way to Greece with his troops, he received word that Marius had transferred command of the force to himself. Furious, Sulla turned his army around and marched on Rome. It was the first time a Roman military commander had used his troops against Rome itself, and it would not be the last.

Lucius Cornelius Sulla.
Archive Photos. Reproduced by permission.

The term "civil war," often applied to the whole period from the murder of Tiberius Gracchus in 133 B.C. and the Battle of Action in 27 B.C., is sometimes applied specifically to the events in Rome in 88 B.C. This was not really a war, since the majority of the violence came from Sulla's executions of Marius's allies. Marius himself fled to Africa. Sulla, having destroyed his other enemies in Rome, went on to Greece to fight two bloody, bitter wars with Mithradates (88-85; 83-82 B.C.). During Sulla's absence, Marius had returned to Rome and killed a number of Sulla's friends before dying in 86 B.C.. Therefore Sulla could not take revenge on him when he returned in 82 B.C. Instead, he massacred thousands of Marius's supporters. In at least one case, the killing took place right before the eyes of a horrified senate.

Dictatorship had finally come to Rome, in Sulla's words, "for the reform of the *constitution.*" It had not been established according to the provisions in Roman law, but it had been established just the same, and given those provisions, it is surprising it did not come sooner. Also surprising is the fact that Sulla, after three years as absolute ruler—during which time he packed the senate with supporters—voluntarily stepped down in 79 B.C. A year later, he was dead.

The collapse of the Republic (79–60 B.C.)

In 77 B.C., Rome sent one of its leading generals, Pompey (PAHM-pee; 106–48 B.C.), to put down an uprising in Spain. Only a few years later, Pompey had to rush back to Rome in order to deal with a new force that threatened the very heart of Roman power, both for the *nobiles* and for the *populares:* a slave revolt.

Its leader was Spartacus (SPAHR-tuh-kuhs), a Thracian slave sent to a school in Capua for the training of *gladiators* (GLAD-ee-ay-tohrz). Gladiators were warriors who fought to their deaths in a ring, watched by cheering spectators. The spectators paid good money for this form of "entertainment," and they expected to see the death of at least one of the two combatants in a match. No wonder, then, that Spartacus and the other slaves at the gladiatorial (glad-ee-uh-TOHR-ee-uhl) school revolted in 73 B.C. Within a short time, they had an army of more than 120,000.

Slavery was the foundation of ancient Rome's great wealth. Rome was not about to allow the slave revolt, sometimes called the Gladiatorial War (73–71 B.C.), to proceed unchecked. Not only did Rome call back Pompey, but it sent another army under the control of Crassus (KRA-suhs; c. 115–53 B.C.), an ally of Sulla who had become incredibly wealthy by buying up property confiscated under the dictatorship. In the final battle, Spartacus himself died rather than be captured— a wise choice, since the Romans *crucified* some 6,000 slaves along the Appian Way (AP-ee-uhn), the main road from Capua to Rome.

Pompey went on to deal with a group of pirates threatening the eastern Mediterranean. As the power of Greece had ebbed and Roman control of the region had remained uncertain, the pirates had returned. In 67 B.C., Pompey broke their hold, thus making the area safe for shipping. The following year saw his destruction of the other principal challenge to Roman control over the Balkan Peninsula and Asia Minor: Mithradates. Mithradates had allied with his son-in-law, Tigranes of Armenia, against Rome. The defeat of both men gave Rome lands that stretched from the Black Sea to the Caspian Sea. Pompey's victory in the east was marred at home, however, by a revolt whose leader was Catiline (KAT-uh-leen; c. 108–62 B.C.) Catiline might have overthrown the government in 63 B.C., but the noted orator Cicero (SIS-uh-roh; 106–43 B.C.) helped foil his plan. Catiline was executed the following year.

To prevent the rise of another Catiline, Pompey proposed to form a new government. He had come out of the wars with Spartacus and Mithradates as one of the most powerful men in Rome, but he was wise enough to recognize that he could not rule on his own. Therefore he turned to Crassus, whose wealth, if nothing more, made him a formidable ally. These two formed an alliance with another soldier-statesman,

The Death of Spartacus. Drawing by H. Vogel.
Corbis-Bettmann. Reproduced by permission.

Latin Expressions and Abbreviations from Everyday Life

A.D. (anno Domini; AN-oh DAHM-in-ee): In the year of our Lord.

Ad hoc (AD HAHK): Concerned with a particular purpose.

Ante belleum (AN-tee BEL-um): Before the war; often used to refer to the period before the American Civil War (1861–1865).

Carpe diem (KAHR-pay DEE-ehm): Seize the day.

Caveat emptor (KA-vee-aht EHMP-tohr): Let the buyer beware.

De facto (di FAK-toh): From the fact; that is, in reality.

e.g. (exampli gratia; ex-EHM-play GRAH-shuh): For example.

E pluribus unum (EE PLOOR-i-buhs OO-nuhm): One out of many; found on the Great Seal of the United States and on many coins.

etc. (et cetera): And so forth.

i.e. (id est): That is.

In medias res (IN MEE-dee-uhs REHS): In the middle of things; used to describe the beginning of action in a drama.

Ipso facto (IP-soh FAK-toh): By the fact itself—similar to "obviously."

Novus ordo seclorum (NOH-vuhs OHR-doh say-KLOHR-uhm): A new cycle of the ages; motto on the reverse of the Great Seal of the United States.

Per: For.

Per annum (AN-num): Per year.

Per capita (KAP-ti-tuh): Per head or per person.

Per diem (DEE-uhm): Per day.

Per se (SAY): In and of itself.

Sic (SIK): Thus, used when quoting a person or document, to signify a mistake in the original.

Status quo (STA-tus KWOH): The existing state of affairs.

Sui generis (SWEE JIN-uh-rehs): Of its own kind; a thing unto itself.

Tempus fugit (TEHM-puhs FYOO-jit): Time flies.

Veni, vidi, vici (VAY-nee VEE-dee VEE-chee): I came, I saw, I conquered—phrase attributed to Julius Caesar.

Vice versa: With the order changed, or conversely.

---

a rising star named Julius Caesar (102–44 B.C.) As leader of the *populares,* Caesar would help to balance the patrician Crassus and garner more support for the proposed government of three, a *triumvirate* (try-UHM-vuhr-eht).

First Triumvirate (60–44 B.C.)

Once they found themselves in power, the members of the triumvirate used that power to their own advantage. Caesar went off to Gaul, where he campaigned for a decade and built a strong power base. Crassus went in the other direction, to Syria, which had become a Roman province following Pompey's victory over Mithradates. Eager to prove himself, he went to war against the Parthians in the east. In 53 B.C., Crassus lost his life in a humiliating defeat.

Now there were only two rulers, Caesar and Pompey. They had never been more than uneasy allies. When Pompey started building up his power in the senate, the *populares* called for his resignation. Pompey in turn demanded, in 49 B.C., that Caesar return to Rome immediately to stand trial for corruption. So Caesar began making his way back—with his army. The senate sent him a message that if he crossed the Rubicon River (ROO-bi-kahn), which formed the southern boundary of Gaul, he would be guilty of treason. Caesar chose to move ahead. (Today the expression "crossing the Rubicon" means passing a point of no return.)

Planning to build up his forces, Pompey went to Greece with a sizable army and most of the senate. Caesar was too quick for him. In a series of lighting maneuvers, he defeated legions in Spain, where Pompey had spent many years building up loyalties. Then Caesar marched on Greece, where he defeated Pompey's forces in 48 B.C. Pompey fled to Egypt, whose boy king Ptolemy XIII (TAHL-uh-mee; c. 59–44 B.C.) wanted nothing to do with any Romans. Ptolemy had Pompey assassinated and was prepared to oppose Caesar as well.

When Caesar arrived in Egypt in 48 B.C., his interest was primarily in Pompey's co-ruler, his intriguing sister—and wife—Cleopatra VII (69–30 B.C.; r. 51–30). She was the last of the Hellenistic rulers that had followed Alexander. In 46 B.C., she left her brother and husband Ptolemy XIV (she had married a younger brother) to join the new Alexander, Caesar, in Rome.

Caesar had meanwhile begun to establish his rule and soon became exceeding popular. Rather than conduct a reign of terror against Cicero and other supporters of Pompey, he left them alone and undertook a number of initiatives to improve the republic. But many feared that Caesar, who had declared himself dictator for life, was becoming too powerful. On March 15, 44 B.C., a group of conspirators led by his former friends Brutus and Cassius (KASH-uhs) stabbed him to death in the senate.

Second Triumvirate (44–31 B.C.)

In the upheaval that followed Caesar's murder, two new leaders stepped to the forefront. One was Mark Antony (c. 82–30 B.C.), who had fought by Caesar's side in number of military campaigns and served with him as co-consul. The other was Caesar's grand-nephew Octavian (ahk-TAY-vee-uhn; 63 B.C.-A.D. 14), whom Caesar had adopted as son and heir just a year before his assassination. When Mark Antony tried to seize power, the senate threw its weight behind Octavian, whom they judged (wrongly, as it turned out) to be a mild-mannered figure uninterested in power.

Eventually, Octavian and Mark Antony formed their own uneasy alliance, with Lepidus (LEH-pi-duhs; died c. 13 B.C.) in the balancing role that Crassus had held. This Second Triumvirate quickly dealt with Brutus, Cassius, and the other conspirators. Then they turned to killing personal foes, among them Cicero, whom Antony judged an enemy. With so much blood flowing, it was not long before they turned on each other. Octavian removed Lepidus from power in 36 B.C., setting the stage for a showdown with Antony.

Mark Antony had meanwhile taken up with Cleopatra, for whom he had left his wife—Octavian's sister. By 34 B.C., Antony had moved to Alexandria. When Octavian read before the senate what he claimed was Antony's will—in which Antony promised to leave Cleopatra all of Rome's eastern possessions—the senate removed Antony from power. Rome declared war on Antony and Cleopatra, whose forces it met in a naval battle at Actium (AK-tee-uhm) in 31 B.C. Actium was in Greece, not Egypt, an indication that the two lovers hoped to build a Mediterranean empire; instead, their forces were destroyed. They fled to Egypt, where they committed suicide.

The Age of Augustus (31 B.C.–A.D. 14)

The defeat on Antony and Cleopatra left sole authority in the hands of Octavian, and as it turned out, this event marked the end of the republic. Though Octavian insisted on claiming that he had restored republican rule—that he was the leading citizen among many, not a supreme leader—historians identify him as the first Roman emperor.

This became clear in 27 B.C., when the senate conferred on Octavian a number of formal titles, each of which had a very real meaning. They named him *Imperator,* which meant commander-in-chief of the armed forces but also meant "emperor." They gave him the title *Caesar,* thus turning the family name of the former dictator into a title, just as the ptolemies of Egypt had done. Finally, they bestowed on him a new personal name: *Augustus,* meaning "exalted" or "sacred."

In accordance with his new name, Augustus and the emperors who followed him would come to be treated as gods. Yet he was shrewd enough to assume absolute power very slowly, so that no one became alarmed. He maintained the trappings of the republic, including the fiction that he ruled only with the approval of the senate.

Augustus did not really have to fool the Romans, who were willing to give up a few freedoms in exchange for political stability. He proved a wise and fair ruler. He reformed the military, reducing its size and bringing it back under civilian control, and expanded the empire greatly. In A.D. 9, however, his troops suffered a devastating defeat at the hands of the Germans. From then on, Rome's northern border would be fixed by the Rhine River. After that point, the empire would continue to grow, but more slowly.

The Pax Romana

Despite all manner of troubles in the capital, the two centuries from Augustus to Marcus Aurelius would be a time of prosperity and peace in the Western world. It was an age identified by the term *Pax Romana,* or "Roman peace," a time when no military force on earth could equal the power of Rome. The "barbarians" were out there, of course—in particular the Germans, who had come to be known as Goths—but they did not dare break through the frontiers of the empire itself.

Thus Roman strength ensured the peace, and the grandeur of the Roman Empire spread throughout Europe, North Africa, and the Middle East. It was a time of massive building projects, including the construction of aqueducts that remain today as an impressive reminder of Roman achievements. Across the wide expanse of the empire, the Romans built temples, bridges, and triumphal arches, the latter to mark victories in battle, of which there were many. Roman artists improved greatly on the example provided to them by the Greeks and brought realism to a high point.

Science also flourished in the work of the astronomer Ptolemy (A.D. 100s) and the physician Galen (GAY-lehn; A.D. 129–c. 199) Neither man was a "Roman" in the strictest sense of the word: Ptolemy lived in Alexandria, and Galen lived in Asia Minor. But the name of Rome had long since come to refer to an entire world, not merely to a city.

Perhaps nothing says more about the stability of Rome in this era than its roads. Rome established a highway network so impressive that it can only be compared to the American interstate system of today, but in fact the Roman roads represent much more of an engineering triumph than the interstates. The Romans, after all, had no bulldozers or other machinery; just the labor of work gangs, mostly slaves.

During the years of the Pax Romana, it was possible to start out from Scotland and travel by Roman roads all the way to Rome itself; or if one wished, into Greece and even across to Asia Minor and thence all the way to southern Egypt. The roads were generally safe, protected from bandits—always a problem in ancient times—because outlaws feared the wrath of the empire.

Nor were these roads mere paths: most were 12 or more feet wide, built of stone, clay, and gravel three feet deep. Drainage ditches lined either side, and there were stone markers showing the distance to and from Rome—hence the famous saying, "All roads lead to Rome." It says a great deal about these roads, and about the dismal conditions that prevailed in Europe after the fall of the Roman Empire, that at the beginning of the Renaissance in c. 1500 A.D., the best roads on the continent were still those built by the Romans more than a thousand years before.

The flowering of Roman literature

Rome never produced the wide array of notable thinkers that emerged in Greece, but it did leave its mark in the areas of literature and history. A few of its most important writers and orators, Cato and Cicero, preceded the age of Augustus. The playwright Terence (c. 190–c. 159 B.C.) was known for his comedies. A much larger number of poets, playwrights, and historians flourished under Augustus or in the years soon after his reign.

Among the most prominent of these was Vergil (70–19 B.C.), whose *Aeneid* (ah-NEE-ehd) was the crowning work of a long and fruitful career. As Homer had done in Greece, Virgil wrote a national epic. The legend of Aeneas had existed for centuries, but Virgil gave it form and poetic style, as well as a moral message. He presented Aeneas as the embodiment of all the virtues Romans admired, which could be summed up in the word *faithfulness*—faithfulness to family, to nation, to the gods.

The poetry of Horace (65–8 B.C.) reflected a love of nature. He also wrote *satires,* a form of poetry for which the Romans were particularly noted. Whereas Horace's satires poked gentle fun, those of Juvenal (JOO-veh-nuhl; c. A.D. 100) were more biting. Ovid (AH-vid; 43 B.C.–A.D. 17), perhaps because he lived in a somewhat later age, was not inclined to uphold the gods and the Roman virtues so admired by Vergil; yet his most famous work, the *Metamorphoses* (meht-uh-MOHR-fuh-seez), celebrates the myths of the past with an extensive collection of stories.

The first great Roman historian of note was Livy (LIV-ee; 59 B.C.–A.D. 17), whose *Books from the Founding of Rome* chronicled Roman history from the time of Romulus and Remus up to 9 B.C. Like Herodotus before him, Livy was not inclined to let the facts get in the way of a good story. He tended to bring in legends such as the tale of Lucretia as though they were established historical fact. But also like Herodotus, he was an entertaining writer who enjoyed considerable popularity in his day and thereafter.

Much the same was true of Josephus (joh-SEE-fuhs; A.D. 37–95), whose work provides one of the only accounts of Jesus Christ—born during the reign of Augustus—outside of the Bible's. Josephus was Jewish, but he had close ties with Rome. Similarly, the biographer Plutarch (PLOO-tahrk; A.D. c. 46–c. 120) is remembered as a Roman even though he was Greek. His *Parallel Lives* presented paired biographies of Greek and Roman figures, establishing links between men separated by time and space. His work is highly readable and offers penetrating accounts of personalities ranging from Sulla to Spartacus.

Herodotus, reading history to the Greeks. *Archive Photos. Reproduced by permission.*

The Empire (A.D. 14–476)

Tiberius (r. A.D. 14–37), stepson of Augustus, was an able ruler in his early days, but he came to place too much reliance on a corrupt administrator. He was followed by Caligula (kuh-LIG-yoo-luh; r. A.D. 37–41), who suffered a serious illness and went insane as a result. Caligula was so cruel and violent that his military officers finally murdered him. Afterward the senate considered restoring the republic to prevent another madman from taking power. However, the military overruled the senate and chose Claudius (KLAW-dee-uhs; r. A.D. 41–54). Claudius's stammer and his absentminded behavior, as well as his interest in scholarly pursuits, made him an object of ridicule; but under Claudius, Rome prospered. It added southern Britain to its conquests in A.D. 47.

The next emperor, Nero, also had interests beyond his job as ruler: Nero (r. A.D. 54–68) saw himself as an artist, a performer, and a charioteer. As with Claudius, his pursuits did not win him many admirers, but for years he was guided by his tutor Seneca (SEHN-eh-kuh; c. 3 B.C.–c. A.D. 65), who virtually ran the empire. A Stoic philosopher, Seneca was also a dramatist of note, but he committed suicide after he was accused of conspiracy against the empire.

Suicide frequently ended the lives of leading Romans. In Seneca's case it earned him the lasting respect of others, who saw his self-destruction as an act of heroism on behalf of his nation. As for Nero, his reputation suffered further when he was blamed for a fire that swept Rome in A.D. 64. To clear his name, he in turn blamed the members of a tiny religious sect then gaining a foothold in Rome: the Christians. Thus

The Barbarians Next Door

The term *barbarian* means an uncivilized person, and it most often carries a highly negative meaning. Three great civilizations of the ancient world used the word to describe outsiders: the Greeks, the Chinese, and the Romans. The Romans, in fact, used the term so frequently that it has come to be used as a general name for the Celts, Goths, and others who threatened Rome.

The word comes from Latin, but it ultimately originated with the Greek *barbaroi*. Obviously the Chinese did not use "barbarian" or even a variation, since their language is completely unrelated to Greek; however, their own word for the nomadic tribes beyond their borders had much the same meaning.

Though it is not very "politically correct" to call someone a barbarian in modern times, it is understandable how the civilized peoples of the ancient world would have looked on outsiders that way. On the one hand, there were the splendid, highly civilized cultures of the Chinese, Greeks, or Romans; on the other hand, there were the tribes of northern China and northern Europe, who wore animal skins and slept on the ground. Worse, they often invaded the cities of the civilized world, where they would rape and loot and burn.

The barbarians *were* uncivilized, of course, meaning that they did not build cities or develop a written language; but many adapted to city life and learned civilized ways, including reading and writing. Yet to the Chinese and later the Romans, that was when the barbarians truly became a threat.

From the beginning, the understandable fear of barbarian invasion was mixed with a heavy dose of prejudice against outsiders. In fact the Greek word *barbaroi* really just meant someone who was not Greek. Later, white Europeans would use words such as "barbarian" and "savage" to describe black Africans, many of whom were highly civilized. Therefore, it is a word to use carefully.

began the persecutions of Christians, which would continue off and on for nearly 300 years. Nero himself committed suicide after revolts against the empire broke out in a variety of places, including Palestine.

Vespasian (vehs-PAY-zhee-uhn; r. A.D. 69–79) began restoring order to the empire. In A.D. 70 his son Titus (TIE-tuhs) captured the city of Jerusalem and destroyed its temple. Titus

Ruins of Hadrian's Wall.
Corbis/Robert Estall.
Reproduced by permission.

was practically a partner in his father's reign, then served as emperor himself from A.D. 79 to 81, during which time a volcano destroyed the city of Pompeii (pahm-PAY). Titus was followed by his brother, the tyrant Domitian (doh-MISH-uhn; r. A.D. 81–96), who quarreled with the senate and demanded that he be addressed as "God."

After the brief reign of another emperor came a series of four able rulers. In fact, the historian Edward Gibbon (1734–1794), whose *Decline and Fall of the Roman Empire* is the most important historical work about Rome, described the period from A.D. 96 to 180 as "the period of the history of the world during which the condition of the human race was most happy and prosperous."

First of these four "good" emperors was Trajan (TRAY-juhn; r. A.D. 99–117), who added several provinces, including Mesopotamia, to the empire. In 116, in fact, the empire reached its greatest extent, stretching from the borders of Scotland to the mouth of Tigris and Euphrates rivers. Among the notable figures in his empire was Pliny the Younger (PLIN-ee; c. A.D. 61–113), a statesman and orator whose uncle, Pliny the Elder (c. A.D. 23–79), had been a famous naturalist.

The emperor Hadrian (HAY-dree-uhn; r. A.D. 117–138) gave the first evidence that Rome had grown too big for its own good. He gave up the recently acquired province of Mesopotamia. He built a large stone border, Hadrian's Wall, between Roman Britain and Scotland. His reign also saw the construction of the Pantheon, a huge temple to the gods covered by an open dome. Another great Roman historian, Tacitus (TAS-i-tuhs; c. A.D. 55–117) flourished under Hadrian. Like others before him, Tacitus, author of a noted work on the German tribes beyond the Roman borders, criticized the moral direction Rome was taking. He was among the last Roman writers of note.

Hadrian was followed by a minor emperor, and then by one of the greatest rulers in Roman history, Marcus Aurelius (oh-REEL-ee-uhs; r. 161–180), who is also famed as a Stoic philosopher. Certainly the events of Marcus's time must have influenced the brave approach to life that he recommended in his writings. Not only did soldiers fighting in Asia bring back the *plague,* but Rome was subjected to invasions from several German tribes. Marcus became the first of many emperors to allow barbarians to settle inside Roman borders as a means of protecting the frontier from *other* barbarians.

The Middle Emperors (A.D. 180–337)

When Marcus died, a golden age died with him. The gap between rich and poor, always wide, began to widen further. The middle class all but died out. In its place were two extremes: *honestiores,* who were the very rich and powerful, most of whom had lavish homes both in the city and countryside, and *humiliores,* who lived in crowded slum dwellings that often collapsed or caught fire.

Romans both rich and poor turned increasingly to entertainment, the rich out of boredom and the poor out of a desire for escape. They watched chariot races in the Circus Maximus, a huge racetrack, and battles between gladiators in the Colosseum (kahl-uh-SEE-uhm). The latter, part of which still stands today, was one of the most impressive structures of ancient Rome. It seated some 45,000 spectators and was the model for the sports arenas of modern times. The Colosseum, of course, became the site of even more cruel "sporting" events, as Christians, slaves, or prisoners were put in the ring unarmed against wild animals.

Marcus's son Commodus (KAHM-uh-duhs; r. A.D. 180–192) imagined himself both a god and a gladiator, but before he got a chance to compete in the ring, he was assassinated. Septimus Severus (SEP-ti-muhs seh-VEER-uhs; r. A.D. 192–211) tried to restore order, but after A.D. 235, the empire went into a period of severe decline.

During the next forty-nine years, no fewer than twenty emperors reigned, many of them promoted to their positions by the army. Emperors who inspired the disfavor of the military or the senate had a way of winding up dead, and they would

An aerial view of the Colosseum. *AP/Wide World Photos. Reproduced by permission.*

simply be replaced. For a time, a rival dynasty of emperors ruled Gaul, and plenty of other would-be rulers contended for power. Zenobia of Palmyra led a revolt in Syria, as did other leaders in other parts of the empire. One emperor, Valerian (vuh-LEER-ee-un; r. A.D. 253–260), was murdered by the Persians—an event which was as humiliating as it was terrifying to the Romans.

A number of other disturbing trends began to emerge during these years. Slavery actually declined, but not for good reasons: rather, the distinctions began to blur between slaves and the poorest of peasants, marking the beginnings of the feudal system that would characterize Europe during the Middle Ages. As political freedom declined, sexual freedom increased, and this helped lead to a drop in the population. Not only did family life began to fall apart, but the practices of abortion and infanticide (in-FAN-tih-side), or killing of unwanted children, spread. As society crumbled, people looked for someone to blame, and Christians made an easy target: thus began a series of persecutions.

The persecutions later decreased under the reign of Gallienus (gal-ee-AY-nuhs; r. A.D. 253–268), Valerian's son and co-ruler, who began a period of slow recovery in the empire as a whole. He built up the military on the borders and prevented senators from holding command positions in the army. Aurelian (oh-REEL-ee-uhn; r. A.D. 270–275) crushed the revolts in Syria and Gaul, but like other Roman emperors, he proved ineffective against the most serious threat to Rome's power: the barbarian tribes. His building of a wall around Rome, which had never had one in all its years, was a sign of the empire's increasingly defensive posture. A bizarre feature of Aurelian's rule was his adoption of the cult of Mithra (MITH-ruh), a Persian sun god whom the Romans called Sol Invictus (SOHL in-VIK-tuhs), as the state religion.

Aurelian was assassinated in A.D. 275, and the army—which had increasingly taken over from the senate the decision-making power in naming new emperors—chose Diocletian (die-oh-KLEE-shuhn; r. A.D. 284–305). Diocletian dealt

Arch of Constantine, illustration. *The Granger Collection, New York. Reproduced by permission.*

successfully with a whole range of problems from the barbarians to the steady decline of the economy, but he resumed the persecution of Christians. Up to his time, attacks on Christians had been a local matter, not something directed by the emperors themselves: his persecution, which began in A.D. 302, was particularly severe.

A number of men contended for the throne after Diocletian, but in A.D. 307, the last truly powerful Roman emperor took control. This was Constantine (KAHN-stan-teen), who would reign for the next thirty years. In striking contrast to Diocletian, Constantine became a Christian and presided over the religious Council of Nicaea (niy-SEE-uh) in A.D. 325. This marriage of church and state would have a corrupting influence on the church, which assumed vast political power. In the meantime, the adoption of Christianity as the official religion of Rome seemed to breathe new life into the empire.

The Late Emperors (A.D. 337–476)

In a reversal of the former persecutions, several of Constantine's successors actively discriminated against believers in the old religion, whom they now condemned as *pagans* (PAY-guhnz). The term pagan simply refers to someone who worships many gods, but in newly Christianized Rome, it became a term of severe disapproval. Paganism made a last stand under the emperor Julian (r. A.D. 361–363), who tried to bring back the old religion, but it was a doomed effort. Romans had stopped believing in the old gods long before, as the popularity of the Mithra cult had proved.

Soon after Julian's death, the empire gave up claims to Persia. This move freed its soldiers to deal with a more immediate challenge, that of the Germans. The problem of the barbarian tribes reached a new level with the appearance of the Huns in about A.D. 355. Setting in motion a domino effect that would ultimately bring down the empire, they pushed the Sarmatians out of the Caucasus and into the Balkan Peninsula, which in turn pushed a Germanic tribe called the Visigoths (VIS-i-gahths) into the eastern part of the empire.

As early as Diocletian's time, it had already been clear that the empire could no longer be ruled effectively from a single center in Rome. Therefore he had reduced the number of provinces, and divided the empire into eastern and western halves. The Spaniard Theodosius (thee-uh-DOH-shuhs; r. A.D. 379–395) became the last emperor to rule both halves; from then on, there was a western empire based in Rome, and an eastern empire ruled from the city of Constantinople (kahn-stan-ti-NOH-puhl). Constantinople sat astride the Bosporus, and had already existed for a thousand years as Byzantium (bi-ZAN-tee-uhm) when Constantine renamed it for himself in A.D. 330.

With the empire thus divided, the eastern empire became stabilized and increasingly cut off from the western half, which continued to decline rapidly. The Visigoth chieftain Alaric (AL-uh-rik; c. A.D. 370–410), driven out of the east in 401, marched his troops into Italy. On August 24, A.D. 410, the Visigoths sacked Rome, an event that some historians consider the true end of the Roman Empire. Certainly the people of the time viewed it as a crisis much greater than the "official" end of the empire 66 years later. For thoughtful people such as the early Christian philosopher Augustine (A.D. 354–430), the sacking of Rome caused deep soul-searching, and in Augustine's case resulted in the writing of *The City of God,* one of the most important works of early Christianity.

Under their new leader Attila (A.D. 406?–453), the Huns were on the move again. Rome could not prevent them from invading Gaul in 451. Rome had meanwhile given up Britain, which would soon be invaded by a number of Germanic tribes, including the Angles; hence the name England. Spain had been overrun by a tribe called the Vandals, who in the 430s took over Carthage and other Roman possessions in North Africa—except for Egypt, safely under the control of the eastern empire. In A.D. 455, the Vandals sacked Rome, and their destruction of property was so severe that their name, too, became a part of the language.

After the Vandals came through, the western empire dwindled quickly. Power was in the hands of generals, and the so-called emperors controlled little more than their palaces, if that. In A.D. 475, a Roman official named Orestes, who had formerly served as secretary to Attila, put his son on the throne and gave him a magnificent title that called to mind both Rome's mythical founder and its first emperor: Romulus Augustulus. He "ruled" for a year: then on August 23, 476, a barbarian chieftain named Odoacer (oh-do-AY-suhr; c. A.D. 433–493),

The Importance of Realistic Art

Historians can learn a great deal about a culture from the ways in which its visual artists and sculptors depicted the human figure. For centuries, artists had been struggling to capture the appearance of human beings realistically. The Sumerians showed people who all looked more or less the same. Although the Egyptians managed to portray a variety of human types, they were confined by their two-dimensional treatment of space.

This development of realism in a particular culture can be compared with the way that a child learns how to draw people: first with scribbles, then stick-figures. Ultimately, something that looks like a person appears. Along the way, the child picks up all kinds of details: eyes are not just dots, nor mouths just lines. To draw a face requires careful study. As the child matures, his or her ability to "see" matures as well.

So it is with a civilization. Western realism in art reached its height in Greece and Rome but would decline along with the Roman Empire. As the glory of Rome gave way to the Middle Ages, portraits of people again began to take on an unrealistic appearance: already by the 300s and 400s, human figures in sculpture were starting to look more or less the same. This also signified a loss of individual identity that came with the "Dark Ages," a time when the great masses of people were subject to the church and to feudal lords.

with the support of what remained of the army, declared himself king of Italy. He sent the imperial standard, a symbol which had once meant a great deal in Rome's glory days, to the eastern emperor Zeno. Zeno recognized him as a vassal king, and the troubled history of the late Roman Empire ended.

The Greco-Roman legacy

It has been said that the two greatest questions in history revolve around how Rome came to conquer the world and how it came to lose it. A number of explanations have been put forward, but one thing is clear: the population of Germans and other barbarians was growing, while the Roman population—along with the vitality of its culture and civilization—declined.

Though the Roman Empire was gone, a remnant of its former glory remained in the Roman Catholic Church, whose supreme leader, the pope, would become a power on a level with the most influential kings. On Christmas Day, 800, Pope Leo III received a visit from a descendant of the barbarians, Charlemagne (SHAHR-luh-main; 742–814), the leader of a nation called the Franks. It was the first visit to Rome by an important monarch in three centuries. The pope crowned Charlemagne emperor of the Holy Roman Empire.

In spite of its impressive name, this empire existed primarily on paper, but it was an important step in the revival of Europe. Once again, Rome had become a center for civilization, a rallying point for all the kingdoms of Europe. Christianity itself became a rallying point as well, sometimes in violent ways such as the Crusades (1096–1272). But the Crusades also exposed Europeans to the civilization of the Arabs, which was much more advanced than that of Europe.

Civilization had also survived in its ancient eastern European center: Greece. There the eastern empire had become the Byzantine Empire (BIZ-un-teen), which embraced its own form of Christianity, the Greek Orthodox Church. For a time, under the emperor Justinian (jus-TIN-ee-un; r. A.D. 527-565), the Byzantines even managed to retake Rome and much of Italy; but the victory did not last long.

A new force was on the march: Islam, which originated in Arabia in the A.D. 600s. The Arabs took over much of the Byzantine Empire, and later the Turks seemed prepared to finish the job after defeating the Byzantines in a battle in 1071. Therefore, during the late A.D. 1000s, partly at Byzantine urging, the Pope launched the Crusades; but in the end, the Crusades led to a falling-out between the western and eastern portions of the old Roman Empire. The Byzantines drifted farther and farther from the west, and preserved civilization in a very rigid form that changed little over time. Their empire, sometimes referred to by historians simply as the Eastern Roman Empire, would remain intact until it was overrun by the Turks in 1453.

A new birth

Meanwhile, the state of constant change and upheaval that had once been the downfall of western Europe became its salvation. During the next centuries, in fact, this tendency toward restlessness—in particular, restlessness to learn and discover—would characterize the West, those countries influenced by the Greco-Roman tradition. In Italy there was a rebirth of learning, but this time, Rome was not its only center. There was Venice, for instance, the home of the journeyer Marco Polo, and Florence, where Dante (DAHN-tay; 1265–1321) virtually established Italian literature with his *Divine Comedy,* in which Vergil played a central role as a character.

The movement that began in Italy in about 1300 spread over the next two centuries to all of Europe, where it would become known as the Renaissance (REHN-uh-sahnts), or rebirth. This rebirth was accompanied by an interest in exploration. Another Italian from another city—Christopher Columbus of Genoa (GEHN-oh-uh; 1456–1506)—quite literally opened up a New World.

Another type of rebirth began to the far north, in Germany, where Martin Luther (1483–1546) and others launched the Reformation (REHF-uhr-may-shuhn.) Luther broke with the Roman Catholic Church over a number of issues and helped begin the Protestant (PRAH-tehs-tuhnt) movement. Protestantism took hold throughout northern Europe among the descendants of the "barbarians" who had been a part neither of Rome nor of Greece. In contrast to the Roman church, Protestants believed that people should be able to read the Bible in their own language, a process aided by the invention of the printing press in about 1450. The printing press in turn led to the spread of learning throughout Europe.

Another center of culture developed in England, which established its own brand of Protestantism, the Church of England. There, literature flourished, producing one of the greatest writers of all time, William Shakespeare (1564–1616), whose *Julius Caesar* honored the Roman leader. Government by the people, an idea begun in Greece and developed in Rome, began to take hold in England with a revolutionary movement in the 1600s.

In France, quite a different movement took hold. The French Revolution of 1789, which replaced a monarchy with a republican government, drew heavily on the symbolism of Rome. Out of that revolution would ultimately come a leader who saw himself as the inheritor of Roman emperors: Napoleon Bonaparte (1769–1821). As a conqueror, his only

European rival was Alexander. Like Alexander, he counted Egypt one of his greatest prizes when he took it in 1799.

The modern world

Napoleon's downfall would come from two sides: Britain and Russia. The latter, along with eastern Europe, shared in the Byzantine legacy, including the Orthodox church. Thanks in part to the stagnation of Eastern culture under Byzantium, political institutions had not developed in Russia as they had in the West. Its kings were often exceptionally cruel. They called themselves *czars* (ZAHRZ), a Russian version of "caesar." They thought of their civilization as the "Third Rome," after Rome and Byzantium.

Another set of European rulers gave themselves a title based on "caesar": the *kaisers* (KY-zuhrz) of Germany. Germany had taken much longer than the rest of Europe to unite as a single nation; therefore it had not built the great overseas empires of the Spanish and Portuguese in the 1500s or the British, French, and others in later centuries. Germany's rulers demanded a greater share of land both in Europe and abroad. This expansionism along with a number of other issues led to World War I (1914–1918).

One result of the war was the establishment of Communism in Russia in 1917, following a revolt inspired in part by the French Revolution. The Soviet Union would become a highly militarized society not unlike Sparta, ruled by a tyrant named Josef Stalin. Another outcome of the war was widespread resentment in Germany, on whom the Allied nations had imposed what many criticized as a "Carthaginian peace." This discontent helped give rise to another brutal dictator, Adolf Hitler.

Hitler had long admired Alexander and dreamed of exceeding his conquests. He also looked back with awe at the Roman Empire, adopting Roman symbols such as the war eagle, along with the ancient Indian swastika. Eventually he allied himself with Benito Mussolini (beh-NEE-toh moo-soh-LEE-nee; 1883–1945), an Italian dictator who likewise fancied himself an heir to the Roman emperors. He, too, adopted an ancient symbol, the fasces. When he invaded Albania (ancient Illyria) and Greece, he must have thought he was repeating the conquests of 2,200 years before.

By that time, World War II (1939-1945) had begun, and when it was over, the world was an utterly different place. Israel became a nation after more than 2,000 years; China became Communist and ultimately emerged as a world power. The former colonies of Europe gradually became independent. The center of power had shifted away from Europe, chiefly to the Soviet Union and to a country that many saw as the heir both of Greece and of Rome, the United States.

Over the next decades, the Cold War between those the Soviet Union and the United States would be the focal point of world events. As America and western Europe prospered, Russia and eastern Europe stagnated. All of the east, except Greece itself, had come under the sway of Communism. By the late 1980s, as in the 400s A.D., a sharp dividing line had developed between what had been the western and eastern halves of the Roman Empire. Only now it was the west that was better off.

Eventually Communism would end, but that end would bring troubles of its own, most notably in the former nation of Yugoslavia, where the Orthodox Serbs waged war on their Catholic and Muslim neighbors in the 1990s. Greece, which had a region named Macedonia, waged a war of words with the newly formed nation of Macedonia over which had the right to the name.

All over Europe, the lines drawn by ancient culture are vivid, far more important than the many magnificent Roman structures that dot the towns of France, Spain, and Italy. Those three countries all speak languages derived from Latin, as do the Spanish- and Portuguese-speaking peoples of Latin America. North of the Rhine, as in ancient times, people speak the language of the Romans' ancient foes, the Germans. Across the English Channel and the Atlantic Ocean, millions more speak a language derived in part from both German and Latin: English.

For More Information

Books

Bardi, Piero. *The Atlas of the Classical World: Ancient Greece and Ancient Rome*. Illustrations by Matteo Chesi, et al. New York: Peter Bedrick Books, 1997, pp. 34-59.

Bombarde, Odile and Claude Moatti. *Living in Ancient Rome*. Translated by Sarah Matthews, illustrated by François Place. Ossining, NY: Young Discovery Library, 1988.

Burrell, Roy. *Oxford First Ancient History*. New York: Oxford University Press, 1991, pp. 206-315.

Caselli, Giovanni. *The Roman Empire and the Dark Ages*. New York: P. Bedrick Press, 1985.

Harris, Jacqueline L. *Science in Ancient Rome*. New York: F. Watts, 1988.

Martell, Hazel Mary. *The Kingfisher Book of the Ancient World*. New York: Kingfisher, 1995, pp. 76-87.

McKeever, Susan. *Ancient Rome*. New York: Dorling Kindersley, 1995.

Poulton, Michael. *Augustus and the Ancient Romans*. Illustrations by Christine Molan. Austin, TX: Raintree/Steck-Vaughn, 1993.

Richardson, John. *Roman Provincial Administration, 227 B.C. to A.D. 117*. Basingstroke, England: Macmillan, 1976.

Steele, Philip. *Food & Feasts in Ancient Rome*. New York: New Discovery Books, 1994.

Web Sites

Armamentarium: The Book of Roman Arms and Armour. http://www.ncl.ac/uk/~nantiq/arma/ (June 28, 1999).

"EAWC: Ancient Rome." *Exploring Ancient World Cultures*. http://eawc.evansville.edu/ropage.htm (June 28, 1999).

Imperium Romanorum. http://wwwtc.nhmccd.cc.tx.us/people/crf01/rome/ (June 28, 1999).

Resource Pages for Biblical Studies. http://www.hivolda.no/asf/kkf/rel-stud.html (June 28, 1999).

Roman Emperors: De Imperatoribus Romanis: An Online Encyclopedia of Roman Emperors. http://www.salve.edu/~romanemp/startup.htm (June 28, 1999).

Rome Resources. http://www.dalton.org/groups/rome/ (June 28, 1999).

Roman Sites—Gateway to 1,849 Websites on Ancient Rome. http://www.ukans.edu/history/index/europe/ancient_rome/E/Romn/RomanSites*/home.html (June 28, 1999).

Where to Learn More

The following list of resources focuses on material appropriate for middle school or high school students. The list is divided into two sections: Books, and Web Sites. Please note that the web site addresses were verified prior to publication, but are subject to change.

Books:

Barber, Richard W. *A Companion to World Mythology.* Illustrated by Pauline Baynes. New York: Delacorte Press, 1979.

Bardi, Piero. *The Atlas of the Classical World: Ancient Greece and Ancient Rome.* Illustrations by Matteo Chesi, et al. New York: Peter Bedrick Books, 1997.

Bowra, C. M. *Classical Greece.* New York: Time-Life Books, 1965.

Breuilly, Elizabeth; Joanne O'Brien; Martin Palmer. *Religions of the World: The Illustrated Guide to Origins, Beliefs, Traditions & Festivals.* New York: Facts on File, 1997.

Brumbaugh, Robert S. *The Philosophers of Greece.* Albany, NY: State University of New York Press, 1981.

Burrell, Roy. *Oxford First Ancient History.* New York: Oxford University Press, 1991.

Davidson, Basil, and the Editors of Time-Life Books. *African Kingdoms.* Alexandria, VA: Time-Life Books, 1978.

Dijkstra, Henk. *History of the Ancient & Medieval World,* Volume 2: *Egypt and Mesopotamia.* New York: Marshall Cavendish, 1996.

Dijkstra, Henk. *History of the Ancient & Medieval World,* Volume 3: *Ancient Cultures.* New York: Marshall Cavendish, 1996.

Dijkstra, Henk, editor. *History of the Ancient & Medieval World,* Volume 11: *Empires of the Ancient World.* New York: Marshall Cavendish, 1996.

Dué, Andrea, editor. *The Atlas of Human History: Civilizations of Asia: India, China and the Peoples of Southeast Asia and the Indian Ocean.* Text by Renzo Rossi and Martina Veutro. New York: Macmillan Library Reference USA, 1996.

Dué, Andrea, editor. *The Atlas of Human History: Civilizations of the Americas: Native American Cultures of North, Central and South America.* Text by Renzo Rossi and Martina Veutro. New York: Macmillan Library Reference USA, 1996.

Dué, Andrea, editor. *The Atlas of Human History: Cradles of Civilization: Ancient Egypt and Early Middle Eastern Civilizations.* Text by Renzo Rossi. New York: Macmillan Library Reference USA, 1996.

Ganeri, Anita. *Religions Explained: A Beginner's Guide to World Faiths.* Marcus Braybrooke, Consultant. New York: Henry Holt and Company, 1997.

Harker, Ronald. *Digging Up the Bible Lands.* Drawings by Martin Simmons. New York: Henry Z. Walck, 1972.

Hunter, Erica C. D. *First Civilizations.* New York: Facts on File, 1994.

Langley, Myrtle. *Religion.* New York: Knopf, 1996.

Leonard, Jonathan Norton. *Ancient America.* Alexandria, VA: Time-Life Books, 1967.

Martell, Hazel Mary. *The Kingfisher Book of the Ancient World.* New York: Kingfisher, 1995.

Percival, Yonit and Alastair. *The Ancient Far East.* Vero Beach, FL: Rourke Enterprises, 1988.

Putnam, James. *Pyramid.* New York: Knopf, 1994.

Smith, F. LaGard, editor. *The Narrated Bible.* Eugene, OR: Harvest House, 1984.

Swisher, Clarice. *The Ancient Near East.* San Diego, CA: Lucent Books, 1995.

Tubb, Jonathan N. *Bible Lands.* New York: Knopf, 1991.

Whitehouse, Ruth and John Wilkins. *The Making of Civilization: History Discovered through Archaeology.* New York: Knopf, 1986.

Web Sites

Archaelogy's Dig. http://www.dig.archaeology.org/ (accessed on June 16, 1999).

"Bulfinch's Mythology." http://www.webcom.com/shownet/medea/bulfinch/welcome.html (accessed on June 21, 1999).

Exploring Ancient World Cultures. http://eawc.evansville.edu (accessed on February 14, 1999).

Mr. Donn's Ancient History Page.
http://members.aol.com/
donnandlee/index.html
(accessed on February 25,
1999).

Resource Pages for Biblical Studies.
http://www.hivolda.no/asf/
kkf/rel-stud.html (accessed
on June 28, 1999).

*Roman Sites-Gateway to 1,849
Websites on Ancient Rome.*
http://www.ukans.edu/
history/index/europe/
ancient_rome/E/Roman/
RomanSites*/home.html
(accessed on June 28, 1999).

Index

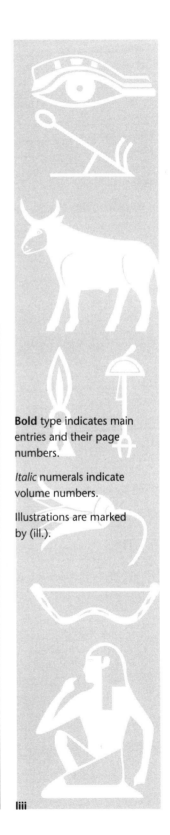

Bold type indicates main entries and their page numbers.

Italic numerals indicate volume numbers.

Illustrations are marked by (ill.).

Q

Quetzalcóatl *2:* 273 (ill.)

R

Ra *1:* 7, 14
Ramses the Great (See Ramses II)
Ramses II *1:* 38, 142 (ill.)
Reincarnation *1:* 195
Rig Vega 1: 189
Roman alphabet *2:* 374
Roman numerals *2:* 394
Rome *2:* **373-420**
Rosetta Stone *1:* 42 (ill.)
"Royal Road" *1:* 165
Rubicon River *2:* 401
Rule of law 2: 382

S

Sadat, Anwar *1:* 44
Sahara *1:* 2; *2:* 286, 287
Saharan rock art *2:* 287
Sama-Veda 1: 191
Samnites *2:* 385
San Lorenzo *2:* 268
Sarah *1:* 90-91
Sarai (See Sarah)
Sarcophagus 1: 22, 32 (ill.)
Sargon *1:* 58
Sargon II *1:* 74
Sassanians *1:* 170
Saul *1:* 99-100
Saul of Tarsus (See Paul)
Savanna *2:* 286 (ill.)
Schliemann, Heinrich *2:* 316, 319
Scipio the Younger *2:* 390
Scythians *1:* 147
Sea Peoples *1:* 142
Second Intermediate Period of
    Egypt *1:* 29
Second Triumvirate *2:* 402
Selassie, Haile *2:* 302 (ill.)
Sennacherib *1:* 125
Set *1:* 6, 15
"Shah of Iran" *1:* 172
Shamash-shum-ukin *1:* 75
Shamshi-Adad I *1:* 71
Shang Dynasty *2:* 222
Shiite Fundamentalism *1:* 171, 175
Shu *1:* 14

Shudras *1:* 190
Silt *1:* 3
Sinai Peninsula *1:* 2
Sixth Cataract *1:* 3
Slavery *2:* 301
Socrates *2:* 234 (ill.), 357
Socratic Method *2:* 357
Sophocles *2:* 360
Sparta *2:* 335, 353
Spartacus *2:* 398, 399 (ill.)
Sphinx *1:* 11 (ill.), 19, 37
"Spring and Autumn Period" *2:*
    230
Stairs of the Jaguars *2:* 275
Stalin, Joseph *1:* 151 (ill.)
Stargate 1: 45
Step Pyramid of King Zoser *1:* 14,
    17 (ill.)
Stoics *2:* 371
The Story of Sinuhe 1: 26
Stupas *1:* 202 (ill.)
Suez Canal *1:* 44
Sulla, Lucius Cornelius *2:* 397 (ill.)
Sumer *1:* 50
Sumerians *1:* 51
Sun Yat-sen *2:* 250
Syria *1:* 126, 131

T

Taharqa *2:* 291 (ill.)
Tai-ping Rebellion *2:* 249
Taj Mahal *1:* 212 (ill.)
Taoism *2:* 235
Tao te Ching 2: 235
Tefnut *1:* 14
Temple of Artemis at Ephesus
    2: 361
Ten Commandments *1:* 45, 97-98
"Ten Lost Tribes of Israel" *1:* 74
Ten Plagues of Egypt *1:* 96
Teotihuacán *2:* 269, 272
The Testament of Amenemhet 1: 27
Thales *2:* 341
Thebes *2:* 321, 334
Theogony 2: 322
Thermopylae, Battle of *2:* 333, 345
Thucydides *2:* 356
Thutmose III *1:* 33-34
Tianamen Square *2:* 254 (ill.)
Tiglath-Pileser I *1:* 72, 125
Tlachli 2: 274
Toltecs *2:* 273